The Coping Stone

The First English Soccer Tour of Australia 1925

The Coping Stone

The First English Soccer Tour of Australia 1925

PAUL NICHOLLS

FAIRPLAY
PUBLISHING

First published in 2025 by Fair Play Publishing

PO Box 4101, Balgowlah Heights, NSW 2093, Australia

www.fairplaypublishing.com.au

ISBN: 978-1-923236-07-3

ISBN: 978-1-923236-08-0

© Paul Nicholls 2025

The moral rights of the author have been asserted.

All rights reserved. Except as permitted under the *Australian Copyright Act 1968* (for example, a fair dealing for the purposes of study, research, criticism or review), no part of this book may be reproduced, stored in a retrieval system, communicated or transmitted in any form or by any means without prior written permission from the Publisher.

Design and typesetting by Leslie Priestley.

Front cover photographs of the Australian and England teams via *Soccer News* (State Library of New South Wales).

Other photographs: *Mark Boric, Sam Calvert, Travis Faulks, Paul Nicholls, Australian National University, South Australian State Library, State Library of New South Wales, Trove Newspapers (National Library of Australia).*

Edited by Craig Lord.

Printed in Australia

All inquiries should be made to the Publisher via hello@fairplaypublishing.com.au

A catalogue record of this book is available from the National Library of Australia.

Contents

Prologue	1
Destiny	2
Part I: An Enduring Obsession	**11**
1 The Coping Stone	12
2 On the Cusp	19
3 The International Era	23
4 Rushing for the Post	29
5 A Capable Party of Players	34
Part II: From Fremantle to Bundaberg	**41**
6 More British Than The People in Britain	42
7 Law One	48
8 'Is he Jealous?'	54
9 Soccer at the MCG	62
10 Rarefied Air	74
11 A Mighty Roar	82
12 'At the point of a Pistol'	93
13 Law One Again	101

14	A Wembley Moment on the Hunter	108
15	Bush Rats and Pineapples	117
16	That Murray Boy	124

Part III: The Test Matches — 136

17	The First Test	137
18	'The Greatest Test Match in Australia'	151
19	Judy's Back	163
20	Daylight Robbery	173
21	Distractions by Sea	181
22	The Vics Stand Tall	188
23	Once More, for The Lads	194
24	A Breath from Heaven	201

Epilogue	211
Appendix	213
Test Matches	213
Other Tour Matches	215
England Player Statisticis	223
Australia Player Statistics	224
All Tour Matches Appearances and Goal Scorers	226
Acknowledgements and Bibliographical Notes	228

"Although the game is now permanently established in Australia, the required coping stone, in the shape of a visit from Britain, will thoroughly cement affairs, and put Australia in the forefront in the most universal game in the world"

Stephen Lynch,
Secretary of the New South Wales Football Association, 1914

Testimonial

Football in Australia has its data, statistics and narratives. However, *The Coping Stone* is a new phenomenon: a book that mythologises the game in Australia, embeds it in the hearts and minds of Australians and reveals a moment in which the game was culturally central.

The great Frank Hardy once joked, *"Of course my story is true; I made it up myself!"* Paul Nicholls might say something along those lines. Rather than simply listing sequences of facts and secondary analyses, his method also involves using imagination to get inside the minds of the players, administrators, and spectators to intimate feelings and emotions beyond the simple statistics. We know, as we read, that these aspects are invented, but we also know they are true.

Working outside institutional structure and support and leaning into his passion for creative writing, Nicholls has hit upon the genre that football in Australia needs: mythological narrative. While all around us, other sports have created legends aplenty, we have stuck to bare bones narratives and maybe wondered why these stories get little purchase. We have our great tales, individuals and events from the past.

Let's take several leaves out of Paul Nicholls' *The Coping Stone* and emulate his brilliant work and place football at the heart of Australian culture.

Dr Ian Syson
Melbourne, Australia

Prologue

Destiny

22 December 1923, Mt Pleasant Colliery near Wollongong

"Is he dead?"

"No. He's still breathing. Has someone called the ambulance?"

"They're on their way."

Choking on the thick coal dust the miners work frantically in the darkness to free their colleague from the rubble. The man had been filling a skip moments before the rockfall.

Eventually they bring the injured miner to the surface.

"What's his name?" the ambulance officer asks.

"Judy Masters."

"*The* Judy Masters? The soccer player?"

"Not just any soccer player. The Australian captain no less."

The ambulance speeds off to the hospital.

The injuries are severe. A fractured skull, broken jaw and numerous cuts and bruises. Judy Masters is lucky to be alive, his football career almost certainly over.

But they breed them tough in the Illawarra…

* * *

Situated on the coast roughly 85 kilometres south of Sydney and centred on the city of Wollongong, the Illawarra district has produced countless Internationals and national league players.

Looming over the narrow coastal plain is the Illawarra Escarpment, a range of steep sandstone cliffs. The slopes of the escarpment were once covered in forests of *toona ciliate,* or red cedar. Its timber was a prized building material in colonial New South Wales and it didn't take long for most of the red cedar forests to be wiped out.

Settlers next turned their attention to the outcrops of coal that protruded from the lower slopes of the escarpment. The first mine in the area was established at Mt Keira in 1849. By 1900 there were fifteen mines operating in the Illawarra district. Townships formed around the pitheads in places such as Thirroul, Corrimal, Balgownie and Bulli.

Many of the coal miners were recent migrants from Britain. Along with their worldly possessions, they brought with them their favourite sport. Rugby might have been popular in Sydney but around the coal mining townships of the Illawarra it was the football played predominately with the feet that held sway. Newspapers, for the sake of a diverse readership, called

James 'Judy' Masters

it 'association football', 'British football', or, from around 1910, 'soccer', but under the escarpment everyone knew it as 'football'.

A team called North Illawarra first competed against Sydney clubs in 1887. From the 1890s clubs such as Helensburgh Boomerangs and Balgownie Rangers began competing for the Gardiner Cup, the premier knockout football tournament in New South Wales.

One of the new arrivals was Alexander Masters, a coal miner from Nova Scotia, who with his wife Frances settled in Balgownie towards the end of the 19th century. They produced a brood of 13 children: eight sons and five daughters.

James William Masters, the seventh child, was born on 21 May 1892. At an early age he was given the nickname 'Judy', which stuck with him throughout his life. With 12 siblings Judy was never short of teammates for a backyard game of football. He took his backyard form to Balgownie Public School where he became captain of the school team.

At the age of 12 he started playing junior football with Balgownie Rangers. At 13 he was working alongside his father and brothers at the Corrimal coal mine. The work was hard and dangerous - an explosion at the nearby Mt. Kembla mine in 1902 killed 96 miners and devastated the community.

Football was a welcome relief from the tough grind underground. Young Judy Masters made good on his talent, joining his brothers in Balgownie's senior team in 1907 at the age of fifteen. Balgownie Rangers reached the semi-finals of the Gardiner Cup in 1911 with a team that featured Judy and his older brothers Bob and Charlie. The following season Judy got his first taste of representative football, playing alongside Charlie for the South Coast (another name for Illawarra) in a 2-2 draw with Sydney at Wentworth Park. The journalist 'Volunteer', writing in the *Arrow,* labelled Masters "a promising colt". Later that year the two brothers played in the South Coast team that hammered Queensland 8-2 in Wollongong. Volunteer called Masters "the most promising forward I have seen in years", and wrote that "he exhibited the skill, speed and stamina which stamps the born footballer."

Masters played the classic centre-forward's role of the time, controlling the ball with his back to goal then sending a pass out to a winger while racing forward to meet the expected cross with head or foot. His strengths were his tenacity, a great ability to read the game, and an instinct for goal. Of slight build - in his prime weighing 64 kilograms and standing just 170 centimetres tall - he was tough and wiry and like most players from the Illawarra appeared to be hewn from the Hawkesbury sandstone of the escarpment.

Grabbing any opportunity he could to improve his game, Masters would turn out for rivals Corrimal in the Gardiner Cup in the years when Balgownie didn't enter a team. In 1913, he joined Newtown in Sydney and made his first appearance in a Gardiner Cup Final, albeit on the losing side. His stocks rose further when he was selected to play for New South Wales against Queensland that same year. Despite losing 3-2, Masters scored both his team's goals including a spectacular effort from distance.

In 1915, Masters was coaxed into playing with Granville, the strongest club side in Sydney. He settled in immediately, banging in five goals in an early season match. But war came calling. On 30 May 1915, Judy Masters enlisted, joining the ranks of the 19th Battalion of the Australian Imperial Force (AIF).

Masters served in Gallipoli and on the Western Front. In July 1916, he was wounded near Pozières. In June 1918 at Mourlancourt, the 19th Battalion came under heavy shellfire. In the engagement, Private William Williams, a coal miner from the Illawarra, copped a shrapnel splinter to the head and was killed instantly. Masters, who witnessed the death of his mate, wrote a touching letter to a friend about the incident. "I wish you to convey to his dear home folk my heartfelt sympathy in the loss." He signed off with, "Kindly remember me to my old chums. I often think -

even muse over - the bonnie South Coast, which from childhood was my home."

Away from the trenches, Masters squeezed in games of football whenever and wherever he could by playing in AIF teams. There is some evidence to suggest he played for an Australian army team that defeated Chelsea at Stamford Bridge near the end of the Great War. If there was a silver lining to his time in the army it was meeting his wife to be, Anne Barraclough from County Durham, who he married in Australia in 1920.

On his return to Australia, Masters went back to work in the mines and resumed playing for his old club Balgownie Rangers.

On 6 May 1922, the 30-year-old Judy Masters took the train to Sydney along with 14 teammates from the Illawarra district. They were headed to Wentworth Park to play a trial against a Metropolitan X1. This was not your run of the mill inter-district game. At stake, for a good performance, was a chance to represent your country.

c 1906, Newcastle-upon-Tyne, England

A group of boys were playing football in the street with plenty of energy and imagination. In their heads they were the next Colin Veitch, Bill McCracken or the flying winger Jock Rutherford - all stars of the powerful Newcastle United side that would win three League Championships, one FA Cup, and be three times FA Cup runners up between 1905 and 1910. The ball the boys played with, a 'clouty baall' made of rags wrapped around sheets of paper and tied with string, may not have been a regulation one but it served. As did the hard surface of the street that in the boys' minds was St James' Park.

In the football education system that was Newcastle-upon-Tyne, the next step was the 'playing fields'. Small boys watching from behind the goals would retrieve the wayward shots of the bigger boys. Sometimes the ball-retrievers were invited to join in.

One boy, big for his age, took up the offer and proved himself a gifted player. His name was Tom Whittaker. Born in Aldershot in 1898, his family moved to Newcastle when he was a youngster and he grew up every inch a Geordie. A technically minded student, Whittaker was offered a position in a Newcastle firm of marine engineers upon finishing school.

Whittaker was also offered a trial with Newcastle United Swifts, a team created during the First World War to provide a talent pool for Newcastle United. Playing outside right, he achieved every Geordie schoolboy's dream by playing and training at St James' Park.

Whittaker was called up for military service in 1918 and served as an army engineer. He was posted to Shoreham and while playing wing-half for the Brigade football team was noticed by a scout from Arsenal.

Still tossing up a career as an engineer, Whittaker, almost reluctantly, signed a professional contract with Arsenal in January 1920. He made his Arsenal debut at the close of the season in a 1-0 loss to West Bromwich Albion. Over the next five years he was in and out of the first team, notching up a total of 64 appearances.

In the 1924/25 season, Whittaker was in the best form of his career. Coming back after a heel injury, he played right fullback against Reading. He had a good game and became a regular in the position. Near the season's end he signed a new contract. Despite Arsenal finishing one off the relegation places, Whittaker felt secure about his future. Then he got an intriguing request. England were short of fullbacks for their upcoming tour of Australia and asked if Whittaker was available. It sounded like a good adventure. Yes, why not?

Tom Whittaker

2 September 1920, Olympisch Stadion, Antwerp

He was never meant to referee this game. John Lewis had come to the Antwerp Olympics solely as a linesman. At age 65, his best days of refereeing were behind him. He could no longer keep up with the play as he had done. But this tournament, the first international tournament since the end of the First World War, had raised passions to an extraordinary degree.

The standard of refereeing had been patchy. Organisers cajoled John Lewis into officiating first a semi-final and then the final itself. Lewis had an impressive reputation but hadn't officiated regularly for 15 years.

Lewis was known as a stickler for the rules. Just the thing for a potentially volatile match. The Olympic final, pitting the hosts Belgium, against Czechoslovakia, would require a firm hand.

The Olympisch Stadion was like a cauldron when the teams took the field. Nearly 50,000 spectators had forced their way into the 35,000-capacity venue. A large contingent of soldiers ringed the field.

The crowd of patriotic Belgians were in a frenzy just minutes into the game when Lewis awarded the home team a penalty for a hand ball, a decision the Czechs fiercely disputed.

At the 39-minute mark, Czech defender Karel Steiner violently fouled Belgian star Robert Coppée. Lewis immediately ordered Steiner from the field. The Czechs were incensed and the entire team walked off in protest. Lewis pleaded with the players to come back but they refused. He called off the game and awarded the gold medal to Belgium.

* * *

John Lewis was born in Market Drayton, Shropshire in 1855. He attended Shrewsbury School, where he first fell under football's spell. In 1868, he moved to Blackburn in Lancashire to work as a coach builder. Concerned that little football was being played in the area, Lewis and another Shrewsbury School alumni, Arthur Constantine, formed their own club in 1875, giving it the name Blackburn Rovers.

Lewis played centre-forward but a leg injury soon ended his playing career. He then became a referee, proving himself a natural. In 1895, he was appointed to the biggest club fixture in the country, the FA Cup Final, between Aston Villa and West Bromwich Albion at Crystal Palace in London. He refereed two more FA Cup Finals, in 1897 and 1898, a period where he gained the nickname 'Prince of Referees'. Perhaps his biggest achievement as a match official was refereeing the final of the 1908 London Olympics between Great Britain and Denmark that went to the hosts 2-0.

John Lewis was a founding member of the Lancashire FA and had administrative roles in the Football League and the Football Association (FA). Prior to his controversial performance at the 1920 Olympic Games he was manager of the FA team that toured South Africa earlier that year.

A strict teetotaller, non-smoker and anti-gambling campaigner, Lewis' reputation as a man who wouldn't take nonsense from anybody was an admired trait within the halls of power. When the FA agreed to send an English team to tour Australia in 1925, they didn't have to scout

John Lewis

too far for a manager. They needed someone who would ensure the Aussies played by the rules and not get their own ideas. Although he would be 70 years old by the time the ship sailed, from the FA's point of view, John Lewis was the perfect man for the job.

* * *

7 October 1921, Sydney

Some said the city itself was draped in a scarf of mourning. Over a period of just two hours, nearly 10,000 people shuffled past the coffin in the chancel of St Andrew's Cathedral in George Street. Outside, thousands more lined the streets. The death of John Storey from nephritis at the age of 52, the first New South Wales Premier to die in office, struck a chord with the people of Sydney.

Schools and public offices closed for the day. Business leaders and Trade Unionists, political allies and foes came together for the funeral. Also paying their respects were staff from the consulates of Great Britain, Japan, Sweden and the United States.

John Storey was a genuinely popular politician. An opponent of conscription, he helped heal the rift in the Labor Party caused by the conscription referenda during the First World War. In 1920, he led the Labor Party to victory in the New South Wales state elections and became premier. Among his personal qualities was his geniality, a common touch and a reputation for honesty.

Storey had been a boilermaker and was a staunch trade unionist. His own United Society of Boilermakers led the lengthy funeral procession. Four vehicles loaded with floral tributes followed the hearse. Behind them a motorcade of nearly 100 vehicles stretching for nearly two kilometres made its way down George Street. Nearly 100,000 people lined the streets as the cortege headed to the Field of Mars cemetery in Ryde.

The outpouring of respect for John Storey was not lost on his family and friends, including his brother Tom, a fellow Labor politician and trade unionist. Tom Storey's son, Sydney Storey, a 25-year-old draftsman in the Railways department, was in awe of the public adulation of his uncle. Syd had only recently returned from his own taste of public administration, managing the New South Wales football team on their tour of Queensland. Syd liked to be at the centre of things. And he loved football.

* * *

Syd Storey

Syd Storey was born in the Sydney suburb of Balmain on 27 February 1896. He went to school at Rozelle and Cleveland Street. He was a good cricketer and was partial to both rugby union and rugby league. But it was football that captured his imagination. The Balmain district had a strong football tradition and it was an easy thing to get a game going.

After finishing school, Storey helped form the Balmain Fernleigh club in 1914. Most of the players were old schoolmates and the team competed in the junior league for players under 18 years of age. Balmain Fernleigh won the junior league two years in a row and were promoted to the Second League. Two years later they gained promotion to Sydney's premier competition, the First League, and in 1919 won the league and Gardiner Cup double, a feat they repeated in 1920. Storey wouldn't hesitate to drop himself if he felt his form wasn't up to scratch. He sat out the 1919 cup final and 1920 would be his sole Gardiner Cup triumph as a player.

Storey was secretary of Balmain Fernleigh and represented them at New South Wales Football Association (NSWFA) meetings. He gained valuable experience in football administration and served on the management committee. When the secretary of the NSWFA stepped down temporarily in 1921, Storey took his place.

When New South Wales toured Queensland in July 1921, for the first time since the war, 25-year-old Syd Storey was appointed manager. According to *The Sun* it was a "fitting recognition to a zealous officer". Storey managed the team well, even filling in as a player in some of the minor games. He became close to the players and must have been stunned to hear of the death of the team's captain, Bill Lambert, in a mining accident at Hebburn Colliery in November 1921.

Storey became permanent secretary of the NSWFA in 1922, a position he would hold for many years. The added responsibilities took up much of his time and his on-field involvement became less frequent. But there was a real buzz around football in Australia in 1922. International football was on the horizon at last.

As he headed to Wentworth Park on 6 May 1922, Syd Storey still felt he had something to offer as a player. He was going as a reserve for the Sydney Metropolitan team in one of two trials taking place that day. And although he would only play if someone was injured, it gave him the chance to mingle with the best players from New South Wales. Eight good performers would join eight players from Queensland on Australia's first international football tour, to New Zealand.

Syd Storey would give anything to be involved in this exciting new era for football. It had been a long road for Australia to get a national team on the playing pitch. Now, all sorts of possibilities opened up. There'd been renewed talk of an English team touring, long regarded as a kind of Holy Grail for Australian football. If that happened, it could be a pivotal moment in the sport's history. And that history went back a long way.

Part I
An Enduring Obsession

1
The Coping Stone

23 December 1861, the colony of Victoria

Atop the Cape Otway lighthouse on the windswept southern coast of Victoria, a lookout sweeps a broad expanse of Bass Strait with a telescope. He spies something on the horizon. A ship!

This is a long-awaited vessel. On board are the cricketers of the 'All England XI', the first English sports team to visit Australia. Almost the entire population of the colony of Victoria has taken a keen interest in the ship's progress.

At the nearby telegraph station, an operator hurriedly taps out the following message in morse code:

>2:40pm: *Great Britain* sighted, fifteen miles distant, SSW

Next morning, enormous crowds converge on Melbourne's waterfront. Bunting hangs from the balconies of houses facing the harbour. People wave from dangerously overcrowded small boats. The players of the All England XI are almost mobbed when they step onto the wharf and have to be manhandled into a nearby hotel, where they are revived with liberal quantities of sparkling Moselle.

The players re-emerge and clamber on top of a giant Cobb & Co coach pulled by eight grey horses. Up goes a cheer so loud "it made the blood tingle", according to one witness.

As they enter the city proper, the swelling crowds make the footpaths impassable. People wave hats and handkerchiefs from windows and balconies. Shops and offices empty spontaneously as workers and patrons rush out to the street to greet the English team.

The carriage comes to a halt in Bourke Street outside the elegant Café de Paris, owned by the tour's promoters, Felix Spiers, a British restaurateur, and fellow hotelier Christopher Pond. People reach out and try to shake hands with the players. Senior-Sergeant Kelly and a detachment of police struggle to hold back the crowd long enough for the Englishmen to enter the café without anybody being injured in the crush.

Melburnians are star-struck by this England team. Not everyone thinks it's healthy. According to *The Argus*, "We are in some danger of passing into burlesque, and of making the colony ridiculous, by the excess of the emotions which have been excited by the arrival of the English cricketers."

* * *

The All-England XI toured Victoria and New South Wales. The visit was an unqualified sporting and financial success. It cleared the way for a succession of incoming cricket tours from England.

Two members of the All-England XI settled in Australia and coached local cricketers. One of them, Charles Lawrence, travelled with the first Australian sports team to tour England, a group of Aboriginal cricketers from the Western districts of Victoria, in 1868.

In March 1877 a combined cricket team from Victoria and New South Wales played England - for the first time featuring an equal number of players on each side. Played in Melbourne and later recognised as cricket's first Test match, Australia won in a surprise result. Australians had at last proven their worth against the 'mother' country. The Australia vs England cricket series, known after 1882 as The Ashes, became the premier international sporting fixture in Australia. The notion of competition with England as being the pinnacle of sporting endeavour was firmly planted into the Australian psyche.

Australia's footballers watched the development of international cricket with a touch of envy. The unity of cricket only served to highlight the disunity between the football codes played in the colonies. In Victoria they played the locally invented game, known today as Australian Rules football, and in New South Wales they played rugby. Neither colony was willing to give up its code for the sake of football unity. But by 1880 rugby in New South Wales was coming under threat from the Victorian code.

All England XI arriving in Melbourne, 1862

3 August 1880, Sydney

On a cold winter's night in 1880, Sydney schoolmaster John Fletcher entered Aaron's Exchange Hotel on Gresham Street with a meeting to attend and much on his mind. He couldn't fail to notice the huge mirror in the dining room, reputed to be Australia's largest. He was perhaps considering more than just his own reflection; Fletcher had been closely following the debates in the Sydney press about whether the game from Victoria should supplant rugby in Sydney.

Fletcher was no mere spectator but an active participant in the debates. In a letter to *The Sydney Morning Herald,* he advocated a different kind of football altogether, the one played under the rules of the Football Association in England. Fletcher said: 'We are rather late in writing for the advocacy of the English Association game, inasmuch as a large section of the football players of New South Wales, dissatisfied with Rugby rules, appear to have committed themselves to the adoption of Victorian rules.'

Another letter writer, 'An Old Etonian', argued against the limited scope of Australian Rules, noting: "I cannot agree to the bastard game now played in Victoria… if the Victorian is to supersede the Rugby game, then goodbye at once to all hope of International contests, for neither the English Football Association or the Rugby Union would ever consent to play under such rules as those in vogue in the neighbouring colony."

The organising body for rugby in Sydney, the Southern Rugby Football Union, sensing an ally in their battle against Australian Rules, sent delegates to Fletcher's meeting at Aaron's Exchange Hotel. One of them was William Burkitt, schoolmaster at The King's School at Parramatta.

Aarons' Exchange hotel, c. 1885

With the endorsement of the rugby delegates, John Fletcher established Australia's first association football club, the New South Wales Wanderers. Boys from Burkitt's King's School provided the opposition for the club's first match.

Rugby gave the new code a leg-up by supplying some of the Wanderers' opponents in the early years. By 1882, with more clubs established, Fletcher formed the New South Wales Football Association (NSWFA) and affiliated it with the Football Association (FA) in London. More encouraging news came in 1883 when enthusiasts in Melbourne, led by businessman Arthur Gibbs, established association football in Victoria. The first inter-colonial fixtures were held in Melbourne that year between New South Wales and Victoria. The good news kept coming: an association football competition had also commenced in Queensland, one featuring three Scottish-influenced clubs in Brisbane.

At a function in Melbourne at the end of the 1884 season, football officials confidently predicted an Australian team could be sent to England as early as 1886. The players would come from Queensland, New South Wales and Victoria, and no doubt with a nod to the Aboriginal cricket tour of 1868, selectors declared that there would be 'two or three aboriginals' in the Australian team.

But the proposed tour never got off the ground. By the end of the 1880s, football had all but died out in Victoria.

Queensland offered an alternative for inter-colonial contests, and in 1890 they toured New South Wales for the first time.

The NSW team in Victoria, 1885

16 August 1890, Botany, Sydney

On the eve of the first football match between New South Wales and Queensland, an excited audience gathered at Sydney Town Hall to welcome the visitors. J. Wallace, secretary of the NSWFA, wished both teams the best of luck. Encouraging young Australians to take up the game, he assured everyone that football was "very free from accidents".

The next day, 16 August 1890, New South Wales and Queensland were locked in a tight struggle at Sir Joseph Banks Park in Botany.

With the visitors leading 3-1 and just ten minutes of the game remaining, Queensland centre-forward Menzies ran on to a well-placed through ball. Jack Logan, the fearless New South Wales goalkeeper came off his line to intercept. A collision came with a thud and a sickening crack. Menzies was helped to his feet before being taken to Prince Alfred Hospital with suspected broken ribs. Jack Logan joined him at the same hospital, his leg fractured in two places. The game was called off.

The snap of Logan's femur was something of a metaphor for the immediate future of inter-colonial football. Despite a one-off tour of Queensland by New South Wales in 1898, it would be 22 years before Queensland returned to New South Wales. Football went into a period of decline across Australia. Outside of Sydney and Brisbane the game was kept alive in the coal mining centres of Newcastle and Illawarra in New South Wales, and Ipswich in Queensland.

* * *

In 1901, when the colonies federated to become states in the new Commonwealth of Australia, football was again showing signs of life. In Western Australia, a viable competition had commenced in 1896. In South Australia, a three-team league kicked off in 1902.

Enterprising officials in Western Australian wrote to the FA in London asking them to send a team out to Australia, although nothing came of it. Western Australia hosted an 'international' football match of sorts in 1902 when they played and beat the touring English cricketers transiting through Perth on their way home from an Ashes series.

In 1903, a group of New Zealand football officials visited Sydney. One of the New Zealand delegates was Arthur Gibbs, the stalwart of early football in Victoria. At the meeting it was decided to send a team from Australia to tour New Zealand. New South Wales offered Queensland places in the team but they declined as the costs would be too great. The subsequent tour, in 1904, was made by a team representing New South Wales only.

New Zealand reciprocated the visit in 1905. The matches in New South Wales were not well patronised. What could get the public interested in international football? A national approach to the sport's administration might help. A visit by England would certainly help.

In 1907, Australian football received a great boost when the sport was revived in Melbourne. In 1909 a football association was also established in Tasmania. Twenty years after football had reached its nadir, the sport was now being played in every state in the Commonwealth.

In December 1911, an Australasian football conference was held in Sydney. Delegates attended from all the Australian states and New Zealand.

The main topic for discussion was how to entice the English FA to send a team to Australia and New Zealand. At the end of the conference a national body, the Commonwealth Football Association (CFA) was established. Although New Zealand remained separate from the CFA, they agreed to work together to bring out a team from England.

Fred Barlow, a New South Wales delegate, called the formation of the CFA "the most important step ever taken in connection with the game. It brought nearer the day when they would see a soccer match between the old country and Australia."

Opportunities for international football began to pop up in unexpected quarters. One was a football tournament as part of the Panama-Pacific Exhibition in San Francisco in 1915. Another was the 1916 Berlin Olympic Games.

When the CFA next met in Melbourne in 1913, they voted against participating in the San Francisco tournament so as not to upset the FA, which didn't recognise the organising body. The delegates were much more open to the Berlin Olympics but there was a hitch to their participation. The Olympic football tournament was organised by the Federation of International Football Associations (FIFA). Australia was concerned that taking part in the Olympics could put their FA affiliation at risk. Unable to make up their own minds, they referred the matter to London. The response from FA secretary Fred Wall was that Australia could compete as one of four British nations invited to the tournament.

Meanwhile, Arthur Gibbs, who had been posted to the Colonial Mutual Society's office in London, was appointed as the CFA's representative to the FA. When Gibbs got a seat on the Football Council, the chances of hosting an English tour seemed a whole lot brighter.

A number of issues stood in the way of the FA sending a team to Australia. The FA were not prepared to lose money on a tour and insisted that all costs be borne by Australia. Another obstacle was the attitude of England's professional clubs. As the English football season lasted nearly nine months, a tour of three months duration would mean players being unavailable for crucial end of season and early season matches. Touring players missing out on an off-season break would likely return to their clubs jaded. Besides, the clubs didn't want their players risking injury on a tour they saw little value in. After all, Australia was good at cricket, not football.

In 1914, after the FA turned down yet another request from Australia to send a team out, an exasperated Stephen Lynch of the NSWFA said that "although the game is now permanently established in Australia, the required coping stone, in the shape of a visit from Britain, will thoroughly cement affairs, and put Australia in the forefront in the most universal game in the world."

The outbreak of the First World War put all international plans on hold. The 1916 Berlin Olympics would never take place. The 1915 CFA conference at Hobart was postponed from Easter to Christmas before being abandoned altogether. The coping stone would have to wait.

2
On The Cusp

17 September 1921, Sydney Cricket Ground No. 2

They were out to 'get' him. The Gardiner Cup semi-final featuring Sydney's two best supported teams, Granville and Pyrmont, was a chance to show who was top dog in Sydney football. The clubs had shared the honours in their two league matches and this cup tie would act as a decider. All eyes were on Alf Jennings, Granville's classy centre-forward - and the man Pyrmont were allegedly out to get.

Pyrmont fans had not forgotten Jennings running rings around them in their recent 4-2 league defeat. They felt Granville had an unfair advantage in fielding a new player so late in the season.

Tall and slender, 18-year-old Jennings was a fine footballing talent. An English schoolboy International, he had come under the scrutiny of several professional clubs in London before his family migrated to Australia. In Sydney, he began his football career at Second League club St George. *The St George Call* said Jennings "had more tricks than a conjurer".

Granville had secured his services mid-way through the season. With his accurate passing, clever footwork and goal-scoring prowess, he destroyed opposing defences. After one match where he scored a hat trick, the newspaper *Referee* said, "it was a treat to witness the ex-International English schoolboy dash through the thickest of tangles always with the ball".

As the semi-final began, some of the Pyrmont supporters jeered and taunted Jennings. Clearly ruffled, he was down on his form. Pyrmont took an early 2-0 lead before Granville clawed a goal back to go into the half-time break 2-1 down.

Jennings was a new man in the second half. He started to dominate the Pyrmont defence. His cracking shot just after the interval was parried by the Pyrmont keeper into the path of Henson who tapped it in to level the scores at 2-2.

It was Jennings who set up Henson's second goal to give Granville the lead. Jennings then helped himself to a goal. Granville went 5-2 up when Bill Dane scored from another Jennings assist.

On the stroke of full-time Jennings took off downfield with the ball at his toe. He beat one defender after another. He slotted the ball into the net past Pyrmont's onrushing goalkeeper James Cornwell. The pair collided and Jennings fell heavily to the ground. Granville fans claimed foul play by Cornwell and screamed their disapproval.

The trainers ran out to attend Jennings. They wasted no time carrying him to the dressing sheds. He lost consciousness and was rushed to Sydney Hospital.

Jennings' condition deteriorated. The family came to the hospital and kept a bedside vigil. Twelve hours later he opened his eyes. X-rays revealed a splintered vertebrae. It would keep him all but paralysed for a month. Fortunately, he recovered enough to leave hospital after a six-week stay. He told his friends he had no intention of giving up football.

NSW vs Australia, July 1922, after Australia's first international tour to New Zealand

In the ensuing court case, a jury found Cornwell guilty of common assault and ordered him to pay compensation to Jennings.

This was Australian club football in the 1920s. It was a mixture of playing styles, none of them pretty. Some teams opted for a short passing game while others favoured a kick-and-rush style where speed was the most valuable asset. Playing surfaces were often rutted, rock hard when dry, or mud heaps when wet. Skilful players like Alf Jennings were rare and could make all the difference to a team's performance. They also carried a target on their backs.

* * *

The First World War took a heavy toll on football and footballers. Competitions in Victoria, Western Australia and South Australia were suspended and those in the other states limped on with clubs struggling to field teams. Many players lost their lives on the battlefields of Gallipoli and the Western Front, and many more came back suffering physical and psychological trauma.

Judy Masters returned to Australia from active service in June 1919. He was soon running around the football pitch again for his beloved Balgownie Rangers. Like many Australian servicemen, Masters was astonished to see the hold football had over the common people in Britain. The Tommies were mad for the game and matches played near the battle zones on the Western Front were cheered on by scores of enthusiastic supporters. It was difficult for Australians to play against British units at any sport other than football.

With a post-war Australia likely to feature an influx of British migrants, there was a good chance they would bring this love of football with them. To the more diehard followers of the entrenched codes of Australian Rules and rugby league, football was viewed as a threat. Before long, particularly in the Australian Rules states of Victoria, South Australia and Western Australia, local councils were being called on to adjudicate on competing claims between the codes for access to playing fields.

* * *

Rugby league wasted no time in returning to international competition following the war and hosted a tour by Great Britain in 1920. Cricket followed with England contesting the Ashes in Australia during the summer of 1920/21. Football was slower to establish an international footprint.

The desire for international football was felt keenly in Australia. Supporters of the game noted that the 1920 Olympic Games featured teams from Europe, including Great Britain, and Egypt. When Norway knocked out tournament favourites Great Britain in one of the biggest upsets in world football, it made news in Australia. Local fans read with interest how the gold medal match was awarded to host nation Belgium after their Czechoslovakian opponents walked off the field in protest at a decision made by English referee John Lewis.

Interstate football made a comeback in 1920 with New South Wales and Queensland exchanging tours. Encouraging news arrived on the international front when England sent a team to tour South Africa in 1920. This led to a renewed focus on bringing an FA team to Australia. Football officials from New South Wales, Queensland and New Zealand banded together to invite an English team out in 1921 but the request fell on deaf ears.

Calls mounted for the reformation of the national association. Brisbane's *Daily Standard* said that "until the Commonwealth Football Association is again formed with a live and capable executive, there is simply no hope for the future of the game in Australia".

The CFA duly reformed at a meeting in Melbourne in August 1921. The delegates included some of the most famous names of early Australian football: Ernie Crawford and Harry Dockerty from Victoria; Wolfram Bellis from South Australia; Fred Barlow and Ern Lukeman from New South Wales; John Hildreth from Queensland and Jack Storr from Tasmania. Two office holders were elected: Harry Dockerty as president and Ern Lukeman as secretary and treasurer.

The CFA asked England to send a team to Australia in either 1923 or 1924. The CFA also agreed to a proposal to send a combined team from New South Wales and Queensland - playing as Australia - to tour New Zealand in 1922. Australia was on the cusp of an exciting new era of international football.

3
The International Era

6 May 1922, Wentworth Park, Sydney

All club matches had been cancelled. Players, spectators and selectors descended on Wentworth Park for two important trial matches. The formula for the New South Wales selectors was simple: choose eight players from the 44 on show to join the eight Queenslanders already selected for Australia's inaugural tour of New Zealand.

Much of the interest focused on the centre-forward position. It was likely only one would be selected and it would come down to a choice in three. From the South Coast it was Judy Masters, the experienced goal scorer from the Balgownie Rangers club. Bill 'Podge' Maunder from the West Wallsend club carried the hopes of the Newcastle district. The Sydney hopeful was Alf Jennings, the star forward from Granville, now fully recovered from his neck injury.

There were many other current and future stars of the sport on display. There was goalkeeper George Cartwright, halves Peter Doyle, Harry Spurway and Gil Storey, as well as the pint-sized outside left from the South Coast, Tom 'Titch' Thompson. Some well-known football personalities took their places on the reserve benches: Syd Storey, the newly installed acting secretary of the NSWFA, and Bondi Neal, the indigenous goalkeeper from the South Coast.

In the first game, South Coast were too good for the Sydney Metropolitan team, running out winners by 2-1. Masters and Thompson scored for the South Coast and set up each other's goal.

Newcastle beat their Metropolitan opponents 3-1. Maunder scored twice for Newcastle while Jennings scored for the opposition.

The selectors opted for Bill Maunder. Jennings and Masters could count themselves unlucky. *The Newcastle Sun* felt Jennings had been harshly treated: "The omission of Jennings is hard to understand. The clever Granville pivot would have been an excellent utility forward, as he can play equally well at inside right or left, in addition to the centre. Always a prolific goal-getter, his clever footwork and anticipation make him a favourite among keen judges."

25 July 1922, Circular Quay, Sydney

Crowds of well-wishers lined the wharf. One group fussed over a tall young man about to embark on a grand adventure. The group consisted of family, friends and football people. There were representatives from Granville and St George as well as officials from the NSWFA. The tall young man was 19-year-old Alf Jennings. Recently passed over for the New Zealand tour, one of the shining lights of Australian football took his leave and made his

Top Row (left to right).—D. Ward, J. B. Bryant, T. Thompson, W. McBride, W. Dane, G. Cartwright, D. Cumberford. Middle Row.—J. Cumberford, P. Doyle, A. Fisher (Vice-Capt.), A. Morgan (Manager), A. Gibb (Capt.), S. A. Storey (Assistant Manager), G. W. Brown. Front Row.—W. Maunder, C. Shenton, W. Bratton.

The first Australian team to New Zealand, 1922

farewells. Clutching a bag containing a silver boomerang gifted to him by the Granville football club, he made his way up the gangplank of the P&O liner *Orvieto*. Also in his suitcase was a signed contract to play professional football with English club Tottenham Hotspur. With him went the best wishes of the entire football community of Sydney.

* * *

Shortly before Australia sailed to New Zealand, Newcastle's Bob Henderson withdrew from the squad. Somewhat controversially, the man chosen to replace him was Syd Storey, who had only been on the bench at Wentworth Park. But there was a dual purpose in his selection. He could assist Alf Morgan of Queensland in managing the team, and as acting secretary of the NSWFA, he was well placed to sound out New Zealand about an English tour.

Australia received a bloody nose in New Zealand.

The match between Australia and New Zealand in Dunedin on 17 June 1922 was notable for a number of firsts. It was Australia's (and New Zealand's) first full International. Tough tackling right-half Alec Gibb from Ipswich in Queensland became Australia's first captain. Bill 'Podge' Maunder became Australia's first goal scorer. Being on the wrong end of a 3-1 scoreline, Australia also suffered its first international defeat.

Borrowing from cricketing terminology, the Australian press labelled the match a 'Test' match. It would become standard practice to refer to soccer matches played between Australia and any nation as a Test match. Although the term has long since gone out of fashion, it was still in common usage in Australia up to the 1950s.

Australia lost two of the three Tests with one being drawn. There were a few feeble excuses trotted out for the poor results: the fields were wet and slow; the weather was too cold. But the main gripe was the refereeing, in particular New Zealand's interpretation of the charging rule.

The Chinese team that visited Australia in 1923

The rule allowed for a defender to edge out an attacker with their shoulder even if not directly playing at the ball, provided the contact was not dangerous. In Australia, referees usually deemed any charging as dangerous and the practice was almost non-existent. New Zealand, however, followed the English FA's practice of tolerating such challenges. Storey believed Maunder's effectiveness was reduced because of the physical pounding he received from New Zealand's backs.

In Wellington, Storey met with his New Zealand counterparts to discuss the hoped-for English tour. New Zealand disagreed about the timing. They didn't want the Englishmen in 1923 as it would take the gloss off their own visit to Australia. Storey explained that 1924 wouldn't work as it clashed with the Great Britain rugby league tour. The two sides did agree that an English tour was essential and they would continue to work towards making it happen.

Even if New Zealand had consented to an English tour in 1923, a letter from FA secretary Fred Wall to Ern Lukeman of the CFA in Sydney dashed any hopes. Wall wrote: "I may assure you that it will be as great a disappointment to ourselves as to our Colonial friends if we are unable to send a representative team to our Australasian colonies. [but] … the difficulties in the way of arranging the tour were insurmountable."

New Zealand's 1923 tour of Australia confirmed the potential of international football. A record Australian crowd of 10,000 witnessed the first tour match in Sydney. Good crowds watched the matches in New South Wales and Queensland. On the pitch, New Zealand proved too good, winning the Test series by two matches to one. The final Test of the tour in Newcastle was notable in marking the international debut of Judy Masters.

After the first Test, the ashes of cigars smoked by the captains of each team, Alec Gibb (Australia) and George Campbell (New Zealand), were placed in a razor case that had been carried ashore at Gallipoli by Queensland footballer William Fisher. The razor case was housed in a small wooden casket and – with a nod to cricket's Ashes series – became known as the 'Soccer Ashes'. The trophy was to be contested every time Australia and New Zealand met on the football field.

Suddenly there was a glut of international football. The Chinese team that represented their country at the Far East Asian Games in 1921 arrived in Australia in August 1923 just as the New Zealanders were finishing their tour.

When the Chinese team ran out onto the Sydney Show Ground to play New South Wales in front of a record-shattering attendance of 40,000, football supporters were over the moon. The size of the crowd came to the notice of the FA in London, proving that big gates were possible in Australia. At the end of the Chinese visit the financial backers of the tour realized a healthy profit. That some of the people making money from the tour were football officials was a point not lost on the players who were paid expenses only.

Australia won the six-match series against China 4-1 with one of the games being drawn. The Chinese played an entertaining brand of football. The matches were spread around the country with well-patronised games being played in Victoria and South Australia. The tour was a watershed moment for Judy Masters, who made his Australian captaincy debut and scored seven goals in his three appearances.

The success of the Chinese tour made some Australian Rules and rugby league people nervous. Football's international dimension had brought home the threat that it could pose to their sport. The idea of locking football out of the best venues took hold in certain circles.

* * *

On 9 April, 1924, the wonder of the age, the battle cruiser *HMS Hood*, glided into Sydney Harbour with hundreds of thousands of people watching from the foreshore. Following closely behind was the battle cruiser *HMS Repulse* along with five light cruisers of the Royal Navy's Special Service Squadron. The ships were visiting Australia as part of a ten-month world cruise, showing that Britain was still capable of projecting power across the globe.

As was usual with visiting British warships, the squadron fielded a number of good football teams. A few weeks before, a squadron team had drawn 2-2 with Victoria in Melbourne. The crews were looking forward to playing matches in Sydney where the standard of football was rumoured to be higher.

On Saturday, 12 April, nearly 10,000 people jammed into Wentworth Park to see a match between Sydney's finest players and the squadron's top team. Sydney won an exciting game 4-2 after trailing early.

On the same day at Woonona, near Wollongong, the squadron's B team was handed a 9-0 thrashing by Illawarra, Judy Masters accounting for five of the goals.

Also on the same day, a solemn ceremony was enacted in the waters off Sydney. In the morning, tugboats towed the Royal Australian Navy's (RAN) first flagship, *HMAS Australia*, down the harbour on its final journey. The ship was being scrapped as part of the naval disarmament treaty of the Washington Conference (1922).

Four cruisers from the visiting Special Service Squadron joined Australian warships to escort the *Australia* out to sea. The event received intense media coverage and a description of the scuttling was broadcast live on radio from one of the escort vessels. Accompanied by a booming 21-gun salute, the *Australia* rolled over and sank at 2:51pm.

Not every part of *HMAS Australia* ended up on the seabed. Many of the brass fittings and internal timbers had been removed and crafted into souvenirs. Some of the teak decking was purchased by Sir Samuel Hordern, director of the sprawling Anthony Hordern and Sons Emporium on George Street. The teak was fashioned into a flagpole and adorned with an Australian flag. It was destined to end up in the offices of the Football Association in London.

* * *

The CFA continued with their attempts to convince England to tour, requesting the FA make a 'supreme effort' to send a team out in 1924. The response was: we can't go in an Olympic year, there are far too many hurdles, insurmountable difficulties. Frustrated, Ern Lukeman sent a message to the Canadians agreeing to their request to visit Australia.

It was a tall order to sell the Canadian tour to the public. Most sports fans in New South Wales and Queensland had saved up their hard-earned cash to watch Great Britain's rugby league tour at the same time. The Australia vs Great Britain rugby league Tests proved hugely popular, drawing crowds of 50,000 and 40,000 in Sydney, and 40,000 in Brisbane.

The Canadian footballers played a competitive and somewhat aggressive style. Despite drawing a crowd of 20,000 for the first game, attendances dropped off alarmingly. When the Test series finished tied at 2-2 (with one drawn) a decider was hastily organised in an attempt to get the turnstiles clicking.

It was a rather gloomy Ern Lukeman who received a telegram a few days out from the sixth Test match. More than likely it would be bad news about the mounting costs of the Canadian tour. But the telegram was from Arthur Gibbs in London. They were always of interest. Lukeman read it. He put it down. Rubbed his eyes. He picked up the telegram and read it again. He could barely believe it. England was offering to send a team to Australia in 1925.

4
Rushing For The Post

That the tour would actually take place was not set in stone. Australia had to meet stringent financial conditions before the FA would formally sign off on the enterprise. The entire cost had to be borne by Australia, which included raising a substantial guarantee and paying for first-class steamship fares for a 23-man party prior to the team leaving England.

The CFA's initial itinerary was for England to arrive in Western Australia, make their way eastwards around Australia before heading to New Zealand and returning to England via a short tour of Canada. New Zealand wasn't keen on a three-country tour as the Canadian leg would curtail England's time in New Zealand. It was the FA themselves that scotched this idea, cabling that they had no intention of touring Canada.

In London, the FA presented a silver trophy to Arthur Gibbs for competition between the Australian states. Gibbs described it as one of the great moments of his life. He forwarded it to the CFA where it was put on public display at Prouds the Jewellers in King Street, Sydney.

The arrangements for the English tour were the main item for discussion when the CFA met in Sydney in late December 1924. Syd Storey chaired the meeting, described by the *Evening News* as "the most important meeting in the annals of soccer history in Australia".

Delegates arriving at the Sports Club in Hunter Street might have felt compelled to genuflect in front of the FA trophy, set up like a shrine at one end the room. Besides Storey, attendees included Ern Lukeman and Stephen Stack from New South Wales, John Hildreth from Queensland and Harry Dockerty from Victoria.

Stephen Stack

The finances for the Canadian tour were sobering. The tour posted a loss of £343. The CFA asked England if they could travel second class on the voyage to Australia so as to save £1,500. The FA refused. More concerning was that after a lot of soul searching, New Zealand pulled out of the tour.

Lukeman cabled the news to London of New Zealand's withdrawal. Without New Zealand on the itinerary, he was worried the FA might cancel the whole venture. It was a nervous wait for a reply. When it came, on 30 December, the news was good: "Happy to tour Australia only."

A torrent of telegrams passed between Sydney and London. One compromise the FA did make was to reduce the size of the touring party from 23 to 21. The squad, consisting of 18 players and three officials, was to leave London on board the P&O liner *Orsova* on 4 April, arriving at Fremantle, Western Australia on 5 May. The tour was scheduled to take three months. The guarantee Australia needed to raise was set at £8,500 and the CFA dictated the amounts each state's football association must raise as follows:

New South Wales	£4,000
Queensland	£1,800
Victoria	£1,200
South Australia	£1,000
Western Australia	£500

Tasmania was left off the tour as they were reluctant to raise a guarantee. Cheekily, but rather pertinently, they posed the question: If the FA was so keen to spread the football gospel to Australia why didn't they fund it themselves?

Determined not to repeat the mistakes of the Canadian visit, the CFA formed a six-man standing committee to control the tour, consisting of Dockerty, Hildreth and four members from New South Wales. Regular meetings were held in Sydney to sort out any problems that might arise. A selection panel for the Australian Test team was created with the four members coming from different states.

A key role for CFA was a tour manager who would escort the English team around the country. The manager would communicate with the football associations in each state about finances, selections and advertising of the games. They would need to resolve any disagreements with the tourists and not be afraid to raise concerns of their own. The person should be ambitious, be an experienced football administrator, and considering the amount of work and travel involved, the role would suit a younger person. Syd Storey was seemingly born to take it on. The 28-year-old accepted the offer immediately and secured time off work for most of the duration of the tour.

Officials in each state began to raise their share of the guarantee and organise the staging of the matches. They immediately hit a hurdle when trying to access venues. The major tenant of the best enclosed grounds in each state were the popular football codes of Australian Rules or rugby league. And not all of them were eager to lend a hand to a sport that appeared to be on the rise.

In Queensland, football had a good relationship with rugby league and the two codes had helped each other with grounds in the past. The Queensland Rugby League happily gave up the Exhibition Ground in Brisbane for football on two consecutive Saturdays. In Victoria, football authorities met with mixed success. They secured the Melbourne Cricket Ground (MCG) for two matches early in the tour, including one on a Saturday, but were denied use of the venue later on. An interstate Australian Rules match scheduled for the MCG meant that the fifth Test would be played at the Brunswick Street ground in Fitzroy.

Australian Rules associations in Western Australia and South Australia were reluctant to give up their grounds. In Sydney, the New South Wales Rugby League flatly refused to allow football to be played on the Sydney Cricket Ground. Syd Storey and Ern Lukeman could only hope that public pressure might yet bring about a change of heart.

* * *

Australian football fans waited impatiently for any news about the English squad. The first person named in connection with the tour was the manager, John Lewis. He was known in Australia as a respected authority on the laws of the game. He'd occasionally been quoted in newspapers and sports journals on the subject of refereeing and rule interpretations. Apart from once being called the 'Prince of Referees' his straight-talking manner also earned him the nickname 'Honest John'.

English football clubs were lukewarm about sending their players to the other side of the world. Each club was asked to nominate a few players who could take part, giving the selectors a reasonable-sized pool to choose from. Initially, only a trickle of names arrived at the offices of the FA. One of the first was Alf Jennings, currently playing for Tottenham's reserves in the London Combination. He was in good form having twice scored four goals in a match but had yet to force his way into the first team.

The clubs did have an excuse in the early stages of the season. The FA didn't expect clubs in the race for titles, chasing promotion, facing relegation battles or on long cup runs to nominate players. But as the season wore on, the response was underwhelming.

The attitude of the clubs was viewed with concern in Australia and parts of the English press. 'Sentinel', writing in the Newcastle (UK) paper the *Evening Chronicle,* speculated that only amateurs or players nearing retirement would be nominated. Clubs didn't want their best players injured or worn out after a long tour that would see footballers playing nearly two years straight without a rest. Sentinel opined: "It will surprise many people if the playing strength of the tourists is at all representative of England's best."

Australia's senior football officials in Sydney, January 1924

CE Sutcliffe writing in the *Tropical Times* (UK) supported the tour and made a patriotic call to the clubs. During the war, Australia had sent its best men to fight on the battlefield to help the British cause and it was the least the English clubs could do to send out a good team. Of the clubs he asked, "Are they even in the least degree less grateful to the country that stood by us when battle was thickest? We cried, 'send us more men' - and so they came. Now they ask for a mere eighteen or twenty, who shall go, not to the risk of their lives, but to help in popularising the game of which they have many experts."

In Australia, anticipation was building with each passing milestone. In February, the CFA paid the steamship fares for the 21-man touring party. Next, they sent a £3,000 cheque to the FA as part of the tour guarantee. A second name was added to the touring party, that of Mark Frowde, who was appointed assistant manager to Lewis. Frowde, a 54-year-old shipping company executive from Weymouth, played a leading role in establishing football in the county of Dorset. A representative of the amateur side of the game, he was, like Lewis, a vice-president of the FA. Frowde would prove a good foil for the abrasive Lewis. Tactful and convivial, Frowde would look after much of the day-to-day organisation while leaving Lewis to do most of the talking.

The trio of non-playing members of the squad was complete when Moses 'Mo' Atherton, trainer and groundsman for Lewis' Blackburn Rovers club, was chosen as the team's fitness trainer.

When the FA representatives met to select the team, they had a list of just over 100 names to choose from. In early March 1925, the squad was announced. Some of the players chosen were unaware their club had even nominated them. Subsequently four players, Bobby Turnbull and Alf Quantrill of Bradford Park Avenue, Harry Storer of Derby County, and Dick Forshaw of Liverpool withdrew from the tour. Last-minute replacements were organised and the squad was finalised on 21 March.

Ivan Sharpe, an editor with Manchester's *Athletic News* quickly put together some biographical notes on the players and sent it to his Australian contact, Alec Boyd from Sydney's *Referee* newspaper. Aware of Australia's hunger for news on the team, Sharpe's typewritten note hums with energy:

"I am rushing you off today some comment on the team to visit Australia as promised. I think you will have all you require. I am sure you will forgive a hurried note, as I am rushing for the post."

5
A Capable Party of Players

The English Team to Australia, 1925

The 18-man playing squad consisted of two goalkeepers, three fullbacks, six halfbacks and seven forwards.

TOP ROW.—J. Davison. W. Caesar. W. Sage. J. Elkes. C. Poynton. — Atherton (Trainer).
SECOND ROW.—H. G. Batten. C. Hannaford. L. Graham. C. W. Spencer. S. Charlton. T. J. Whittaker. S. Seymour.
THIRD ROW.—J. Hamilton. J. Hannah. E. Simms. W. Williams. J. Walsh.

The England touring party in playing kit

Goalkeepers

Both keepers had international experience. Thirty-year-old Harry Hardy, Stockport County's regular keeper since 1919, played for England in an FA Friendly against Belgium in 1924 that ended in a 4-1 victory for the hosts, played at West Bromwich Albion's ground. At 177cm, Hardy was rather short for a keeper. The team's other goalkeeper, John 'Teddy' Davison was even shorter - at just 170cm he was (and still is, as of 2024) the shortest goalkeeper to ever play for England. Davison's one England cap was against Wales in 1922. Vastly experienced, he had been at Sheffield Wednesday for 17 years and at the age of 37 was the veteran of the squad.

Fullbacks

Stan Charlton was a 24-year-old first team regular at Division 3 (South) club Exeter City. Tottenham's Cecil Poynton was a pacy left-back with flaming red hair. Rounding out the trio was Arsenal's recent convert to the fullback position, Tom Whittaker.

Halfbacks

Charlie Spencer was the provider for Newcastle United's first goal of the 1924 FA Cup Final. At 25 years of age, he was at the top of his game and one of the star players in the squad. He gained his first international cap in 1924 against Scotland and a second against Wales just a few weeks before being selected for the Australian tour.

Joe Hannah played fullback and halfback for Norwich City, a club he would eventually rack up over 400 appearances for.

Len Graham, captain of Millwall, was a classy left-half as well as being a handy batsman for Essex County Cricket Club. He made his international England debut against Wales in February 1925.

Billy 'Julius' Caesar was the team's only amateur player. He played for Dulwich Hamlet and gained an amateur international cap against the touring South Africans in 1924. A civil servant, the cheery Billy Caesar was a popular member of the squad. Not a fitness disciple like some of the professionals, Caesar was the heaviest member of the team.

Jimmy Hamilton was an up and coming player at Crystal Palace. At just 21 he was one of the youngest players in the squad.

Goalkeepers

Fullbacks

Harry Hardy (SN)

John Davison (SN)

Stan Charlton

Cecil Poynton

Halfbacks

Charlie Spencer (SN)

Joe Hannah

Len Graham (SN)

Billy Caesar (SN)

Jimmy Hamilton (SN)

Bill Sage

Forwards

Stan Seymour

Jack Elkes (SN)

Billy Williams (SN)

Ernie Simms

Charlie Hannaford (SN)

Bert Batten (SN)

Jimmy Walsh

Rushed into the team after Turnbull's withdrawal was Billy 'Sapper' Sage of Tottenham Hotspur who had toured South Africa under John Lewis in 1920. He was known as a workhorse (although some unkind pundits referred to him as a cart horse).

Forwards

Stan Seymour, Newcastle United's outside left, was playing some of the best football of his career. He could land crosses on a penny and score goals as well. He scored Newcastle's second goal in their 1924 FA Cup Final triumph over Aston Villa at Wembley. Known as one of the best outside lefts in England, he had played one war-time international in 1918.

John (Jack) Elkes from Tottenham Hotspur, was a specialist inside left. Tall, gangly and with a strange but effective dribbling technique, he was bound to entertain Australian audiences.

Nineteen-year-old William 'Billy' Williams was the baby of the team. An England schoolboy International, in 1921 he became West Ham's youngest ever signing, aged only 15. He had been in and out of West Ham's first team during the 1924/25 season, scoring four goals in 21 appearances. Away from football Williams was a talented singer.

Ernie Simms of Stockport County initially made his name as a centre-forward for Luton Town, scoring 109 goals in 160 matches. He sustained a leg wound during the First World War but resumed his football career for Luton. In gaining his first international cap against Northern Ireland in 1921, he became the first player from a Third Division club to play for England.

Charlie Hannaford was an outside right for Second Division club Clapton Orient. He was another schoolboy International.

Bert Batten was another who joined the team as a last-minute replacement. He was centre-forward for Third Division (South) club Plymouth Argyle. He possessed strength and speed and a hunger for scoring goals.

Liverpool's Jimmy Walsh was a young player with a big reputation. He was Liverpool's leading scorer in 1923/24 with 19 goals but in the current season had been plagued by injuries. At only 23 years of age, the tour was expected to be a valuable learning experience.

* * *

This was nowhere near England's best team. Nobody with any real knowledge of English football expected it would be otherwise. The squad drew plenty of criticism in England and Australia. England's *The Daily Chronicle* described the team "as unequal to present day Third League teams", and was "no compliment to Australia". Many critics were disappointed by the attitude of the English clubs. A letter writer known as 'Another Laddie' wrote to Sydney's *Evening News* pointing out that there were no players at all from famous clubs such as Aston Villa, West Bromwich Albion, Sunderland or Manchester City.

There were some positives about the team, however. First Division players accounted for the biggest contingent, with eight, ahead of the Second Division's five and the Third Division's four. There was only one amateur in the team, not the four or five anticipated. The players were not all ready to be put out to pasture, the average age being around 26, with just four of the tourists being over the age of 30. In Seymour, Elkes, Graham, Spencer and Hardy there was a core of quality players.

English sports writer James Catton, aka 'Tityrus' of the *Athletic News,* put a positive spin on the team. He told Alec Boyd in Sydney, "they are not a lot of old crocks on their last legs, and about to be stowed away on a shelf in a collection of damaged goods and has beens". He went on to say: "The Football Association have done their utmost to send out a capable party of players in order to show the possibilities of the code and to help in the popularisation of the game throughout the breadth of your continent."

London's *Sporting Life* made a similar observation: "With a couple of international goalkeepers, three hard working backs, a fine set of middle-line players, and an exceptionally strong attack, we expect them to return undefeated."

* * *

The Englishmen were at least going to look the goods. The players were each forwarded £50 to buy dress suits and in doing so would become one of the smartest dressed sporting teams to visit Australia. On Saturday 4 April, the dapper looking squad assembled at London's King's Cross St Pancras station. From there they caught the train to Tilbury docks on the Thames, where the P&O liner *Orsova* lay at anchor.

Before embarking, John Lewis answered questions from reporters. He was disappointed that more clubs didn't release players for selection. Drawn on what he expected to encounter in Australia he said he had no idea of the standard of play but hoped the visit would be educational for their hosts. When quizzed on who would captain the team, he said a different player would be selected for each match.

At 3pm, the *Orsova* sailed with 19 members of the touring party on board. At the precise moment the team departed, two players were over 500 kilometres away at one of the most intimidating cauldrons in world football. Millwall's Len Graham and Tottenham's Jack Elkes were both at Hampden Park in Glasgow for England's annual match against Scotland. Graham played left-half, while Elkes was a reserve. The 100,000 noisy fans went home in delirium after Hugh Gallacher scored both goals in Scotland's 2-0 victory.

After the game, Elkes and Graham hotfooted it south and crossed the English Channel by ferry. They travelled through France by train, reaching Toulon in time to catch up with the *Orsova*. Their teammates looked a little worse for wear after their rough sea voyage. Stan Charlton had never missed a meal but the rest of the team had been seasick. Most of Liverpool's Jimmy Walsh's meals ended up regurgitated in the Bay of Biscay.

The *Orsova* sailed down the Mediterranean and through the Suez Canal before making landfall in Colombo. The players had a game of cricket against the ship's crew, their only meaningful exercise on the trip. It was while at Colombo that Lewis received a cable from Western Australia asking if England could squeeze in an extra match in Perth two days before their originally scheduled tour opener. Lewis was open to the idea. The players needed some game time in their legs. He cabled back in the affirmative. England would now open their tour on Thursday 7 May, just two days after stepping off the boat.

After leaving Colombo, the ship was buffeted by rough seas. The heat was stifling. Walsh still suffered from seasickness and had lost about six kilograms. In the Indian Ocean, the *Orsova* passed the liner *Maloja* sailing in the opposite direction carrying the English cricket team on their way back from Australia after they'd suffered a 4-1 defeat in the Ashes. Lewis sent a marconigram in welcome. Arthur Gilligan, the English cricket captain, replied: "Many thanks, hope you have better luck than we. Gilligan."

Before dawn on Tuesday 5 May, the *Orsova* steamed through rolling seas under steel grey skies. Passengers up early, including many of the English footballers, strained their eyes eastward towards the dark land mass that was the Western Australian coast.

Lights were spotted on the shore. Fremantle. Rain began to tumble down. The English football team had arrived Down Under.

Part II
From Fremantle To Bundaberg

6

More British than the People in Britain

Tuesday, 5 May 1925, Fremantle, Western Australia

Syd Storey stands on Fremantle Wharf peering westwards into the pre-dawn darkness. The now 29-year-old football administrator from Sydney, dressed in a suit and sporting his trademark bow tie, is not alone. Around him, a crowd of Perth's football players and supporters are also eagerly scanning the grey horizon for any sign of the P&O liner *Orsova*.

Despite the inclement weather and early hour, the crowd are here as witnesses to history. Their hope is that football's many ills in Australia can be put right by this tour. Once Australians see football as it should be played, there will be no stopping the growth of the game. In their minds, these English players that have journeyed over 20,000 kilometres promise to be the sport's deliverance.

Then someone shouts from the wharf: "There she is!"

A ripple of excitement goes through the gathering. The golden glow of the *Orsova's* cabin lights can be seen through the grey gloom.

The rain begins to fall in buckets. Nobody gives a damn.

* * *

Storey had done a considerable amount of travelling himself. He'd left Sydney by train on 26 April, and after meeting with South Australian football officials in Adelaide, checked in to the King Edward Hostel in Perth on 1 May. It was an interesting time to be a traveller in Western Australia as unions representing hotel workers and bar staff had been taking industrial action. The hotels were kept running by family members of proprietors and sometimes by the guests themselves.

Almost as soon as John Lewis set foot on Australian soil, Storey was in his ear about a pressing issue. It concerned the very first of the official 'Laws of the Game', in particular, the use of substitutes in non-competitive matches. The part of Law One in question was:

"By arrangement made before the commencement of a match (but not in a match played under the Rules of a Competition) substitutes may be allowed in place of injured players."

In Australia for the past few years, arrangements had been made with touring teams to allow for the substitution of injured players. The practice had become so commonplace that substitutes were even permitted in competitive matches in New South Wales. Referees haphazardly enforced the rules. In some instances referees had allowed players to be replaced and let them back on the field again after receiving treatment.

For Storey, the use of substitutes was critical to the success of the tour. He argued that professionally trained English players would be better able to absorb knocks and it would be the amateur Australians who were more likely to get injured. Without substitutes, Australian teams playing a man down would have no chance to compete against their more experienced opponents. Too many mismatched games would adversely affect gate takings.

Lewis, weary after the long voyage, was taken aback by Storey's abrupt request. The two had a sharp discussion. Their exchange went something like this:

LEWIS: Why didn't Australia cable the FA before the team sailed?

STOREY: We didn't expect the FA would agree.

LEWIS: And you thought I would agree to it against the FA's wishes?

STOREY: But you have to understand local conditions. Football is a minor sport here. If the public thinks England are getting an unfair advantage by playing against depleted Australian teams, they will call it bad sportsmanship and stop patronising the matches.

LEWIS: No. Law One only applies to charity matches and the like. These games are not mere exhibitions. I will absolutely not allow substitutes in any of the matches!

As Law One required the agreement of both teams, there was little Storey could do about it. It was a long tour and there was still time to impress upon Lewis the importance of allowing substitutes. But as Australia would find out, John Lewis was not a man to change his mind once it was made up.

***

The English team were ferried down the Swan River on board the launch *Dauntless*. The easterly wind blew the clouds away and the water shimmered diamond-like in the sunlight. The players were enchanted by the beauty of the river and the city of Perth.

After disembarking they were paraded before the press. In their dress suits and overcoats, they made a fine impression. All the players were in good shape except Jimmy Walsh, who had a miserable voyage. The players were described as 'nuggety', 'fit', 'intelligent', and, 'a hefty bunch of fellows'. One by one they were weighed like prized cattle. Billy Caesar, the only amateur in the squad, tipped the scales at 90 kilograms. What the press couldn't do was get the players to talk.

One of the Englishmen took out a penny from his pocket. He dropped it, caught it with his foot and flicked it to a teammate who in turn kicked it to a colleague. Soon the players were nonchalantly tapping the coin to each other while keeping it off the ground. It was a neat trick. It caught the pressmen's attention. The players were evidently going to let their feet do the talking.

The tourists headed to Claremont after lunch to practice. They turned out in full kit for the hour-long session. The kit, which they would wear in every game, was a white shirt featuring a badge on the left breast with three lions surmounted by a crown, and navy shorts. Each player's club colours were sewn into the tops of their navy socks.

Newspapers from the eastern states had begged for photographs and the local press were busy getting them done. One of the photos, reproduced in papers around the country and showing all members of the touring party in their playing kit, was from this training session.

On the dry surface at Claremont, the Englishmen struggled to control the light ball yet their skill was undeniable. Stan Seymour, the Newcastle United outside left, pumped cross after cross from the sidelines into the goalmouth with mechanical precision. Syd Storey could hardly keep the grin off his face. "They're the goods, alright," he said.

***

The Perth Literary Institute was bursting at the seams for the first official reception of the tour. Western Australia's acting Premier, William Angwin, welcomed the Englishmen to the city and told them not to be offended if they were called "Pommies… it is a harmless and friendly term. Mr Lewis will find that Australians are even more British than the people in Britain and that the team will get a real welcome everywhere."

Billy Orr, the secretary of the local Australian Rules body, the Western Australian Football League (WAFL), was invited to speak. Being the chief architect of the opposition to football being played on Perth's premier venue, Subiaco Oval, there was an awkward moment as he mounted the podium. His speech was conciliatory, welcoming the team as worthy representatives of English sport. He urged all Australians to make them feel welcome.

When John Lewis got up to speak, he had to wait while the crowd performed a rendition of 'For He's a Jolly Good Fellow', followed by three boisterous cheers. Lewis seemed genuinely surprised at the enthusiasm of his hosts.

Not a born orator, Lewis rattled off details about the strength of football in England. There were 750,000 registered players; 88 professional clubs in three divisions and 22,000 clubs overall; 7,000 full-time professional players earned up to £8 per week. The FA brought in so much revenue that it paid one million pounds per year in entertainment tax. The subtle message was, that if you were serious about your football, then soccer should be your code of choice.

Lewis then presented specially made badges to Angwin, Storey, and some of the Western Australian football officials. The badges, made of enamel and predominantly blue in colour, featured the crest of the Football Association with a crown on top. The little blue enamel badges would become treasured keepsakes in Australia.

* * *

The hotel workers' strike was still in full swing when England prepared to leave the King Edward Hostel for the opening match of the tour. The strikers, led by formidable trade unionist Cecelia Shelley, had blacklisted venues employing non-union labour by pasting sheets over the walls and doors of offending establishments. In one case a proprietor opened the door of her hotel only to have a sheet pasted across the front of her dress.

Outside the King Edward Hostel, incidentally a venue not blacklisted, an intimidating all-male mob tried to force their way in. The English players waited in the foyer, unable to leave. Mr Bannon, the proprietor, decided to take matters into his own hands. Retrieving a pistol from his office, he strode out the front door and levelled the weapon at the crowd, crying out, "Don't come any further!"

The strikers wisely backed off. Bannon later told the press that the English footballers "were quite prepared to act if the necessity arose". Whether John Lewis and Mark Frowde would have allowed their players to get involved in any public fracas was highly doubtful.

Thursday, 7 May 1925, Match 1: England v Perth Metropolitan XI, Subiaco Oval

England and Perth run out onto the muddy field to warm applause. A hasty compromise with the WAFL has allowed this midweek fixture to be played at Subiaco Oval. England are in white, while Perth play in maroon.

Ernie Simms, the Stockport County centre-forward, is given the honour of captaining England for the first game of the tour. He wins the toss, choosing to run towards the Subiaco end. Constant rain has made the pitch greasy. The conditions are more suited to England and go some way to offset their lack of match practice.

As the teams line up, spectators remark on the hefty appearance of the English players. Billy Caesar is the beefiest of the lot. One spectator says: "Australians are not used to seeing the real Englishman out here. But these men, how they satisfy the eye."

England start cautiously, trying to find their feet after such a long time at sea. After just two minutes, Bert Batten, the Plymouth Argyle forward, slams a shot against the crossbar that rattles the whole frame of the goal. This is what the crowd has come to see.

Charlie Hannaford, the Clapton Orient left-half, sends in a neat cross and Ernie Simms heads in England's opening goal of the tour. It has taken the tourists all of five minutes to draw first blood.

The crowd takes a liking to Jack Elkes. At over 183cm tall and weighing around 90 kg,-he has an awkward running style, appearing almost clumsy, but he beats men with ease using a kit bag full of swerves and feints. One spectator says that Elkes "has such rhythm and swing of the body, that he would make a wonderful player under Australian Rules".

Hannaford, the provider for the first goal, centres into the box and the chunky Caesar heads in England's second. The fans are getting a master class in the technique of heading the ball.

As another heavy shower begins, Elkes takes possession and dances through a clutch of defenders. He executes a one-two with Batten before back-heeling to Simms who steers home England's third goal.

The crowd applaud when Elkes himself scores England's fourth with a booming left foot drive. As the teams leave the field at half-time with England 4-0 up, the crowd can hardly complain of a lack of entertainment.

England's passing game gets better after the interval. Ten minutes into the second half, Simms completes his hat trick by heading in another arrow-like cross from Hannaford.

Shortly after, Simms collides with Perth goalkeeper, Alex 'Sandy' Marr. On the touchline, Syd Storey leaps to his feet, his mind going over Law One. Slowly, Marr gets up and the game continues.

Jimmy Hamilton, the Crystal Palace centre-half, puts in a neat run and passes to Elkes, who with another smart piece of footwork sets up Simms for his fourth goal and England's sixth.

Towards the end of the game, an incident occurs which would again try relations between the two football codes when players from the Subiaco (Australian Rules) Football Club begin their training routine in the area between the sideline and the boundary fence.

With the Australian Rules players hand passing and kicking to each other on the sidelines, Elkes sets outs once more on another bamboozling run and plays the ball into a dangerous position. Fine interplay between the forwards sees Bill Sage slam home a perfectly crafted team goal.

Finally, an England breakaway ends with the ball at Simms' feet. He slots it past Marr to make it 8-0 for England and take his personal tally that day to five goals.

* * *

It was a fine opening to the tour by England. Their superb ball control, short passing game and brilliant exhibition of heading enraptured the crowd. Many people new to the sport were surprised the British version of football could be so entertaining. As one spectator commented after the game: "I say without hesitation, that soccer is a finer game of football, than is even our own national game."

7
Law One

The Australian Rules practice session rekindled the war of words between Australian Rules and soccer. One spectator, 'Sportsman', wrote to *The West Australian* saying that the practice "was disconcerting to a degree and savoured of extremely bad manners ... this display of discourtesy, coupled with the veiled hostility evidenced on every hand by the [Australian Rules] League to our visitors, especially in the manner of grounds, should impel every follower of football to forsake their usual games today and see a demonstration of football of another code at the Fremantle Oval."

The Australian Rules supporters contested this, saying that the practice had been permitted as part of the compromise that allowed the match to be played at Subiaco Oval, something that John Lewis publicly acknowledged.

The tourists spent Friday taking in the sights around Perth. They were given a tour of Parliament House and in the afternoon were driven to a vineyard on the upper reaches of the Swan River. The players were encouraged to eat as many red grapes off the vine as they wanted.

Football supporters turned their thoughts towards the game on Saturday featuring Western Australia's best eleven. General admission for the match was one and sixpence, higher than the one shilling charged for Australian Rules club games. Western Australian football officials were worried that the high cost of tickets could affect the attendance. Advertisements for the game were almost apologetic about the prices:

'Owing to enormous expense involved in the tour, prices of admission will be...'

It was, however, stressed that patrons would be watching:

'THE FLOWER OF ENGLAND'S SOCCER PLAYERS'

The big game was played at Fremantle Oval since the WAFL refused to let soccer be played at Subiaco Oval on a Saturday even though there were enough playing fields to accommodate a full round of Australian Rules club fixtures. Western Australian soccer officials also had their request for local Australian Rules matches to be suspended for the weekend turned down. Billy Orr of the WAFL said his organisation "were not there to foster the soccer code".

For the match against Western Australia, John Lewis included six players rested for the first game. The other player, Jimmy Walsh, was still sick from the sea voyage. Turning out for their second match in three days were Charlton, Elkes, Hannaford, Hannah and Simms. Charlie Spencer of Newcastle United would play centre-half and captain the side.

Among the leading players for Western Australia were brothers Jimmy and Andrew Gordon from the Casuals club, who both scored in an early season fixture against the touring English cricketers. The promising right half, Harold Boys of Claremont, the only Australian born player in the team, was also hoping for a big game. An extra incentive for the locals was the chance to earn selection in the Australian XI team to play England in Adelaide the following week.

The weather that coming Saturday was perfect. There would be no rain excuse to keep crowds away. An hour before kickoff, both teams attended a civic reception at the Fremantle Town Hall. If the late hour had Syd Storey on edge, his demeanour must have lightened considerably when he stepped outside.

People were hurrying to Fremantle Oval by trams, buses, motor cars - and on foot. When Storey entered the arena, filling fast with spectators, he would have been far more comfortable with his decision to charge high ticket prices. For a moment, he could afford to put his concerns about Law One out of his mind.

* * *

Saturday, May 9 1925, Match 2: England v Western Australia, Fremantle Oval

Western Australia, in dark green jerseys with a gold swan monogram on their chest, walk out first onto Fremantle Oval to warm applause. England come out next to a thunderous ovation from the big crowd. Dick Utting, the Western Australian captain wins the toss and elects to run to the Hospital end with the wind at their backs.

Ernie Simms kicks off for England and the second tour match is underway.

The dry surface has England wary. The light ball proves difficult to control. Stan Seymour takes the first shot of the match, forcing a good save from Western Australian goalkeeper Boland. For the next few minutes, England hammer the goal and force a succession of corners. Jack Elkes and Ernie Simms come close with headers but the locals' defence holds firm. Elkes dazzles the crowd with his unorthodox footwork. Every skilful move of the Englishmen is greeted with applause.

Western Australia's defence works hard and holds up well. Harold Boys stops one English attack and sets his team on the counter. Stan Charlton, the right back from Exeter City is able to stop the move and set England underway again. England's clever use of the three-man offside rule, allowing one fullback to patrol behind the other, helps snuff out many of the attacks by the locals.

Elkes comes close for England, his shot thundering against the crossbar. The ball rebounds to West Ham's Billy Williams whose follow up shot is saved brilliantly by Western Australian keeper Boland.

The programme for the second match between England and Western Australia

Boland is called into action again when Elkes puts Simms through on goal. Boland dives at the attacker's feet and they collide. Syd Storey watches on with dread as the trainer runs onto the field. After treatment, Boland gets back to his feet and the game continues.

Just before half-time, Western Australian fullback Boys inadvertently plays the ball to Billy Williams, who taps it in to give England a 1-0 lead. At half-time, the spectators give the local team a great ovation for their heroic defensive play.

Shortly into the second half Elkes receives a pass from Simms, dummies to shoot, then passes to Williams just as a defender closes in. Williams scores from close range to make it 2-0 to England.

The second goal spurs Western Australia to play their best football of the match. Jimmy Gordon has the locals' first shot of the game and England's keeper Harry Hardy tips the ball over the bar.

England regains control and a long-range effort from Williams sails over Boland into the top corner for a spectacular goal that makes the scorer the second Englishman to register a hat trick on tour.

Jack Elkes cleverly sends Norwich City's Joe Hannah through on goal. Boland advances and dives bravely at Hannah's feet. The Englishman gets a toe to the ball just as the pair collide with a sickening crash. The ball rolls into the vacant net but all eyes are on the two players lying on the ground.

Syd Storey can barely watch.

Hannah is helped to his feet and hobbles back to his position. Boland, however, remains prone and in agony. There's a lot of head shaking by the trainers. They signal for a stretcher. Boland is taken to hospital, where he is diagnosed with a compound fracture of the left leg. Unable to make a substitution, Western Australia are forced to play out the match a man down. Right fullback Finlayson dons the goalkeeper's jersey.

England stroll through the final ten minutes of the game. Finlayson can do nothing to save a fearsome shot from Williams that puts England up 5-0. Ernie Simms makes it six when he turns in a cross from Hannaford and shortly after heads in a pinpoint cross from Seymour. The full-time whistle sounds with the score 7-0 to England.

* * *

Three of England's goals had been scored in the final ten minutes after Boland's injury. John Lewis sportingly entered the home team's dressing room after the match to congratulate them on their outstanding first half effort and inquire on the health of Boland.

Although still finding their land legs, there were signs England were starting to click. Their teamwork had been sharper than the first game and they were adapting to the unfamiliar conditions.

For England, Len Graham played a fine game. An elegant player with a knack of making the right pass at the right time, he possessed speed and superb ball control. Elkes proved to be a crowd favourite, at one time beating three men in the one movement.

One of the few tourists who didn't play up to their reputation was Stan Seymour. He put it down to over indulging on red grapes the day before.

Nearly 11,000 people ventured to Fremantle Oval, paying a premium to watch football despite a full round of Australian Rules club fixtures being played in Perth. Many in the crowd were unfamiliar with the game but the quality of the football had everyone talking. The match was fast and spectacular from beginning to end.

After the game, Storey announced that he would take two Western Australian players, Boys and Gardner, across to Adelaide to play for the Australian XI the following Saturday.

Storey had much to be pleased about from the first leg of the tour. Almost 14,000 spectators had witnessed the two matches, paying over £700 at the gate.

Press commentary on the quality of the English team and their style of play was overwhelmingly positive. Even the conflict with the WAFL over the use of grounds had brought publicity to the tour. Most of this commentary cast Australian Rules as the villain.

John Lewis' post-match comments about England not yet hitting their peak were food for thought. Storey hoped that New South Wales and Australia would be capable of putting up a fight but if England continued to improve that couldn't be guaranteed. And this was why Storey was so disappointed with Lewis' inflexibility over Law One. With no substitutes, a local team's goalkeeper going off injured was the worst possible outcome. Fans would watch pretty football up to a point, but if the tour became a series of drubbings the crowds would stop coming.

There were signs the tour was having some positive effects in promoting football. In an article in *The West Australian*, 'P.S.R.' said he witnessed a group of boys playing in the park:

"On Monday, some lads playing with a soccer ball, which was obviously new, caught my eye, and it was very amusing to watch them endeavouring to attain proficiency in the art of ball control without using their hand. This then is what the Englishmen are here for, to popularise the game of all nations in this country, so that Australia will be able to take her place not only at Inter-Dominion trials of strength, but at international games too. By international I mean the word to be used in its broadest sense, for it is unfortunately a fact that Australia is one of the few nations who have not up to date become proficient at this game which numbers its adherents by the million."

At 9pm on 9 May, the tourists boarded the Transcontinental Express for the trip to Adelaide. Among the well-wishers at Perth railway station were a group of well-dressed young 'flappers' waving autograph books at the players.

Also on the train was Syd Storey and the two Western Australian footballers. The trip would take three days. In the close confines of the train, Storey hoped he could still make John Lewis see sense over Law One.

On Sunday, the train made a brief stopover at the gold mining town of Kalgoorlie, where the tourists were welcomed by the Mayor, Fred Allsop. Lewis hoped the team could see more of the town and maybe play a match the next time they passed through.

    The tourists set off on the next leg of the trip. The train, carrying English footballers from places such as Stockport, Plymouth, Exeter and London, headed east across the vast and ancient saltbush scrublands of the Nullarbor Plain.

8
'Is He Jealous?'

March 1925, Adelaide

Hundreds of shoppers in Victoria Square, Adelaide, stare up at the roof of Moore's Department Store. They gasp when something round and colourful rises above the building. It's followed by another similar object. Soon there are dozens of balloons, in silver, orange and green, floating over the city. It's not so much the balloons that people have come for but what is attached to them. Affixed to each one is a package containing a Moore's product sample, and as they fall gently to the ground eager hands grab at them.

Some of the balloons drift across the road and as people follow them, seemingly oblivious to the traffic, motorists shout and blast their horns. Then some of the car windows are wound down and motorists try to catch the little gifts from above. Other balloons float far across Adelaide's suburbs or away to the distant hills. No matter, for everywhere they land someone will read the name: Moore's Department Store.

As an advertising gimmick, it's a masterstroke. One of the architects of the stunt, looking down from the store's rooftop garden, is Campbell Campbell-Smith, Moore's general manger. He's a busy man, full of ideas. It's not just the retail trade he applies his many talents to. The one-time football player, now recently installed as chairman of the South Australian Soccer Football Association (SASFA), has his hands full. As anyone involved in football in Australia will tell you, 1925 is the most important season in the history of the code.

* * *

Recent tours by China and Canada had raised football's profile in South Australia but the visit by England was something altogether different. At the early summertime meetings held in the rooftop gardens of Moore's, while guests admired the sun setting over the Adelaide Hills, Campbell-Smith talked up England's visit and how it would lead to a new era of international football.

Moore's Department Store

Changes were already afoot in 1925. An eight-team district-based competition would get underway in the city that season.

'Wing-Foot', writing in *The Register,* called the visit by the English FA "second only to the tour of England's cricketers in importance, this 'missionary' tour should firmly establish the game in all the Australian states." He also said "the importance of the trip, from a sportsman's point of view, cannot be overestimated. An interchange of international fixtures between the two countries will be given birth."

South Australia would host two tour matches. The first in midweek would feature the South Australian state side, while the second on a Saturday would see England play an Australian XI consisting of players from states other than New South Wales and Queensland. The SASFA had hoped to use South Australia's premier enclosed ground, Adelaide Oval, for both matches but the oval's chief tenants, the South Australian Football League (SAFL) (Australian Rules), refused to give up the venue on the Saturday.

A war of letters broke out in the newspapers over the attitude of the SAFL. One contributor wrote: "For a lot of correspondents, including many who also labelled themselves as Australian Rules fans, it felt disrespectful not to allow a team representing England to play at the best ground in the state."

Not everyone opposed the SAFL decision. 'Australian' said he "commended the delegates to the Football League on their attitude", and complained that the soccer authorities were "trying by every means to supplant our national game".

In reply, a correspondent to *The Advertiser,* referring to herself as 'An Australian born woman', tells 'Australian' that he "must remember that soccer is played all over the world, and our game in Australia only. Is he jealous?"

In truth, Australian Rules was in rude health in South Australia. The 1924 Grand Final between West Torrens and Sturt had drawn a crowd of 44,345 to Adelaide Oval. Yet two tour games by England had the SAFL spooked.

* * *

The train carrying the English footballers pulled into Adelaide railway station on the evening of Tuesday 12 May. As the weary players stepped onto the platform, they were astonished to hear cheer after cheer ring out through the station's buildings.

The English tourists, along with Syd Storey and the two Western Australians, were taken to their accommodation at the Grosvenor Hotel, where another large crowd attended the welcoming reception. Long-serving South Australian football administrator Bob Holiday told the excited audience the English tour would "place soccer in an unassailable position in the Commonwealth". His comment was met with loud applause. John Lewis rattled off his mind-boggling figures of the growth of football in England and when he predicted "the advance of the game in Australia to be equally rapid", he nearly brought the house down.

The next morning, the touring party was given a civic reception at Adelaide Town Hall. There was a tense moment when one of the speakers, Councillor McEwin, remarked that football "would never supplant the native game [Australian Rules]".

Never one to back down from a challenge, John Lewis pointed to football's spectacular rise around the world. Lewis said that football being included in the Olympic Games was evidence that it had every chance of prospering in Australia. It was a soccer-friendly crowd and Lewis was roundly applauded.

In the afternoon, the players attended Morphettville race course. Somewhat uncomfortably, owing to John Lewis' distaste for gambling, the players witnessed the gelding Stralia take out the Adelaide Cup. The race meeting was a relief from the formal receptions and the drudgery of their three-day train journey. There was certainly no time for any practice. And as some of the players remembered late in the day, they had a football match to play tomorrow.

Thursday, 14 May 1925, Match 3: England v South Australia, Adelaide Oval

England makes several changes to the team that defeated Western Australia. Len Graham has been ruled out with a knee injury. Whittaker, Caesar, Hamilton, Sage, and Batten come into the side. Starting for the first time on tour is Jimmy Walsh, the Liverpool forward who has finally recovered from sea-sickness.

The South Australian team has been selected after two trial matches. Their gun players are the Port Adelaide pair of Jock McQueen, at inside left, and Jack Mitchell, at right-back, and the hard-tackling centre-half Jimmy Gore, from the West Torrens club.

Four days of unsettled weather have made the Adelaide Oval surface greasy, conditions suited to the tourists. England's captain for the day is goalkeeper Harry Hardy, while Gore captains South Australia. A moderately sized midweek crowd of around 4,000 looks forward to seeing England in action.

After a slow start, England warm to their task. Fifteen minutes into the game, South Australia's Gore is dispossessed by England's Charlie Spencer, who plays a ball down the right wing to Bill Sage. He whips in a cross to centre-forward Bert Batten, who slots it past South Australia's keeper Sid Gibson to put England 1-0 up.

Batten's next effort is parried by Gibson to the feet of Billy Williams, who plays it back to Batten to tap in England's second goal.

A cross from Spencer sees Batten and goalkeeper Gibson challenge hard for the ball. The players hit the ground with a thud. Batten is able to get up but Gibson stays down. The trainers are called for. Gibson has badly injured his thigh and cannot continue.

Campbell-Smith gets off the bench and approaches John Lewis and asks if South Australia can make a substitution. No, says Lewis, substitutes will not be allowed. For the second tour match in a row, the local team is forced to play one man short and without a specialist keeper.

Jack Mitchell, the right-back, is drafted in as goalkeeper.

Stan Seymour, England's outside left, crosses to Batten. The Plymouth Argyle centre-forward heads the ball into the net to become the third touring English player to notch up a hat trick in as many games. Half-time arrives with the score 3-0 to England.

In the second half, Mitchell is in action early, tipping Batten's header around the post. Then he performs a sensational save to deny Walsh his opening goal of the tour. Eventually, Mitchell can't hold onto a shot and Seymour slams the rebound along the ground to put England 4-0 ahead.

Shortly after, a smart piece of play by Walsh sends Seymour down the left wing and his cross picks out Batten, who loops his header over Mitchell to make it 5-0 to England.

Seymour again takes off down the left flank and his cross, like a magnet, finds Batten, who scores his fifth and England's sixth goal of the match. Then, from a scramble in front of goal, Williams smashes home England's seventh.

A superb piece of defensive play by England's Tom Whittaker breaks up a rare attack from the locals and he feeds Bill Sage, whose cross finds the ever-reliable Batten to head in England's eighth goal.

Whittaker is also the provider for England's ninth goal when his long clearance finds Williams and the West Ham man's low shot is too good for Mitchell.

Crystal Palace's Jimmy Hamilton scores his first goal of the tour with just a few minutes to go. At full-time, the score reads: England 10 South Australia 0.

* * *

It was a masterful performance by England. They had found their land legs and despite a lack of practice were combining well as a team. Bert Batten's first game as a centre-forward proved fruitful, with six goals in the bag. The unofficial top scorer's race for the tourists now stood at: Simms 7, Batten and Williams tied at 6 each.

* * *

If dancing to the latest jazz music was your thing, the Maison de Danse in Glenelg was the place to be. Located a stone's throw from the seaside, the venue boasted a fine dance floor, a large balcony upstairs, and a lighting system said to be the best in Australia.

The Glenelg soccer club had been busy organising the dance since early in the year. Eight hundred people attended the sold out event. They were not disappointed. The resident band, led by Walter Barratt, belted out dance numbers that got the toes tapping. It seemed all Adelaide was there to see if the English team were as nimble on the dance floor as they were on the football pitch.

Also tripping the light fantastic was Syd Storey, still stewing following the injury to Gibson and Lewis' refusal to allow a substitute earlier that day. Storey had intimated to reporters that he would consider contacting the FA directly to overrule Lewis.

Storey's conga-line of Australian footballers included four players from interstate. They would be part of Saturday's Australian XI team that would hopefully take some of the wind out of England's sails. With 25 goals scored and none conceded in three games, England were in danger of taking the enjoyment out of the tour.

The interstate players included Harold Boys and Wally Gardner, who travelled with Storey from Western Australia. They were joined by a pair of Tasmanian players: Les Honeysett and Len Norman. Honeysett was an astute football administrator as well as being a special talent on the field. The previous Saturday, he had scored eight goals in a club match in Hobart. Norman had represented Australia against Canada in 1924.

The new players displayed some pleasing initiative by practicing among themselves on the morning of the England vs South Australia fixture.

On Friday, winger Joe Grieves and fullback William Aiken from Victoria arrived in Adelaide bringing the interstate contingent to six.

The tourists passed a pleasant Friday morning on the rooftop of Moore's Department Store. As the guests took in the fine views of Adelaide, Campbell-Smith reminded them of their roles as pseudo immigration agents. He hoped the Englishmen "would return to their home land and speak to their friends of what they had seen, as this was one of the best means of advertising Australia".

John Lewis replied that visits such as this were the key to "strengthening the bonds of unity of the Empire".

Saturday, 16 May 1925, Match 4: England v Australian XI, Thebarton Oval

Locked out of Adelaide Oval by the SAFL, the two teams prepare to walk out onto Thebarton Oval under overcast skies. The Hindmarsh Band plays 'Song of Australia' as The Australian XI come out followed by 'Hearts of Oak' when England enter the arena to generous applause.

Among the five South Australians playing for the host XI is goalkeeper Edward Pilgrim, who replaces the injured Sid Gibson. Gibson cuts a lonely figure as he watches on from the stands.

With three easy wins under their belts, England experiment by playing Tom Whittaker, the Arsenal fullback, at centre-forward.

The home captain is Jimmy Gore of South Australia, while goalkeeper Teddy Davison captains England.

Jack Elkes is soon up to his old tricks, taunting the defence and amusing the crowd. After an interchange with Whittaker, Elkes looks certain to score but his shot goes just wide. At the 12-minute mark Elkes shimmies past Gore and Mitchell then back-heels to Jimmy Hamilton, whose strike from 20 yards beats Pilgrim to put England 1-0 up.

The Australians do their best to hit back. Les Honeysett sets up Jock McQueen only for him to blast the ball over the bar. Honeysett also plays in Grieves but he's pulled up for offside.

At the other end of the pitch, Elkes controls the ball and sends it out to Hannaford. The Clapton Orient winger goes around two players then scores from close range to put England 2-0 up.

Another English attacking move starting with Elkes sees Billy Caesar in the clear. His clever pass finds Whittaker, who makes no mistake to notch up his first goal on tour. England are now three goals to the good.

Desperate to salvage some respectability, Syd Storey tries his hand as a tactician. At half-time, he makes some positional changes, shifting Western Australian Wally Gardner to centre-forward.

In the early going of the second half Australia's defence plays with more resolve. Both Norman and Mitchell throw themselves into their work and England are stymied. Up front, Honeysett and Grieves begin to combine well. Grieves even forces a save from England's keeper Davison.

Playing into the wind, England struggle with their passing game. Up front, Tom Whittaker's shortcomings as a centre-forward are evident. Whittaker and Batten both miss good opportunities, each of them heading over the crossbar. Bill Sage does get through but his shot only rattles the side netting.

Australia's attack improves in the second half and a good chance is squandered when Grieves is pulled up for offside after being set up by Honeysett. Shortly afterwards, Davison is forced off his line to clear, only for the ball to ricochet off one of his own men and nearly end up in England's net.

England's left half Len Graham puts the ball in the back of the net but is pulled up for offside. The leg injury he sustained in the collision with Boland in Fremantle flares up again and he plays on with a limp. The football becomes scrappy, with England content to wind down the clock.

Fifteen minutes before full-time Australia goes on the attack. Honeysett's clever pass to Denman is then played into the path of Gardner. England's Billy Caesar makes a strong challenge and Gardner hits the turf. Mr Childs, the referee, awards Australia a penalty. Caesar throws up his hands in puzzlement over the decision.

Wally Gardner places the ball on the penalty spot. He walks back a few paces and Thebarton Oval goes quiet.

He runs in and strikes the ball sweetly. The net bulges and a raucous cheer goes up from the stands. England's almighty defence has been breached at last. England now leads 3-1.

The goal wakes England from their lethargy. Three minutes before time, Batten receives a pass from Sage and blasts home from the edge of the area.

The final score is England 4, The Australian XI 1.

* * *

The penalty was the biggest talking point of the game. Billy Caesar had been perplexed by the ruling. Most of the press felt the decision was harsh. Wally Gardner, the man who was fouled, could only shrug his shoulders when asked what the penalty was for.

Despite conceding a goal, England were rarely troubled. Apart from Whittaker, playing out of position at centre-forward, most of the Englishmen were a class above their Australian counterparts. After the game, Syd Storey awarded the prize of a Woodrow hat to Jack Elkes.

For Australia, Honeysett was the most dangerous attacking player and was well supported by Grieves and Gardner. Jack Mitchell was superb in defence and was awarded the Woodrow hat by John Lewis. To cap off Mitchell's day he was selected for the Australian XI team to play England in Melbourne the following week.

The fine performance in the second half by the Australian XI was just the tonic the tour needed. Syd Storey could breathe a little easier. Here was proof that a motivated team playing in their correct positions could compete for at least part of a game. With a bit of luck, who knew what could happen. The breaking of the scoring duck by Australian teams had proved England's defence was not infallible.

Pundits gushed over England's performances in South Australia. They marvelled at the ball control, superb technique and clever positional play. Tactics such as the offside trap, headed passes, switching play by passing backwards, even as far back as the goalkeeper, were new to Australian audiences.

The modest crowd of 3,658 was hardly anything to strike fear into the hearts of the Australian Rules diehards. In the end, the decision to deny football the use of Adelaide Oval seemed mean-spirited.

On Sunday, the English team were given a tour of the Adelaide Hills and had afternoon tea in the pleasant surrounds of the village of Gumeracha. In the evening, the touring party boarded the Overland Express for Melbourne. The train had been covered in streamers by South Australian football supporters.

9
Soccer at The MCG

1 April 1890, the mean streets of Melbourne

In the early months of 1890, thirty-two-year-old Robert Amson was struggling to make ends meet. The hay and corn exchange he was a partner in had gone bust. A sharp recession was starting to bite and jobs were scarce. Amson could do with some cash. He mulled over an idea.

Over the previous ten years, Amson had been one of the finest soccer players in Melbourne. He'd regularly represented Victoria in their intercolonial matches against New South Wales. He'd even captained them a few times. He was still very much involved in the sport. As the current captain of the Carlton club, who had won successive league and cup championships in 1888 and 1889, he had custodianship of the two trophies, the Beaney Cup and the George and George Challenge Cup.

A desperate Amson took matters into his own hands. On April Fool's Day 1890 he brought the two football trophies to a shop in King Street, Melbourne, where he pawned them for the grand sum of seven pounds.

A year later Amson was arrested on charges of larceny. The magistrate ruled Amson "acted without felonious intent" and he was acquitted of the crime.

The Victorian British Football Association, which brought the charges, had all but disappeared by 1891. Nobody could rightly say who the items should be returned to.

The pawning of the cups was a symptom of the demise of football in Victoria in the early 1890s. The sport was struck by other blows around the same time. Arthur Gibbs, the man who had done so much to organise football in the 1880s, was transferred by his employer, the Colonial Mutual Society, to New Zealand. James George Beaney, the eccentric diamond and ruby ring-wearing Melbourne surgeon who had been a patron of the sport and donated the Beaney Cup, died in 1891.

Melbourne became a football wasteland for nearly 20 years.

* * *

In 1907, Harry Dockerty, a tailor from Scotland who had spent some time in Sydney, moved to Melbourne and set up his business. He was shocked to find that football was not played in the city. Knowing there must be old players from England and Scotland around, he set about re-establishing the game in Melbourne.

The new organisation began in 1908 with six clubs playing for a league championship and a cup. He personally donated the Dockerty Cup for the knockout competition.

To capture some of the spirit of the game back home, an annual match between players representing England and Scotland was played at the enclosed Brunswick Street ground in Fitzroy. These matches were among the highlights of the season and drew sizeable gates.

The skill of local footballers improved to such an extent that Victoria defeated New South Wales in 1914.

Although the First World War ravaged the game in Melbourne, football was strong enough to rebound. Post-war immigration gave the game a growth spurt and the 1925 season commenced with 32 senior clubs spread across four divisions featuring promotion and relegation.

England vs Australian XI, Melbourne Cricket Ground

* * *

Although soccer had made progress in Melbourne, it was completely overshadowed by Australian Rules football, which had immense popular appeal and garnered the majority of inches in newspaper sporting columns. The club culture that had evolved since the 1860s was every bit as strong as the football cultures of England and Scotland.

For the 1925 season, the main Australian Rules organisation in Melbourne, the Victorian Football League (VFL), added three new clubs to its competition, its biggest expansion since the inception of the league. The VFL was so popular that organisers had seriously contemplated raising ticket prices for finals matches to reduce the size of crowds that were expected to exceed the capacity of the Melbourne Cricket Ground (MCG).

Dominant as the local code was, some Australian Rules supporters were concerned by the spread of football. The dazzling sums of money quoted by John Lewis reinforced the notion that football was a juggernaut of world sport. Football's growing international presence also gave some Australian Rules supporters sleepless nights.

Melbourne's *The Herald* complained that "immigrants from England do not renounce soccer football when they step ashore at Port Melbourne". This was a worrying sign for the future, the paper opined, since "as we get more young immigrants, soccer gets a stronger hold on Australian footballers."

Just before the English team arrived in Melbourne the same newspaper posed the following question: 'That Soccer Game. Will it Sweep Australia?'

* * *

In February 1925, Harry Dockerty addressed a meeting of Melbourne's football community about the arrangements for the English tour. England would play two matches in May: one in midweek against Victoria and a Saturday game against an Australian XI. Melbourne would also host the fifth and final Test match between England and Australia in July.

Victoria needed to raise £1,200 towards the cost of the tour. Dockerty reminded the delegates that fundraising efforts needed to be stepped up. Despite the apparent enthusiasm, only £450 had been raised by the start of April. *The Sporting Globe* reported: "There has been a regrettable lack of enthusiasm among the various clubs, and it behoves them to get to work, otherwise it may be necessary to curtail a portion of the programme, owing to lack of funds."

The start of the club season was brought forward in order to get players match fit for the big games ahead. A squad of 20 players was selected on the basis of the previous season's form and began training two nights a week at Albert Oval.

Dockerty and the Victorian organisers had mixed success gaining access to venues. They secured the premier stadium, the Melbourne Cricket Ground, for the first two matches of the tour, but the fifth Test would have to be played at the Brunswick Street ground in Fitzroy.

The mood among football people was positive as the arrival of the English team grew nearer. Journalist J.O. Wilshaw, writing for *The Herald,* captured the anticipation: "Never in the history of soccer football in Australia has such enthusiasm prevailed as at the present moment."

* * *

It was a wet and cold day when the Overland Express pulled into Melbourne's Spencer Street station. Eager football supporters burst into applause when the English players got off the train. One of the first men to shake the hand of England manager John Lewis was Harry Dockerty, a moment captured by one of the news photographers on duty.

England's assistant manager Mark Frowde, known as the 'Father of Football' back home in Dorset, told reporters he was overwhelmed by the welcome the team had received and the opportunity the tour provided for Australians to appreciate soccer.

A chirpy Syd Storey talked up the tourists: "The Englishmen have displayed wonderful form, and their exhibitions are going to be a revelation to every football enthusiast."

After settling in at the Windsor Hotel, the English team practiced at the Melbourne Cricket Ground. Despite expressing disappointment at the distance the stands were from the pitch, Lewis said it was one of the finest grounds he'd ever seen.

The following day, the players were given a tour of Parliament House by a representative of the federal government. Melbourne was Australia's temporary capital and would only relinquish that status to Canberra in 1927. Despite being received by the federal government, no civic reception was provided by Melbourne, the only city in Australia not to afford the visitors this courtesy.

None of that mattered that evening when the players arrived at the Oddfellows Hall in Latrobe Street for a rowdy

Harry Dockerty (right) meeting John Lewis (left) in Melbourne

welcome function put on by the football community. Over 700 guests packed the venue. Among the musical highlights was a delightful vocal performance by the tourists' own songbird, Billy Williams of West Ham United.

Wednesday, 20 May 1925, Match 5: England v Victoria, Melbourne Cricket Ground

Victoria runs out first onto the MCG in dark blue jerseys with a white 'V' and white shorts. Besides the honour of representing their state, they are playing for a spot in the Australian XI team on Saturday. Victoria suffers a pre-match setback when Grieves, who played so well in Adelaide the previous Saturday, is ruled out with a knee injury. His place is taken by Hubbard of Footscray Thistle.

England come out to hearty cheers from a small crowd. The Dulwich Hamlet amateur player, Billy Caesar, captains England and wins the toss from Victoria's George Raitt. England run towards the Richmond End.

Among the press tables on the sidelines is a rather unusual sight for both sets of players. Reporters from Melbourne radio station 3AW are busily setting up their equipment. It will be the first soccer match in Australia (and possibly anywhere in the world) to be broadcast live on radio. Football coverage had moved into a new era. The match in Melbourne marked a pioneering moment that the visitors would not witness until 22 January 1927, when Arsenal and Sheffield United played the first football match to be covered live on radio in England three weeks after the BBC received its first licence to broadcast sport.

To most people's surprise it's the local team that gets away early. Church, Victoria's inside right, intercepts a pass from England's centre-half Charlie Spencer and sends a ball down the wing. Templeton suddenly finds himself in open territory. He takes the ball down the sideline, cuts back in and fires a shot that forces a diving save from England's keeper Teddy Davison.

England soon begin to exert pressure of their own. Controlling a clearance from Davison, Jack Elkes turns, and with his characteristic jinking style beats several defenders before hitting a low shot that is palmed away for a corner by Victorian keeper Jim Robison. The corner is swung in and Robison punches clear but only as far as Stan Seymour. The Newcastle United outside left sends a cross over that is deftly headed in by Ernie Simms. England lead 1-0.

After a sustained spell of defensive play, Victoria brings the ball into England's half. From a free-kick, Ritchie passes to Johnny Orr, who crosses to Barrett. From about 15 yards out, Barrett hits a powerful shot. Davison is caught off balance and can only watch. The ball hits the post and Victoria are denied an equaliser.

Dusting themselves off, England gain possession through Simms, and Seymour is sent away down the left. Controlling the ball deftly on the run, he cuts inside, beats a handful of defenders and side foots it into the net for England's second goal.

Nearly 35 minutes into the game Charlie Spencer has the ball in midfield and plays it to Seymour on the wing. Seymour switches the ball across the field to Jimmy Walsh. The Liverpool man sends in a perfect cross for the part-time tenor Billy Williams to head cleverly over Robison for England's third goal.

A few minutes later a pass by Billy Caesar releases Simms down the right wing. He turns Raitt and Aiken inside out and crosses to Williams, who makes no mistake from close range. It's now 4-0 to England and the Victorians are grateful to hear the half-time whistle.

It's a quiet start to the second half, with England coming out a little flat. Elkes gets England rolling again with a scything pass to Walsh who plays it to Simms in the outside right position. A floating cross is met by Williams who heads in England's fifth goal and brings up his hat trick.

Victoria's keeper Robison makes a fine save off Elkes then pulls off a double save from Simms that gets a tremendous ovation from the crowd. Robison is called into action again to save from Walsh but from the ensuing melee Stan Seymour pokes in England's sixth. In the goalmouth scramble, Robison cops a stray boot to the face and is taken off for treatment. He is the third Australian goalkeeper to be injured in just five games. Fortunately for Victoria, he is able to come back after treatment.

The final minutes of the game see England passing the ball around with Elkes performing a bunch of tricks for the crowd. Shortly before full-time, Billy Williams finishes the day's scoring with a shot from distance to make it 7-0 to England.

* * *

Elkes had been the crowd favourite and his dazzling skills on the ball kept Victoria on the back foot. Stan Seymour, after some indifferent form earlier, played his best match of the tour. Charlie Spencer, Seymour's Newcastle United teammate gave a commanding performance at centre-half.

But the kudos of the day belonged to Billy Williams. Fresh from his virtuoso vocal performance the night before, the West Ham songbird brought up his second hat trick in three games and with ten goals was now England's leading scorer.

* * *

On Thursday morning the tourists were driven to the Royal Australian Navy's training base at Crib Point in Western Port Bay. The sailors and officers gave England a hearty welcome and showed them around the base. John Lewis celebrated the occasion by turning back the clock and refereeing a match between the young sailors.

That evening, Melbourne's social set had the chance to put England's hot-stepping footballers through their paces on the dance floor. The Wattle Path Palais de Danse & Cafe on The Esplanade in St Kilda was another of the purpose-built ballrooms that had sprung up around Australia after World War 1. Designed by Geelong architect Arthur Purnell, Wattle Path boasted the largest dance floor in Australia. Made of Kauri wood secretly nailed every 40 centimetres, the rubber-lined dance floor enabled dancers to literally bounce across it. Members of the English team could quench their thirst from one of the illuminated soda fountains, or be dazzled by the kaleidoscopic crystal balls and 'scientifically operated' light show. If they took a break from dancing, they could take a seat and admire the gaudily coloured murals and drapery adorning the walls. In the barren words of the promoters, the design was "so artistic and truly wonderful that words are barren of description". The fourteen-piece band, conducted by Maurice Guttridge and powered by four saxophones, played a set list of foxtrots, waltzes and the newest music craze from America sweeping the world: jazz.

While the England players jazzed the night away at Wattle Path, one member of the touring party was conspicuous by his absence. John Lewis, a lifelong teetotaller and member of the Band of Hope Temperance Society, spent the evening lecturing on the evils of alcohol at a function put on by the local branch.

* * *

Seven Victorians were selected to play for the Australian XI. Only four of them had played against England on Wednesday. Robison kept his place in goal while Aiken at left back would face the tourists for a third game in succession. William Ritchie in the halves and Johnny Orr at inside left were the other survivors from the midweek game.

Jack Mitchell, the South Australian who had performed well in Adelaide would play right fullback and Tasmania's Les Honeysett was brought in at outside left. Making up the eleven were two players from New South Wales, Bill Maunder and Roy McNaughton.

Bill 'Podge' Maunder, was a centre-forward from the West Wallsend club in Newcastle. He was one of the most experienced players in Australia against international opposition. He had scored Australia's first goal in a full international, against New Zealand in 1922. Maunder played against New Zealand and the Chinese in Australia in 1923 and the Canadians in 1924. Still only 22 years old, Maunder was pacy and had a good nose for goal. In just four seasons at West Wallsend, he'd helped the club win the Gardiner Cup twice.

Roy McNaughton played for the Cessnock club in Newcastle. Just 20 years old and one of the fastest wingers in the country, he had been overlooked for the New South Wales team to play England the following week and would be out to prove the selectors wrong.

Victorian football officials had done a good job getting the message across about the matches. Ads appeared in the newspapers explaining the rules of this strange sport from Britain. Members of the English touring party were caricatured by cartoonist Sam Wells in *The Herald*. On the eve of the match, radio station 3LO broadcast a talk on football by John Lewis and the Australian XI captain Bill Maunder.

Saturday, 23 May 1925, Match 6: England v Australian XI, Melbourne Cricket Ground

A good crowd, including a contingent of sailors from the Royal Navy's *HMS Concord*, give a rousing cheer as the teams step out onto the MCG. The players are introduced to Lord Stradbroke, the Governor of Victoria. Stradbroke performs a ceremonial kickoff to polite applause and manages to avoid slipping on the greasy surface.

Australia runs into a strong breeze and as the clouds start to clear they will have the sun in their eyes. The non-playing members of the teams take their seats on the benches near the pitch. The announcers for radio station 3AR begin another live broadcast. The match, labelled in one newspaper as 'the most important soccer game that has ever been played in Victoria', gets underway.

The Australians burst out of the blocks. Johnny Orr sends Roy McNaughton down the flank. Showing great pace, McNaughton leaves Tom Whittaker floundering. England's captain Cec Poynton has to scurry across and clear. The crowd applauds the home side's enterprising start.

The action soon moves to the other end. Jimmy Walsh receives a ball from Spencer and his shot skims the crossbar.

Stan Seymour is at the start of the next attacking move for England. He passes to Bert Batten, who sends it across to Spencer. The Newcastle United centre-half shrugs off a couple of challenges and shoots from 20 yards out.

Jack Mitchell (SN)

Robison dives and gets a hand to it but the ball spins back and rolls into the net.

From the restart, the Australians go on the offensive. Jack Mitchell, the right fullback, clears to Ritchie, who finds McNaughton on the left. The Cessnock speedster races down the touchline. His cross finds Bill Maunder, who is through on goal. Just as Maunder lines up a shot, he's brought down in a solid challenge by Whittaker. The Australians claim a penalty but referee A. McLeod waves play on.

McNaughton again finds room on the left and crosses to Maunder. The West Wallsend man cleverly evades two defenders but with the goal at his mercy, hesitates. England's goalkeeper Harry Hardy pounces and just manages to clear the ball from Maunder's feet. For the first time on the tour, England's defence is under pressure. McNaughton's pace and Maunder's skilful play are a step up from anything they've faced in Australia to date. In another fine move, Maunder tries to beat the powerfully built Whittaker but is dispossessed. Maunder comes off second best in the challenge and has to be assisted from the field.

Ten minutes later Maunder returns but is limping noticeably. John Lewis still won't allow substitutes so Maunder will have to stick it out as best he can. At half-time, England lead by just the one goal.

Within minutes of play resuming, England takes the ball upfield in a dazzling passing move. Ernie Simms receives Batten's pass and shoots through a tangle of legs to beat the unsighted Robison and give the visitors a 2–0 lead.

Charlie Hannaford, the Clapham Orient outside right, is finding the greasy surface to his liking. He has been beating the Australians' challenges with ease for much of the game. Now he collects a pass from Walsh near the touchline, about 15 yards inside England's half. He cuts infield. He waltzes past McNaughton with ease. Orr comes across but Hannaford twists past him like a magician. As Hannaford drives diagonally down the field, more defenders are left red-faced. Once inside the area, Hannaford steadies and smashes an unstoppable shot into the top corner of the net. Players on both sides are stunned. The crowd roars their approval. After the game one newspaper says, 'Many people who had witnessed plenty of soccer said they had never seen a goal taken so perfectly.'

It starts to rain heavily. Leading by three goals to nil, England slow the game and the tiring Australians start chasing shadows. Hannaford is not done, and after intercepting a loose pass from Raitt weaves past several defenders. He lines up a shot but has his feet taken out by Aiken. Mr McLeod points to the spot. Bert Batten hammers the penalty past Robison and England are up 4-0.

England close out the game pressing hard. The final act sees a scramble in the goalmouth, with the ball popping up to Ernie Simms who pokes home England's fifth goal.

* * *

Charlie Hannaford was the star performer for England. Not only did he score a stunning goal but set up a few others. Simms, Spencer and Seymour also played well. The Australians showed plenty of spirit but could not match England in the second half. Honeysett and McNaughton on the wings troubled the tourists the most. Far from being overawed by the occasion, McNaughton calmly told reporters after the game that he expected New South Wales and Queensland would give England a tough time. The big blow for Australia was the knee injury sustained by Bill Maunder.

The attendance at the game was quoted at anywhere between 11,000 and 17,000. Rain no doubt kept some fans away but it was a record for a football match in Victoria. Syd Storey would have been particularly pleased with the gate, which exceeded £1,000 for the first time on tour.

* * *

What did the pro-Australian Rules press think of the football match? Would youngsters abandon the Australian game in favour of the British one? Opinion writers found much to complain about. Where was the high marking? What kind of football didn't allow players to use their hands? Where was the physicality in the contest?

"There is no denying the skill of the soccer player, both with his feet and head", said one, "but I think that in any athletic contest which resolves itself into a man-to-man struggle, the prohibition of the use of the hands is robbing it of an essential feature."

Some suggested that goalkeeping would be an easy position to master: "I have no doubt that with a few weeks' practice with the round ball, peculiar to the soccer game, any Australian player could fill this position with credit."

But the message the papers were happiest to get out were opinions like that published in *The Herald* under the title 'AUSSIE AND SOCCER. An Englishman's Comparison'. It was written by a Stanley Grist, who referred to himself as 'an old soccer player'. He'd watched the match with some Australian Rules supporting friends and they could not get enthused about the game. His summary of his experience was: "No. Soccer is not the game for Australians."

The crowd figures and gates for Saturday's football matches were published in *The Australasian*:

Match	Code	Crowd	Takings £
Richmond v South Melbourne	Australian Rules	22,000	430
St Kilda v Fitzroy	Australian Rules	17,000	415
Collingwood v Geelong	Australian Rules	16,000	375
North Melbourne v Essendon	Australian Rules	15,000	350
Footscray v Melbourne	Australian Rules	12,000	290
England v Australian XI	Soccer	10,600	1,004
Carlton v Hawthorn	Australian Rules	10,000	230

The published soccer crowd of 10,600 was only the sixth biggest of the seven Saturday football matches. Because of its much higher ticket prices, the soccer international had the top gate for all matches. It was higher than the top two Australian Rules matches combined.

Among the 22,000 fans at Punt Road watching the Australian Rules match between Richmond and South Melbourne were two very curious spectators. At the invitation of the VFL, John Lewis and Mark Frowde attended the first half of the match. The two English managers were able to get to the nearby Melbourne Cricket Ground in time for the start of their game.

When asked what he thought of his first game of Australian Rules, Lewis was circumspect: "[I] do not consider it possible to criticise any game until it had been witnessed several times."

* * *

A dinner and smoke concert for the English team was held on Saturday evening at Sargent's Cafe in Elizabeth Street. Lewis believed his team would go through the tour undefeated but would congratulate any side that beat them provided they played a clean game. Guests crowding the venue were once again enchanted by the golden voice of Billy Williams.

The rain that had dogged the tour intensified as the team prepared to travel to New South Wales. Word came through that the midweek game to be played in Cootamundra had been called off because the pitch was under water. With no need to break the trip, the tourists left Melbourne a day earlier than planned. Syd Storey had been talking up the quality of football played in his home state. English assistant manager Mark Frowde, perhaps with a roll of his eyes, said: "… we have heard a great deal from Mr Storey about the standard of the game in New South Wales".

The tourists were given a rousing farewell when they left Melbourne. For Storey, the tour was at a critical juncture. He could take issue with what Australian Rules opinion writers said about soccer but he couldn't deny an important point they made - that the matches were not competitive. The next game against New South Wales in Sydney was of crucial importance. If the best-prepared side in Australia was soundly beaten, the tour could turn into a financial disaster.

The train pulled out of Spencer Street station late on a miserably wet afternoon. The 21 members of the English touring party settled down to chat, play cards and look out of the train's rain-spattered windows. As the growing deluge lashed the carriages, one compartment was awash with a different sound: the New South Wales trio of Syd Storey, Bill Maunder and Roy McNaughton were busy plotting England's downfall.

Roy McNaughton

10
Rarefied Air

The rain in New South Wales didn't let up. The train carrying the English football team rattled on through the countryside just ahead of the rising floodwaters. The *Evening News* in Sydney received information from police that the railway viaduct at Wagga Wagga was in danger of being washed away. The express carrying the English team had only just passed over it.

In Cooma and Gundagai, rivers peaked at levels not seen in 50 years. The town of Queanbeyan, near Australia's newly built capital city of Canberra, was cut off by floodwaters. Water overflowed the wall of the still-under-construction Burrinjuck Dam on the Murrumbidgee River. In Cootamundra, where locals had clung to the hope of at least treating the Englishmen to a dance, workers reluctantly pulled down the bunting from the Town Hall.

This was all quite welcome to John Lewis and Mark Frowde. The train trip from Melbourne to Sydney was a long one, over 850 kilometres, made even longer by the necessity of changing trains at Albury, where the broad gauge rail in Victoria met the narrower gauge system in New South Wales. A stop at Cootamundra would have required getting off the train and boarding it again at 2am on two consecutive days. Now the Englishmen would arrive in Sydney with a seven-days break between games.

In Sydney, a severe thunderstorm struck during the evening peak hour. Flash flooding brought trams and trains to a standstill. The city was plunged into darkness when the power failed. To anxious football fans awaiting the arrival of the English team, the tempest felt like a portent of great events to come.

* * *

At 11:30am the express from Melbourne reached Sydney's Central station and three hearty cheers rang out from the platform. As the doors opened, enthusiastic supporters rushed inside. The tourists' hands were shaken and backs were slapped as the players struggled to get off the train.

Old friends and acquaintances were reunited. Harry Hardy was met at the station by his sister-in-law. Mr R.F. Graham, a cousin of John Lewis, who hadn't seen him for over thirty years, was there to greet him. An old Blackburn man, J. Brooks, excitedly told people he remembered watching Lewis playing centre-forward for the Rovers in the 1880s.

Mr Jennings, an official of the St George football club was also there. Though disappointed his son Alf wasn't in the team, he was aware that due to his son's influence, Tottenham Hotspur had the biggest representation of any club on the tour. Ern Lukeman was another man waiting at the station. One journalist said the already broad-chested Lukeman was 'looking broader across the chest every day.'

The team were ushered out like movie stars through the crowd to a fleet of nine Austin motor cars. They were given a mini-tour of the city. At the Royal Botanic Garden, they stretched their legs and got their first view of Sydney Harbour. Told that work had recently begun on the Sydney Harbour Bridge, Jack Elkes quipped: "Do you think it will be finished by the time we return from Brisbane?"

A welcome was held at the Australia Hotel. The compere was a new ally of football in Australia, New South Wales politician Hugh McIntosh, MLC. McIntosh had been a rugby man but experienced a football epiphany in 1924 on a trip to the United Kingdom. He witnessed the England vs Scotland match and after soaking in the incredible atmosphere declared that football really was the game for him.

When McIntosh told the audience that football would surely take over as the main winter sport in Australia, he received thunderous applause. The pro-football crowd cheered everything McIntosh, Lewis and Frowde said. They were particularly vocal when McIntosh criticised the New South Wales Rugby Football League (NSWRFL) over its refusal to hand over the Sydney Cricket Ground (SCG) for the big matches. He assured them he had done everything in his power to overturn the decision and vowed it would not happen again.

* * *

In 1920, the NSWRFL secured the sole winter rights for the use of the SCG for ten years. During the football season, other sports could only use the ground with the NSWRFL's permission. Since the beginning of football's international era in 1923, only three soccer matches had been played on the ground, and only one of those on a Saturday. With the likelihood of large crowds to watch England in 1925, the NSWRFL had reservations about giving up the ground to a potential rival.

Towards the end of 1924, a bill was debated in New South Wales state parliament to raise funds to improve public accommodation at the SCG. At a meeting, Fred Flowers MLC, the patron of the NSWRFL, told Lands minister Walter Wearne in the presence of Syd Storey that rugby league would be happy to give up the SCG on two Saturdays for the football matches against England on the proviso the bill was passed.

Early in 1925, Storey wrote to Horrie Miller, secretary of the NSWRFL, for confirmation of the promise made by Flowers. Miller said he had no knowledge of it and that Flowers had no authority to make it. Besides, the bill didn't pass so any promise was now irrelevant.

The ever-tenacious Storey appealed directly to Lands Minister Wearne, who agreed to a conference between the parties in the dispute. Miller didn't attend, instead telling Wearne that the NSWRFL had no intention of allowing soccer the use of the ground.

Thwarted over the SCG, Storey next tried to ensure the English tour matches in Sydney wouldn't clash with the big rugby league matches. He wrote to Miller a number of times to find out the dates of rugby league's main fixtures. Miller ignored Storey's correspondence. It was like a game of poker but Storey was forced to show his hand by announcing the itinerary of the English tour. The NSWRFL subsequently scheduled their New South Wales vs Queensland interstate fixtures on the same days as the football matches.

The war of words over the SCG had been re-opened when a reporter in Melbourne asked John Lewis, as he boarded the train for Sydney, what he thought of the NSWRFL's actions. "Rotten", he said. He mentioned that football clubs in England had allowed touring Australian rugby league teams to use their grounds and expected the gesture would be reciprocated in Sydney. Lewis appealed to the Sydney public to patronise the England football games as a protest against the NSWRFL.

There was a good deal of public sympathy for football's position. The *Referee* newspaper opined: "All matters of protocol aside, the Rugby League should repay the sportsmanship showed to them by the football authorities in England."

The Sun weighed in with: "Some League enthusiasts may possibly dislike, or even fear, soccer, though there is surely room for both codes in a sporting community like this. They must admit, however, that there is a very large section of the public which wants to see the matches against the English visitors staged under the best possible conditions. And the public is entitled to some consideration."

* * *

If you'd walked up to someone of a sporting bent in 1925 and said to them: "I'm off to Langridge's", they'd know exactly what you meant. The Langridge School of Physical Culture, next to the General Post Office on George Street, was Sydney's go-to gymnasium for sportsmen of all stripes. The owner of the establishment was Tom Langridge, a masseur with magic hands who possessed a seemingly mystical ability to heal niggles, repair ruined muscles and elevate the most reluctant athlete to near superhuman powers.

During the cricket season just gone, Langridge was official trainer to the English team when they were in Sydney. He worked wonders on them. Through a combination of physical exercises, hot baths and massages he raised the fitness of the English players to levels not seen on the cricket field before.

When Maurice Tate complained of a sore knee, a treatment from Langridge would put it right. Herb Sutcliffe's shoulder troubles? No problem for Mr Langridge. Jack Hobbs with lumbago? A hot bath and a rub down from Tom Langridge soon fixed that.

This was on top of Langridge's efforts with the touring Great Britain rugby league team of 1924 that won the Ashes series two games to one. In football, he'd first worked with the New Zealand team after they lost the opening Test to Australia in 1923. New Zealand's remarkable turnaround to win that series 2-1 owed, at least in part, to the work put in by the players at Langridge's School of Physical Culture. Langridge also helped train the Chinese team in 1923.

When Australian football entered its coping-stone season of 1925, Tom Langridge was pressed into service. The great man was first appointed trainer for the Sydney Metropolitan team, then the New South Wales team and finally as the Australian team's trainer.

* * *

For the matches against England, New South Wales selectors chose a squad of 29 players early in the season. By necessity it was chosen on past form, but by bringing forward the start of the season a few weeks, they hoped to unearth more talent. The initial squad were told to start training, and Sydney based members began to meet regularly at Langridge's School of Physical Culture.

Some players were certainties for New South Wales selection. From the South Coast, the deadly forward combination of Judy Masters and Tom Thompson of Balgownie Rangers were obvious picks. In an early season benefit match Masters scored a hat trick and Thompson scored one goal in a 4-1 victory. Although he would be 33 years old by the time of the England matches, Masters was in fine form. The quietly spoken coal miner and World War 1 veteran fitted the mould of a heroic 1920s-era Australian sportsman. To the football administrators, Judy Masters was box-office gold.

Newcastle's Bill Maunder was another who would slot into the forward line. His brother Henry, a fullback, was also selected in the initial squad. Percy Lennard from the Cessnock club was an experienced international inside left, while his teammate Roy McNaughton was an outside left with serious talent - and one of those in on the conversation on the train to Sydney when England's downfall was being plotted.

The Sydney competition had an abundance of good halves. Harry Spurway of Gladesville was in good form while Granville's Alf Edwards was regarded as one of the best centre-halves in Australia. Experienced international George Cartwright was favourite for the goalkeeping position.

On 17 May, the New South Wales selectors announced the following team to meet England on 30 May:
Goalkeeper: G Cartwright (Annandale)
Backs: C Leabeater (Granville); A Druery (Corrimal)
Halves: F Coolahan (West Wallsend); A Edwards (Granville); H Spurway (Gladesville-Ryde)
Forwards: S Bourke (Granville); P Lennard (Cessnock); J Masters (Balgownie); W Maunder (West Wallsend); T Thompson (Balgownie)

Sydney scribes were upset that the diminutive Frank Gallen was not chosen as a fullback but as he'd missed the early part of the season the selectors plumped for the experienced Arthur Druery from Illawarra. There was no room for Roy McNaughton although he was on standby as a reserve.

The Sydney based players, along with those selected for the Sydney Metropolitan team, immediately started training at Langridge's. The entire New South Wales team came together on Thursday 28 May. First League club Balmain were also regulars at Langridge's and who couldn't blame them for pushing their bodies a little bit harder when the New South Wales players were there. Not that goalkeeper George Cartwright was getting ahead of himself. When he asked a teammate whether bending exercises were useful for goalkeepers his mate said: "You need to practice for all the times you bend down to pick the ball out of the net."

For the general public, there was a growing awareness about the big football matches ahead. People were getting to know the names of not just the Englishmen but the New South Wales players as well. Sports fans discussed the relative merits of men like Cartwright, Edwards, Maunder and Masters.

The dispute with rugby league over the SCG had made football many friends among broad-minded sports fans. The undoubted skill of the tourists and the utter novelty of playing England in a sport other than rugby or cricket raised public awareness of football to levels not seen before. There was something special in the air and not just the aromatic herbs in the hot baths of Langridge's School of Physical Culture. Maybe this visit by England really would prove to be the elusive coping stone that would finally establish football's place in the national sporting culture.

On Friday afternoon, Syd Storey addressed the New South Wales players in Langridge's about his grand plan to surprise England. He'd witnessed every minute of the tourists' matches from Fremantle to Melbourne and believed he'd found, if not a weakness, a window of opportunity. Local teams had always allowed England to take the initiative. For the big match on Saturday, he wanted New South Wales to come flying out of the blocks. He told Masters to forgo choice of ends if he won the toss and choose to kickoff. From the kickoff, the ball needed to be sent out to one of the wings. Tom Thompson or Stan Bourke would then use their blinding pace to take the ball down the touchline and cross to Masters. Time was of the essence to shock England. If they scored an early goal, anything could happen.

* * *

8:00pm, Friday, 29 May 1925, Sydney Town Hall

In casual attire, the New South Wales players followed in single file behind captain Judy Masters down the central aisle of Sydney Town Hall. They could barely hear themselves think. This was rarefied air for these amateur footballers. On either side, grinning supporters stood and applauded. Above them in the galleries, people clapped and waved their hats, the sound reverberating around the walls. In front of them, the 9,000-pipe Grand Organ, one of the world's largest, dominated a platform filled with a choir and musicians.

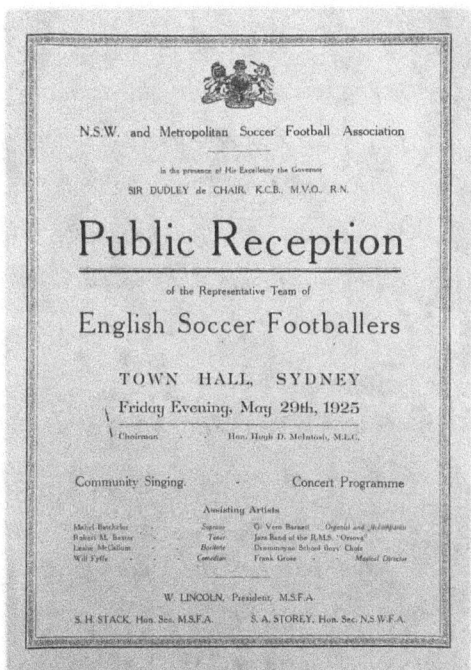

The program for the function at Sydney Town Hall

When the English team entered the hall, the audience could not contain themselves. It felt as if the roof might lift off the place. Resplendent in their dress suits, the athletic looking English players were cheered all the way to the stage. No journalist present could remember such a boisterous welcome for an overseas sporting team.

When the applause died down, New South Wales governor Admiral Sir Dudley de Chair presented John Lewis with an Australian flag. The flag was donated by Samuel Hordern, with its pole fashioned from the timber of *HMAS Australia*.

Australia's newest football zealot, Hugh McIntosh MLC, presided over the event and invited Lewis to say a few words. He was greeted with a standing ovation. Lewis was in his element: "I regard our game as the only true football," (*cheers*); "Our sport is not just a British game but the world's game," (*hear, hear*); "We are not here merely as football pioneers, but Empire pioneers," (*hurrah!*).

The crowd sang the specially penned lyrics with gusto, including this one to the tune of the 1923 song 'Barney Google':

> *Johnnie Lewis had sailed the seven seas,*
> *Johnnie Lewis known to referee,*
> *Thinks a lot of Hardy and Sage*
> *Keen, tho' seventy years of age,*
> *Johnnie Lewis, daddy of them all*
>
> *Judy Masters, captain of our set,*
> *Judy Masters kicks great goals - you bet,*
> *Bucks into it like a Turk,*
> *Gets a lot of help from Bourke,*
> *Judy Masters, the South Coaster's pet*

They were entertained by a musical program of popular songs from the jazz band of the *Orsova* - the ship that brought the Englishmen to Australia. Popular Scottish comedian Will Fyffe, who was performing at the Tivoli theatre, performed his signature act about a downtrodden working man with the song 'I Belong to Glasgow';

I'm only a common old working lad
As anyone can see,
But when I get a couple o' drinks
On a Saturday
Glasgow belongs to me

The evening was a great success. The audience was far more than the 3,000 people who squeezed into the Town Hall. Both of Sydney's radio stations, 2BL and 2FC, broadcast parts of the speeches and musical program live. And if you were at home in front of a fire on a cold Friday night in Sydney in 1925, in the days before television, what better entertainment could be had than listening to a live broadcast from the Town Hall?

As the players and guests left the reception rather late in the evening, perhaps humming 'I Belong to Glasgow', attention turned to the big match the next day between England and New South Wales. There was more to it than just this football game. The rivalry with rugby league had meant the question of which football code would draw the biggest gate had garnered the attention of many people. There was some indication of the popularity of the football match by the groups of people already down in Sydney from the country areas.

There was one other intriguing contest to be held on the Saturday - the New South Wales state election. Political parties had their eyes on securing the vote of football fans, many who would be away from their electorates. Overnight, the Sydney Town Hall was transformed into the biggest polling booth in New South Wales.

The function for the England team at Sydney Town Hall

11
A Mighty Roar

When Syd Storey woke on Saturday to sunbeams streaming through his window, he could almost hear the clicking of turnstiles. So far, the signs were good. He, too, had noticed a number of visitors down from the country the previous evening. Picking up a newspaper, he would have read that one enthusiastic football supporter had come from New Zealand to watch the matches in New South Wales. A Canadian Railway manager who had assisted his country's team in Australia the previous year said he "wouldn't miss it for the world".

Would the fans come, or would the lure of the cheaper interstate rugby league match next door prove too strong? There was nothing for Storey to do now other than concentrate on his master plan of snatching a result against the Englishmen. The performance of New South Wales in today's match meant everything to the success of the tour.

* * *

At 9am, a train pulled out of Cessnock station near Newcastle. On board was a large contingent of football fans, many of them coal miners, bound for Sydney to watch the match between New South Wales and England. More supporters joined the train at stations along the route. It was a football express quite unlike anything experienced in Australia before.

Also on the train was Newcastle referee Tom Crawford, accompanied by the secretary of the Crane Drivers and Trimmers' Union, W. Stanton. Voting in the New South Wales state election was not compulsory, and in a tight race every vote would count. Both men encouraged the fans on the train to exercise their democratic right to vote.

When the train reached Sydney's Central station, Labor party scrutineers picked up the supporters in motor cars and ferried them to the Town Hall to cast their votes. The scrutineers reported a 100% voter turnout from the football fans on these trains. After voting, supporters headed off to the football game. Very few of the Newcastle supporters had come to watch the rugby league match.

The Newcastle fans were disappointed to learn that local hero Bill Maunder had succumbed to the knee injury picked up the previous week and would not play. The blow was tempered by the elevation of Cessnock's Roy McNaughton to the team. In a reshuffle, Illawarra's Tom Thompson was moved to inside left, allowing McNaughton to play in his familiar position of outside left.

Special trains from the Illawarra region brought many more fans to Sydney. They had Tom Thompson and Arthur Druery to cheer for but by far the biggest star in their eyes was Judy Masters, the New South Wales captain. His aggressive style of play and knack of popping up at the right time to poach goals had made him a fan favourite for years. With the amount of publicity football had been getting in Sydney over the last few days, Masters' name was on everyone's lips.

Apart from the polling booth at the Town Hall, the centre of Sydney was deserted. Crowds swarmed around the Moore Park precinct to watch the two big football matches: New South Wales vs Queensland in rugby league and the New South Wales vs England football game. Rugby league spruikers attempted to steer spectators towards the Sydney Cricket Ground. The football fans walked straight past them.

By 1pm, the Show Ground's Coronation Stand was full. At 2pm, all seated accommodation had been taken. Preliminary matches were played to entertain the ever-swelling crowds.

A goal scored for England in a match against NSW

Despite the rain earlier in the week, the ground was firm. The verdant field belied a rough surface. A sheep dog trial - a show where farm dogs display their skills in rounding up sheep - had been held the day before, further compacting the surface. The dry conditions meant the ball would be light and bouncy. The sun was shining, a trifle warmer than the Englishmen liked.

It was becoming a squeeze inside the Show Ground as the time for kickoff approached. With 45,000 tickets already sold, ground staff stopped issuing tickets. With more than 50,000 people packed inside, the gates were shut.

This was a cosmopolitan audience for 1920s Sydney. Accents were heard from all over the British Isles; there were Europeans, especially from ships' crews, as well as members of Sydney's Chinese community who became fans of the game in the wake of the visit by their countrymen in 1923.

It was a busy scene down on the field. Policemen, first aid officers, band members, pressmen and others were milling about. Presenters from radio stations 2BL and 2FC were performing final checks before their live broadcasts of the match. The 40-member Westmead Boys' Home Band entertained the crowd with a selection of popular tunes. Just after 3pm, all eyes turned towards the players' gate near the grandstand.

* * *

Saturday, 30 May 1925, Game 7: England vs New South Wales, Sydney Show Ground

In the New South Wales dressing room, the players are on edge. The younger team members listen to their leaders; experienced goalkeeper George Cartwright, centre-half Alf Edwards, the only English-born player in the team, and of course their Gallipoli-veteran skipper Judy Masters. There are last-minute instructions from coach Bill Carrol. Syd Storey gives them a pep talk and reminds them of the match plan. Strike early, strike hard, kickoff if we win the toss. Referee Wright calls the players and Masters leads his team down the steps and out onto the field.

Blinking in the bright sunlight the players look out onto a sea of faces. It's like something out of dream. People crowd the stairwells, others have clambered onto grandstand roofs. One man has lashed himself to a railing and will spend the entire game dangling above the other spectators. People have taken up vantage points on balconies and roofs of buildings overlooking the ground. The reception is absolutely deafening. The sound of the Westmead Boys' Home Band playing 'Advance Australia Fair' is drowned out by the heaving crowd.

The appearance of the New South Wales team in their sky blue jerseys has brought the 50,000 people in

The crowd at the England vs NSW match, Sydney Show Ground

'Judy' Masters (left) with Len Graham of England

the Show Ground to their feet. They now eagerly await the arrival of the all-conquering Englishmen.

A momentary silence comes over the crowd.

The white-shirted figure of captain Len Graham emerges from the grandstand leading his men out. This is England. A mighty roar goes up around the arena that shakes the timbers of the grandstands like an earth tremor. Finally, after 45 years of waiting, hoping and cajoling, an English football team has stepped onto a pitch in Sydney. The roar goes on and on and on. Bemused patrons at the rugby league match at the Cricket Ground wonder: what the hell is going on next door?

The two teams line up to shake hands with the dignitaries. There is a clear difference in the size of the players. The Englishmen are taller and heavier. How can the lightweight amateurs from New South Wales compete against such hardened professionals as these?

New South Wales officials Syd Storey, Ern Lukeman, Stephen Stack, Tom Crawford, the coaching staff of Bill Carrol and Tom Langridge, and the reserve players take their seats. On the English side, John Lewis, who had delivered a football lecture to schoolboys at the Education Department in the morning, is joined by Mark Frowde and trainer Mo Atherton. The rest of the non-playing members of the English squad take their seats dressed to the nines in overcoats and hats. Unable to contain their excitement, the Westmead Boys' Band keeps on playing.

The attention of the 50,000 spectators now turns to the match that is about to unfold. The actual audience is far bigger than those gathered at the Show Ground, of course: beyond the ticketless with a distant view from their vantage points, many thousands more are home, tuning their wireless sets to the live radio broadcast. And not only in Australia. The signal can be heard loud and clear as far away as New Zealand.

Judy Masters and Len Graham shake hands out in the middle. Masters wins the toss, a small victory for the home team. Completely forgetting the game plan, he chooses to defend the Paddington end, meaning that England will kickoff.

At 3:15 pm, Mr Wright puts the whistle to his mouth.

England centre-forward Bert Batten kicks off and Jack Elkes immediately lights up the crowd with an angular, jerking run that takes him around a couple of the New South Wales players. Elkes threads a ball through to Batten but before he can unleash a shot he is robbed by New South Wales' centre-half Alf Edwards. Edwards is alert to the game plan and looking up to see which winger is free, switches the ball to Stan Bourke on the right.

Stan Bourke

Bourke takes it down the touchline and sends a long ball to the opposite wing. Now it's the turn of the Cessnock youngster Roy McNaughton to show his mettle. McNaughton motors down the sideline, outpacing Stan Charlton. Reaching the ball just inside the byline, he sends a high cross into the goalmouth. England's left-back Cec Poynton doesn't see Judy Masters, who, drawing on all the craft of his 18 years in the game, drifts between the English defenders. Facing the ball, Masters swivels and makes good contact with his head. Harry Hardy, the English keeper, scrambles backwards, eyes on the looping ball. He flings himself full length and gets a hand to it. It's not enough. The back of the net ripples. Masters wheels around to celebrate and the crowd roar in utter disbelief.

New South Wales has scored just 90 seconds into the match. It is the first outfield goal England have conceded. It is the first time they have trailed. In the crowd, hats are tossed in the air, people jump up and down and hug strangers. Some spectators immediately switch allegiances. A man from Glasgow says, "if it's good enough to live here, it's good enough to support the local side".

The crowd stand and applaud Masters all the way until he takes up his position. England look shell-shocked. Hardy has words with Poynton. There's a lot of finger-pointing by the tourists. Conceding an early goal is not what they had planned on.

England looks to slow the play down and adjust to the firm pitch. Elkes in particular does his best to keep the ball away from the locals. Pressure mounts on the home team as England get into their stride. New South Wales face a succession of corners, which George Cartwright and his defence deal with unconvincingly. Edwards is everywhere for New South Wales and is well supported by left-half Harry Spurway, who proves his value in the aerial duels.

After claiming a cross from McNaughton, England's Harry Hardy boots the ball well over halfway. It's skilfully trapped by Graham. He passes to Elkes, who runs at the defence but the ball is put behind by Australia.

Newcastle United's Stan Seymour's corner is deadly accurate. Ernie Simms attacks the ball and heads it into the net. The crowd roar again. It seems they are enjoying the spectacle regardless of which team scores. Twelve minutes in and it's 1-1. A spectator is overheard saying, "you can shut the gate".

Alf Edwards breaks up another of the visitors' attacks and sends the ball out to Percy Lennard. He picks out Masters in the middle and on he boots it to Stan Bourke on the right wing. English hands shoot up for offside against Bourke. Fullback Poynton momentarily stops and appeals to the referee. Masters, sensing an opportunity, glides in behind Poynton. Bourke sends the ball out in front of his captain. Hardy comes tearing off his line. Masters gets a touch on the ball as Hardy closes in. The ball rolls at a snail's pace towards the unguarded net.

There is an agonising moment for the spectators as players from both sides sprint towards the ball. It beats them all into the back of the net. There's bedlam in the stands as people jump and shout and cheer themselves hoarse. The little coal miner from Balgownie has done it again.

Alf Edwards

English protests about offside are waved off by Mr Wright. On the sideline, Tom Crawford jumps in the air and as he lands, knocks John Lewis off his seat. He is helped to his feet and calls the decision "a ridiculous affair". A few pressmen near the play think Lewis might have a case but the goal stands and New South Wales lead 2-1.

Again the Englishmen come on, probing at the Sky Blues' defence. The diminutive inside left, Tom Thompson, continually helps out at the back but gets injured in a challenge and is forced off the field. Without substitutes there is deep concern on the New South Wales bench. Tom Langridge gets to work and Thompson is able to return after a few minutes.

Jack Elkes makes a good run and for once gets the better of Edwards. After an interchange of passes with Simms, Elkes beats Charlie Leabeater before laying the ball into the path of Batten. From close range, Bert Batten makes no mistake. England celebrate the equaliser far more enthusiastically than any goal they'd scored on tour. The half-time whistle blows, the scores locked at 2-2.

The crowd applaud the Westmead Boys' Band as they march around the arena in the half-time break. In the England dressing room, trainer Mo Atherton is kept busy. Charlton has picked up an injury tussling with McNaughton and has a muscle under his ribcage taped up.

England begin the second half throwing everything at New South Wales. Elkes twists and turns, "jazzing as ably as Penny Dawes ever did", according to one press reporter. Hardy clears a ball downfield, Elkes controls it and dribbles past four defenders before being fouled by Druery. Elkes gives him a spray, an indication of England's growing frustration.

The pressure affects England more than New South Wales. Not wanting to end their winning streak, England skipper Graham rallies his men. The game develops into a battle between the skilful possession tactics of England and the occasional counter attacks down the flanks by the home side. Charlie Spencer and Judy Masters have been having a fine battle all day but Spencer finally snaps when Masters slides through and takes out his legs. The big Englishman waves his finger theatrically in the local hero's face. Fifty thousand spectators watch each wag of the finger then give Spencer a razz.

Ten minutes to go and still New South Wales holds out. England launch another raid through Charlie Hannaford. His pass finds Elkes, who drops his shoulder and rounds a couple of defenders. He lays off a beautiful ball to an onrushing Batten, who slams the ball first time. Cartwright makes a despairing dive but the ball rattles the back of the net. It's 3-2 to England.

A completely exhausted New South Wales rally for a final effort. The crowd are in great voice and urge them on. With time nearly up, McNaughton makes a dash down the left. Once more outpacing the defence, his cross has Hardy scurrying across the goalmouth. Stan Bourke from the opposite wing makes a run into the area and stretches to meet the cross. The open goal beckons in front of him. His outstretched leg misses the ball by inches. The full-time whistle blows soon after and England have won an amazing match 3-2. Both teams are given a standing ovation but it is Judy Masters who is cheered all the way back to the pavilion.

* * *

Most critics thought England did just enough to win. Batten and Elkes were outstanding, even if Elkes overdid the clever footwork at times. Len Graham gave a faultless exhibition of halfback play. England's ball control and positional play was much better than New South Wales, even if they were a little slow at times. Hardy's ball distribution from the back was exceptional and far better than Cartwright's.

Besides the all-conquering hero Masters, Roy McNaughton was the pick of the New South Wales forwards. Edwards at centre-half had a brilliant game and all but booked his place in Australia's first Test team in three weeks' time. Cartwright performed well after a slow start, confirming his position as the leading goalkeeper in the country.

The match was a fine advertisement for football. Nobody who witnessed the game would ever forget it.

Crowd figures were very much estimates but the general consensus was that football drew a bigger crowd than the rugby league. One newspaper published the following:

Crowd:
    Soccer: 45,000   Rugby League: 38,000

Gate
    Soccer: £3,750   Rugby League: £2,550

Despite these figures, Horrie Miller of the NSWRFL offered a £100 bet (proceeds to charity) if someone could conclusively prove that football had the bigger crowd. There was no disputing the gate takings though. Football's nearly 50% higher gate was a cause of celebration among the game's supporters.

Football people were in great spirits at Sargent's Cafe in Market Street that night. Stephen Stack of the NSWFA toasted the visitors. John Lewis replied that New South Wales had come out so fast and were so quick on the ball that it gave his team a fright. He was sure soccer would become the most popular sport in the country and urged Australia to enter the Olympic Games. Mark Frowde said New South Wales caught them napping but assured them it wouldn't happen again.

The match had people talking in offices, factories and schools. Caricatures of the players, especially Judy Masters, appeared in the papers. The cover of *The Sydney Mail* was adorned with an image of an archetypal English footballer. The *Arrow* newspaper began a series of weekly articles by a 'renowned British Coach' on the tactics of the game.

Writing in the *Arrow,* Alec Boyd noted: "It was wonderful to see 40,000 people at the Show Ground when Judy Masters led out the thin blue line. A soccer wave has come over New South Wales."

The *Referee* said that "after the missionary work of the English team is finished, soccer enthusiasts expect the game to be played in every hamlet in Australia".

The English footballers were being looked after by their hosts. Captain Turner of the Canterbury Football Club organised a fleet of cars to take the tourists on a day trip to Palm Beach. Alec Boyd took Len Graham, Bert Batten and Ernie Simms to a billiards exhibition by Australia's famous Lindrum brothers.

The team were guests of the Tivoli theatre, where they once again caught up with Will Fyffe. His skit on the horrors of being a teetotaller had everyone in hysterics. Even John Lewis, the ardent temperance advocate, was seen to have a smile on his face.

* * *

England's next game was against a Sydney Metropolitan team. State selectors would be at the match to see if any players could force their way into the New South Wales team for their next encounter with England in five days' time.

The advertising for the game made use of the extraordinary crowd at the weekend:

'Why did 50,000 people see the Englishmen play last Saturday? COME AND SEE FOR YOURSELF'.

To show that no hard feelings existed between football and the Queensland Rugby League, which had allowed football the use of the Exhibition Ground in Brisbane, the Queensland rugby league team was invited to watch the game as guests of the New South Wales Football Association.

Wednesday, 3 June 1925: Match 8 - England v Sydney, Sydney Show Ground

Another fine day with a light breeze greets the tourists as they step on to the hard surface of the Sydney Show Ground. A record midweek crowd of around 12,000,

Frank Gallen

including a few thousand school children, makes for a vibrant atmosphere. The Sydney side take the field in a smart uniform of red and black vertical stripes, England as always in white. The Queensland rugby league players take their seats on the sideline, as does radio station 2FC, whose team is again calling the game due to the popularity of Saturday's broadcast.

The locals make a fast-paced start. Allan Burns gets away down the wing only to be stopped by Tom Whittaker. The powerfully built Arsenal man begins the match well, breaking up most of Sydney's early attacks. He is proving an invaluable member of the team and every bit as good a back as Charlton and Poynton.

Sydney's forwards lack cohesion and England begin to take the game up to the locals. A powerful shot by Charlie Hannaford skims the crossbar early in the game. Jack Elkes, with his tricky body swerves and ability to keep possession under pressure, is the most dangerous player for England. Thirty minutes into the game Joe Hannah receives the ball from a throw-in and passes to Liverpool's Jimmy Walsh who slips it to Batten. Sydney's right-back Frank Gallen makes a challenge but the ball falls to Jack Elkes who sends in a belter of a shot to give England the lead.

A few minutes later, Bert Batten receives a cross from Jimmy Hamilton, takes on a defender and blasts a scorching shot into the top corner. Sydney keeper Ted Atchison can only stand and watch. At half-time, the score stands at England 2 Sydney 0.

England start the second half in style, peppering the goal but Atchison makes some fine saves. In a rare attacking move, Sydney brings the ball into England's penalty area. A melee ensues and Sydney's centre-forward, ex-rugby league player Sid Alewood, goes down in the box. Referee Bates points to the penalty spot. Fred Hancock of the Balmain club converts with ease and the score is now 2-1 to England. The visitors are under

Programme for the function at Bondi on June 3rd

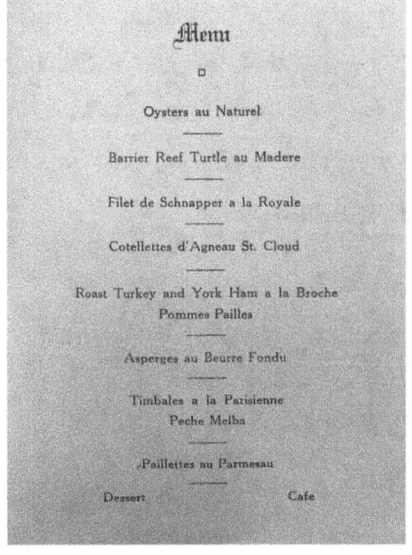

On the menu at the Bondi event

pressure for the second straight match.

For the rest of the game, a nervy England are happy to keep possession while Sydney wear themselves out chasing shadows. With just a few minutes to go, England half Jimmy Hamilton wins a challenge and threads a pass through to Batten. Hands shoot up from the locals and someone yells 'offside'. Despite there being no whistle, Atchison stops and Batten calmly slots the ball into the back of the net. England win the match 3-1.

* * *

That night, the English team were guests of the Eastern Suburbs Football Club. The dinner was held at the Bondi Hotel right on the beachfront. Hugh McIntosh, a patron of the club, gave another of his impassioned speeches on the future of football.

John Lewis replied with thanks and gave out the precious little blue enamel FA badges to Ern Lukeman, Bill Robertson, William Lincoln and Stephen Stack.

The party moved next door to the exotically named Bondi Casino, a jazz dancing hall with views over the Pacific Ocean. With a sprung floor of Tasmanian blackwood, the Bondi Casino could accommodate over 1,000 people. What the strict teetotaller John Lewis would have been unaware of at this supposedly dry venue, was that if you asked the right person in the right way, you could get an order of sly grog delivered discreetly to your table.

Lewis was quite taken with Bondi. The salt air was good for the lungs. The crashing waves of the Pacific were soothing to the soul. Waverley Oval was just around the corner and England could train there. When the tourists returned from their impending trip to the South Coast, Lewis would shift the team's Sydney base to the Bondi Hotel.

12
'At The Point of a Pistol'

Saturday, 28 March 1925, Ball's Paddock, Woonona

Beneath the shadows of the escarpment, the two wrestlers circle each other, probing for a weakness. Sweat pours off Englishman Billy Dutton as he grapples his opponent. The two men writhe about, trying to catch the other off guard. Then Dutton spots an opening and in a flash applies his trademark scissors hold.

The crowd rise. They may not know the first thing about wrestling but these mostly coal miners from the Illawarra are firmly on Dutton's side. Dutton slowly forces his opponent to the canvas, twisting and manoeuvring him so as to pin a shoulder. His opponent, Billy Meeske, a bull of a man born with hazy Russian ancestry, bridges his powerful body but Dutton has a good grip. Gradually, he forces one of Meeske's shoulders to the ground. He now begins to work on the other.

The referee lies flat on the canvas, right arm raised, ready to bring it down if Meeske's other shoulder is pinned. The crowd are mesmerised. Ding! Meeske is literally saved by the bell.

Dutton's supporters take the bell as a signal the bout is over. They hurl their hats in the air and prepare to cash in their betting slips. Spectators mob the arena. One woman gives Billy Dutton a kiss.

But the bell is only for the end of the third round. With difficulty, the event staff clear the ring and the match continues. Although he had once wrestled to a draw for the European Middleweight Championship, Dutton still has to prove himself in Australia. And Billy Meeske, one of the strongest wrestlers Australia has ever produced, is no pushover.

In the fifth round, Meeske goes on the offensive. Applying a headlock, he pins Dutton for a fall. As the lighter Dutton tires, Meeske presses home his advantage. He quickly scores another fall and is declared the winner in the best of three falls contest.

* * *

The mastermind who staged the wrestling bout was Harry Graino, a one-armed boxing and wrestling entrepreneur originally from South Africa. That this unusual sporting contest took place on the South Coast of New South Wales was down to Graino's belief that it would get strong local support. The preliminary attraction was a football match between two local clubs, Helensburgh and Woonona.

Graino knew that the Illawarra miners watching the football would be a captive audience for the wrestling match since Billy Dutton, although in the country for just over a month, was working as a coal miner at Bulli. And it was common knowledge that people from the Illawarra always supported their own. Added to that, a specially organised train bringing wrestling fans, illegal bookmakers and assorted charlatans from Sydney, meant that a good gate was assured.

As the locals left Ball's Paddock at the end of the wrestling match, they were already looking ahead to 6 June. That was the date for the biggest match in the South Coast's football history - the game between their local heroes and England. Not that the upcoming match had everybody's support.

* * *

In 1924, the Illawarra representative team played six matches, including three against Canada. This disrupted the local competition, which had to be extended into the summer months. Some players dropped out of football when the cricket season began.

Illawarra football administrators Bill Cunningham and Jack Hawke had been at loggerheads with their Sydney counterparts over players' expenses. Both men knew intimately the tough conditions that many players faced in the coal mines and how injuries acquired on the football pitch could affect the incomes of men and their families. Indeed, the football year 1925 began with a benefit match between Woonona and Balgownie for Bill Cunningham, who had his hand blown off in a mining accident the previous year.

The 1924 Gardiner Cup Final was another sticking point in relations between Illawarra and Sydney. No South Coast team had ever won the competition but the 1924 final was between Illawarra club Woonona, and Newcastle club West Wallsend. The logical neutral venue would have been Sydney but the NSWFA played the match in Newcastle, where they would get a better gate. Woonona lost 3-0 and this irked many football supporters in the Illawarra.

Another keen supporter of Illawarra football was Sid Cope, who wrote for both the *Illawarra Mercury* and the

South Coast Times and Wollongong Argus. Cope was once the secretary of the Illawarra association and had supplied medals and trophies for the competitions. He not only advocated for the fair payment of players' expenses but pushed strongly for the introduction of professionalism. Commenting on England's chances in the games in New South Wales, he wrote: "It is logical to conclude England will win being trained in the art of soccer not to mention paid also, which is your incentive to produce your best."

* * *

After jazzing the night away at the Bondi Casino, the English team were driven by motor car to Wollongong on Thursday, 4 June. They were given a civic reception at Zander's Hotel in Thirroul, where the team would stay for three nights. Once more displaying the tourists' versatility, Charlie Hannaford provided the piano accompaniment to a number of the songs.

The venue for England's match against Illawarra was Bode's Oval in North Wollongong. It was a private ground close to a hotel owned by publican George Bode. The spectator accommodation was Spartan. There were no grandstands. There were not even turnstiles - spectators were urged to bring the exact change. People were asked not to encroach on the arena, which was awkward because the boundary of the ground was a long way from the pitch. With no embankments, people arriving late would have to crane their necks to see over the people in front.

George Bode was a canny businessman. He applied for a licence to run a liquor stall from 10am to 6pm on the day of the match. The magistrate questioned why so early considering the game would be played in the afternoon. He granted the licence from 12pm to 5:45pm instead.

The Illawarra District Rugby League cancelled all their fixtures on the day of the match to give football a chance at maximising their gate. This move was at odds with the attitude of the NSWRFL.

On the Friday, A. McEvoy, an official of the Illawarra Rugby League, accompanied the tourists to Kiama to see the famous blowhole. With the recent unsettled weather, it was putting on a fine show, the plumes of ocean spray whooshing up over 20 metres in the air.

In his preview of the match, Sid Cope referred to the gutsy display of New South Wales the previous Saturday: "The secret of our wonderful display lay in the determination to do or die, that selfsame spirit which carried our boys up the slopes of Gallipoli, and let it be known that our [South] Coast team is fully imbued with the same spirit."

Part of the reason for Cope's combative talk was his concern over the bustling tactics of the Englishmen.

Cope was firmly in the camp that thought the English charging tactics were illegal and that the heavier tourists were gaining an unfair advantage.

Playing on their home turf and with a good crowd behind them, there were a few optimistic fans who believed the locals could spring a surprise. In Masters, Druery, and Thompson, Illawarra had players with recent experience against the Englishmen.

England's captain for the game was Arsenal fullback, Tom Whittaker. Newcastle United's Charlie Spencer was at centre-half and looking to make amends for allowing Judy Masters too much room in Sydney. Shortly before the game, Bill Sage had to withdraw due to knee trouble. Jack Elkes was summoned and made a quick change out of his suit. News that Elkes would play was much welcomed by the spectators flocking to Bode's. The crowd was in fine spirits. George Bode's liquor stall had been doing a brisk business, as had the illegal bookmakers taking bets out the back of the hotel. There was a rain shower about 15 minutes prior to kick off but as 3pm approached the sun came back out. The crowd waited expectantly for the teams to appear. This serene scene was entirely at odds with the chaos going on inside Bode's Hotel.

Saturday, 6 June 1925. Match 9: England v Illawarra, Bode's Oval, North Wollongong

Alec Boyd, the Sydney football correspondent, is chatting with some of the players inside the hotel, where England are getting ready. He notices Jack Elkes rush in from outside to change into his football gear. The reshuffle required by Sage's injury is worked through quickly and everything is going like clockwork. But there is no movement from where the opposition are getting ready. Common courtesy is that England enter the field second. So, they wait. And still they wait. Boyd goes across to take a look for himself.

He is politely greeted by Judy Masters and Illawarra Soccer Association president Bill Cunningham. But everywhere he looks he sees stony faces. Ern Lukeman, Syd Storey and Illawarra officials are talking earnestly with the players. Boyd soon gets to

Entry pass for England vs Illawarra match

the bottom of the incident. Encouraged by the big gates in Sydney and the disparity in earnings between themselves and England (and perhaps influenced by Cope's public advocacy of professionalism), the Illawarra players refuse to take the field when told their expenses will be ten shillings. Lukeman pleads with them - this is a long-standing agreement; we cannot just alter it willy-nilly; there are thousands of spectators outside waiting to see the Englishmen play.

A deal is finally struck, "at the point of a pistol", according to Boyd. The players agree to take the field for fifteen shillings. It is unclear to Boyd whether this extra money has come from Illawarra officials or from Storey and Lukeman. Judy Masters leads out a rather sullen team of locals a few minutes late to generous applause.

When Tom Whittaker leads England out, the cheers resound like thunder. Masters wins the toss and defends the southern end, where they would have the aid of a light breeze in the first half.

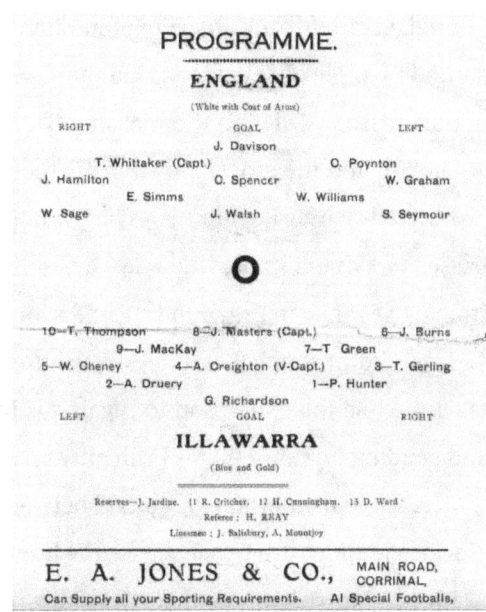

Programme showing Illawarra and English teams

The choice of referee is another bone of contention between Illawarra and Sydney. Illawarra's preferred referee was overruled by the NSWFA, which appointed Mr Reahy. Without the support of local officials and with the 'Prince of Referees' John Lewis watching on, it is a rather nervous Reahy who starts the game.

The pitch is soft underfoot and England spring into action from the kickoff. Elkes in particular is sharp and soon launches an England attack. He brings the ball downfield and slips it through to Ernie Simms on the gallop. Simms' low shot fizzes over the turf and beats Illawarra keeper Richardson pointless.

Illawarra, down in the dumps and down a goal, react with some physical play but against their heavier opponents come off second best. After England half Jimmy Hamilton is fouled for an illegal charge, Arthur Druery, the Illawarra left back, brings down Walsh in a crunching foul.

Five minutes into the game, Jimmy Walsh collects a pass on England's right flank and evades Druery's challenge. He beats Cheney and crosses from near the byline. Big Jack Elkes pounces and hits it first time, the shot flying into the corner of the net. It is now 2-0 to the tourists.

England's left-back Cec Poynton starts another attacking raid. He passes upfield to Hamilton, who waltzes around a couple of defenders. Hamilton passes to Elkes, who hits a first-time screamer that goes in off the underside of the crossbar. One reporter calls it, "The most beautiful shot seen on the ground." Within ten minutes, England are up 3-0 and the crowd are enjoying the spectacle.

The red-haired Poynton is giving a fine display of fullback play. He dispossesses Illawarra winger Burns and passes to Ernie Simms, who takes a shot from distance. Richardson fumbles the ball and Billy Williams converts from close range to bring up England's fourth.

Tom Thompson makes a rare foray into England's half but he is flattened by the much bigger Tom Whittaker. It takes a while for Thompson to regain his breath but when he does he creates another chance, beating Whittaker and sending in a shot that is brilliantly saved by Teddy Davison.

After a neat interplay of passes between Graham and Simms, the ball is played out to Williams, who hits a glorious left foot drive that shakes the home team's net for the fifth time.

Elkes next tricks three defenders on a jinking run and passes to Walsh on the right side. Walsh crosses to Stan Seymour who cleverly heads it in to make it 6-0 to England.

Millwall's Len Graham now turns provider. His pass finds Seymour who slips between two defenders and beats another before hitting a bullet-like shot into the top corner.

The locals have no response. Any forward movement is checked by England's speedy back pair of Poynton and Whittaker. Masters can barely get a touch with Spencer covering him like a blanket. England's keeper, Davison, begins wandering out of goal, sometimes up to the halfway line, a sight rarely seen on an Australian field.

Stan Seymour then breezes around a few players and sprints down the wing. His perfect cross finds the head of Simms and it is 8-0 to England.

Just before half-time, a particularly nasty incident occurs that casts a shadow over the rest of the game. Tom Thompson, who had been having a tussle with Tom Whittaker all match, brings down the Arsenal defender in a crude challenge. Referee Reahy waves play on. John Lewis is furious. English players rush in and jostle Thompson.

The half-time whistle blows as tensions simmer. The crowd invade the field and congratulate England on their great performance. Meanwhile, England's trainer Mo Atherton walks Whittaker up and down the touchline but the Arsenal man is in extreme pain.

The second half gets underway without Whittaker. As Lewis has steadfastly refused to allow substitutes, England have to play the rest of the game a man short. Spencer is taken out of the midfield and moved to the backs. England play on with four forwards.

It is England who are sullen in the second half. With ten men they spend most of their time keeping possession. They wait for an opponent to come to them then pass it to a free player. They show little ambition, partly in protest against the referee's failure to protect their player. There is no change to the half-time score, with England winning the game 8-0.

* * *

England's best player was Elkes, who put on a fine display of clever footwork and shooting. England were also happy with the effort of Seymour, who was getting back to his club form. Most importantly, Spencer did a good job bottling up Judy Masters. But nothing could make up for the injury to Whittaker.

At the post-match dinner in Bode's Hotel, Lewis was ropeable: "I am disgusted with today's match. Foul play went on unchecked, and if our players are assaulted there is a danger of retaliation. Things which happened today were a disgrace to soccer football. These are strong words; but I am in the habit of saying just what I think when I feel strongly about things. For a man who will deliberately hurt an opponent, there is no room on the football field. Had today's incident happened in England the offender would have been sent off the field for a considerable time."

This was quite astonishing for the assembled guests. Generally, these functions were congenial affairs, but Lewis was never one to mince words.

Lukeman, Storey and Masters all said a few words to the stunned audience. The little blue enamel FA badges were duly handed out including one to McEvoy of the Illawarra Rugby League.

In the true tradition of Illawarra folk supporting their own, local journalists turned on John Lewis.

Writing in the *Illawarra Mercury*, 'Centre Forward' called Lewis "One-eyed", adding: "He can see all the dirty work by an opponent, but never by his own team." He also put into words what some of the journalists covering the tour had been thinking: "To me, Mr Lewis is a gentleman who is rather impressed by his own personality, and to treat this side of the world with a shade of contempt."

In the *South Coast Times and Wollongong Argus*, Cope, borrowing a coal-mining metaphor, likened the contest to "a pit horse trying to race a racehorse". His solution was to further advocate for professionalism: "How anybody can expect our boys to be disciplined so they will be forced to train, without receiving monetary inducements is beyond my comprehension."

Alec Boyd, however, was supportive of Lewis. He thought the match was ruined by fouls that went unpunished. He agreed with Lewis that Australia needed to stick to the FA's rule interpretations and that included not allowing substitutes.

This difference of opinion between journalists was another issue that reinforced the view in the Illawarra that Sydney was against them. As England left Wollongong for Sydney, the dispute between the associations was reaching boiling point.

13

Law One Again

Monday, 8 June, 1925, Sydney

The seaplane's engine spluttered into life with a cloud of blue smoke. Taxiing across the surface of Rose Bay, the plane picked up speed before lumbering into the air. The plane flew above the sparkling waters of Sydney Harbour before banking around to the south. There was barely a cloud in the afternoon sky and just a gentle breeze blowing from the south-west. Perfect conditions for flying, perfect conditions for a game of football.

The flight and its payload of paper were a welcome distraction for Lebbeus Hordern, one of the wealthiest men in Sydney. Lebbeus was part of the family empire that owned Australia's biggest department store, Hordern Brothers. This seaplane was one of a number owned by Lebbeus. His pilots had been flying them from Rose Bay since before the war. No longer directly associated with the firm, Lebbeus had splashed out his immense fortune on works of art from Europe, yachts, seaplanes and fast cars. One day he reputedly walked into a motor car showroom, asked to see the most expensive car in Sydney and bought it on the spot with cash. His home at Darling Point on Sydney Harbour was one of the most well-appointed mansions in the country.

The thing he wished to be distracted from was his very public divorce case, settled just a few days before. Newspapers called it a 'High society divorce' and the tribulations of the case were lapped up by the public. The salacious details supplied by Hordern's valet, Edward Fitzgerald, of secret trysts between Lebbeus and a Miss Willis in various swanky hotels in London were read widely, Hordern denounced as immoral - before the tales of his adventures were then read eagerly all over again. There was a child from the relationship that Lebbeus acknowledged as his own. Much to the public's amusement, Fitzgerald testified that Miss Willis used to call Hordern by the pet name 'Lebbie'. The ruling that Mrs. Hordern was granted an annulment was made in front of a gallery packed with the cream of Sydney's party crowd.

Whether Lebbeus Hordern himself was actually in the seaplane or just watching from the shore that day is unclear, but regardless, he was in his element. The sound of an aeroplane engine and the smell of the plane's exhaust was far more invigorating than the goings on in the divorce court.

The pilot veered slightly to the south-east of the city and fixed his gaze on the target a few kilometres away. Up ahead in the Moore Park precinct were the two stadiums, the Sydney Cricket Ground and the Sydney Show Ground, both filled with spectators. The plane levelled off and made its final run. Down below, thousands of arms reached upwards ready for the catch.

* * *

John Lewis was not a happy man when he arrived at England's new digs at Bondi. He knew Arsenal would be furious about the injury to Whittaker. Other clubs could make things difficult for the FA in London. If anything, the drama at Wollongong had hardened his resolve to ensure the Australians played strictly to the FA version of the game.

Both Tom Whittaker and Bill Sage had been originally selected for the second match against New South Wales on the Monday that also marked the King's Birthday holiday. Sage's knee was still causing him trouble and Whittaker could only hobble about. Sage's place was taken by Hannah, and Whittaker's by Charlton. The changes meant England fielded the same team that edged out New South Wales nine days earlier.

New South Wales only made one change from the first game, Percy Lennard making way for Illawarra player Tom Green of the Coledale club.

The first match between England and New South Wales whetted the appetite of Sydney sports fans for competitive football. In expectation of another epic struggle, a huge crowd of around 40,000 packed the Sydney Show Ground. As before, an interstate rugby league match between New South Wales and Queensland was being played at the Sydney Cricket Ground next door.

Monday, 8 June 1925, Game 10: England vs New South Wales, Sydney Show Ground

Judy Masters leads New South Wales out onto the Sydney Show Ground. When England follow behind their captain Jack Elkes, they are given a typically loud reception. Although the players are well received, the reverence for manager John Lewis has diminished. His outburst at Wollongong and his continued refusal to allow substitutes has cooled the relationship between the sporting public and the English team's management.

With state governor Sir Dudley de Chair watching on from the grandstand, Masters kicks off for New South Wales. The Sky Blues advance downfield but the move is intercepted by Len Graham, who passes to Elkes. The England captain has the ball on a string, taking it around a few defenders before testing Cartwright with a good shot.

The early play is all with England but they struggle with their footing on the hard surface.

New South Wales attack on the counter and a rasping shot from Judy Masters is saved well by Hardy. The pattern of England pressure with the occasional New South Wales counterattack has the crowd enthralled. The match looks set to be another classic.

Around twenty minutes into the game, Masters forces another save from Hardy. The English keeper quickly sends his team on the attack.

George Cartwright

Ernie Simms receives the ball in his own half and passes to Elkes, who sets Batten underway. Batten beats a couple of players and bears down on goal. Forty thousand spectators rise as one. The New South Wales left-back Arthur Druery gives chase and catches up with Batten just as he enters the penalty area.

New South Wales goalkeeper George Cartwright has had his fair share of detractors. According to them, he doesn't always gather the ball cleanly, takes too long to get rid of it and his distribution is poor. But one thing they never doubt is his courage. And with the English centre-forward charging towards goal, Cartwright instinctively dives headlong at Batten's feet. Druery, Cartwright and Batten all come together in a sickening pile up. To everyone's astonishment the ball doesn't end up in the net.

Cartwright's brilliant save has come at a cost. He waves for assistance. Spectators can see blood pouring from a gash in his wrist. The game is stopped as an ambulance officer stems the bleeding with a bandage.

Syd Storey and New South Wales football officials look on in despair. Even Tom Langridge can't work his magic and Cartwright is taken to hospital. The 'no substitute' clause of Law One is now in play. After a quick conference between Masters and the New South Wales bench, it is decided to give the goalkeeper's jersey to Tom Thompson, one of the shortest men on the field. New South Wales will now have to play seventy minutes with a man down and a makeshift goalkeeper.

Most of the crowd, unacquainted with the nuances of the substitute rule other than reading criticisms of John Lewis in the newspapers, fully expect a substitute will come on. When they realise it's not going to happen a section of the crowd becomes hostile. The word 'sportsmanship' or rather, the lack of it, is tossed around. They have paid good money to see a fair contest. What had been one of the most interesting matches now appears to be headed for a walkover.

Play starts again between the ten amateurs of New South Wales and the eleven professionals of England in front of a deflated crowd. Judy Masters does his best to rally his men and soon they launch an unlikely counterattack. Tom Green takes possession and skilfully evades Graham's challenge. He looks up to see his captain calling for the ball and guides a pass right at Masters' feet. With his uncanny ability to read a game, Masters utilises the old 'miner's style' tactic of sending the ball out to the opposite wing. Now the crowd sees what's up. Roy McNaughton has made a run down the wing and Masters has brilliantly played him into space. The crowd rise as the New South Wales outside left makes an angled run towards goal. If only McNaughton can get to the ball before the English defenders.

Harry Spurway

McNaughton reaches the ball first and without looking up hits it first time. The shot catches Hardy off guard. Springing to his left, the England keeper throws out a hand but the ball is past him. The crowd see the net ripple and go delirious as New South Wales take the lead. The Show Ground rocks as the spectators go wild.

England don't dwell long on the setback. A typical long clearance from Hardy is controlled by Charlie Hannaford, who rounds Harry Spurway with ease. He takes the ball downfield and passes to Elkes, who plays it out to Seymour on the wing. Dropping his shoulder, Seymour cuts in and hits a shot that speeds across the grass and beyond the reach of stand-in keeper Thompson to level the scores.

With half-time looming, England press forward once more. The ball arrives at Simms' feet with the goal beckoning. Before he shoots, Edwards clatters into him and referee Wright points to the penalty spot. Bert Batten steps up and slams the ball way over the crossbar. Half-time arrives with the scores locked 1-1.

The crowd are annoyed about the match being spoiled by Cartwright's injury and restless, too, since there is no band to entertain them in the interval. But help is at hand. A shape appears out of the sky followed by the faint sound of an aircraft engine. The Hordern's seaplane passes over the ground dropping leaflets from the sky. Fans try their best to catch as many of them as they can. Next day, they can check the newspapers to see if their leaflet has one of the lucky numbers that entitles them to a £1 voucher at Hordern Brothers' George Street store.

When the second half begins, England makes good use of their one-man advantage. Thompson is soon beaten but a last-ditch goal line clearance from Charlie Leabeater keeps the ball out. Elkes, Seymour and Simms then combine to bring the ball into the area and from a scramble the ball bounces to Batten, who volleys from close range to give the visitors a 2-1 lead.

New South Wales become stretched as England starve them of possession. The local players may be speedy but they lack the stamina of their professionally trained opponents. New South Wales' defenders heroically work to keep England from scoring. At the other end, the tourists' keeper Harry Hardy cuts a lonely figure.

Leabeater, who has defended superbly all day, lunges into a challenge and fouls Seymour. Leabeater gets up and tries to walk off the pain in his knee but it's no use. He's forced to retire and New South Wales play on with just nine men.

With only a few minutes left, Elkes sets up Simms, who shoots from the edge of the area, easily beating Thompson. Right on full-time, Elkes sets up Batten to crash an unstoppable long-range shot off the inside of the crossbar and into the net.

The match finishes 4-1 to England. Considering the setback New South Wales had, the result is no disgrace. England's first two goals had been scored against 10 men and their last two against nine.

* * *

Harry Spurway and Roy McNaughton were the best of the local players. They looked to have booked their places in the first Test in Brisbane in three weeks' time along with Judy Masters and Alf Edwards. Two other seeming certainties, Maunder and Cartwright, were under injury clouds. Maunder had not played after picking up his knee injury in Melbourne, while Cartwright needed to recuperate after receiving several stitches in his wrist.

Most of the 40,000 crowd left the venue disappointed. For them the match had been a farce once Cartwright left the field. No amount of technicalities about rules and playing the FA way could shake their belief they'd been robbed of a fair contest. Why pay extra to watch a lopsided football match when they could see a cheaper game of rugby league? Their one consolation was the possibility of cashing in a £1 Hordern's voucher the next day.

Sports fans had long memories. During the Great Britain rugby league tour in 1924, the visitors observed the no-substitute rule but sportingly allowed Australia to use them. The Australian public gave more credence to that precedent than an edict from the FA in London, an organisation that had paid lip service to football in Australia for years.

The *Sydney Sportsman* commented: "If the tour of the English Soccer players is to continue, the financial success it has so far been, some more satisfactory arrangement must be come to with the English manager, Mr Lewis, regarding the replacement of players injured in the first half of the game."

As well as calling the match "a farce, due to the bad sportsmanship of the Englishmen", *The Labor Daily* opined: 'It was not a Test match, and it does not seem fair that the game should be spoilt by the enforcing of such a strict rule, especially when the round ball game is striving for popularity."

The *Evening News* said John Lewis should be more tolerant, especially as football was competing against the rugby codes: "The English managers would do well to meet the desires of the New South Wales public in this matter, for the substitution of injured players seems part of the traditional sportsmanship, and that they should play according to the practice in local soccer, rugby union and rugby league."

One of the few journalists who sided with the English management was Alec Boyd. He argued that Lewis was duty bound to play by the dictates of the FA, and they had decided these games would be treated as competitive matches. Australia needed to play according to the correct laws of the game.

There were anomalies in the way substitute rules were applied in New South Wales. In a match in Newcastle, the goalkeeper had been replaced after being injured. Once he'd been treated he went back on the field and the substitute goalkeeper came off again.

It had also become customary to allow first-half substitutes in league and Gardiner Cup matches. As they were competitive fixtures, the NSWFA was in breach of the rules.

For his part, Lewis said that neither himself, Mark Frowde, or captain Jack Elkes had been approached before the game. His view was that only matches played for a charity or similar purposes were covered by the substitute law. This was also the view in London. If he agreed to anything otherwise he would be going against the wishes of his governing body. He warned that since Australia was affiliated with the FA, they must accept their ruling without complaint.

* * *

With the New South Wales game being played on a Monday, England had some time on their hands before their next game in Newcastle on Saturday. Players took to the Moore Park golf course, looking dandy in their plus-fours and multi-coloured sweaters. Len Graham and some teammates watched Walter Lindrum playing billiards. Lindrum said he would be happy to give the Englishmen some tips.

With the first Sydney leg of the tour complete, it was a good time for Syd Storey and Ern Lukeman to take stock. The 10 matches to date had drawn gate receipts just shy of £10,000, about half the amount needed to break even. With 15 matches left, including the five Tests, there was hope that the tour could make a profit. Negative publicity over the substitute rule was a potential dampener. Frustrated by Lewis' intransigence over substitutes, Storey devised a new plan to force England's hand.

14

A Wembley Moment on the Hunter

Spring 1884, Minmi, Awabakal Country

In the gloaming, eight coal miners gather on a hillside in Minmi. They watch in silence as the last light fades from the western skies, silhouetting the tops of the gum trees. Around them, the air is alive with the night sounds of the Australian bush. The noises might put the wind up a new chum fresh off the boat, but these miners have been here long enough to take no notice. And although their little mining community of Minmi is expanding, they still feel a long way from the rest of the world; a sense of being at the edge of things. The men speak among themselves in broad Scottish accents.

One of the men is Jack Winning, dark haired and the possessor of a luxuriant walrus moustache. He has just collected a newspaper from the post office. His edition of *The Glasgow Herald,* although six months old, represents the latest news from home. A member of the group harangues him: "Come on Jack, we're dying to know what's happening."

Winning obliges and in the dwindling light reads aloud a football article that goes something like this: the Vale of Leven were due to play Queen's Park in the final of the Scottish Cup. A few days before the match, Vale of Leven let Queen's Park know they couldn't make the final and asked for it to be postponed. Queen's Park refused their request. Rules were rules and Vale of Leven should be well aware of them. Queen's Park claimed the cup when their opponents didn't show.

A silence comes over the group, apart that is from the screeches, hisses and shrieks of various owls, frogs, geckos, brush-tailed possums, bats and other creatures of the night. A man named Charlie Fitzpatrick shakes his head and says: "Imagine not turning up for a cup final. Minmi lads would never do that."

It's 'Scones' McCrorie who puts two and two together: "Why don't we form our own team?"

A meeting is held. The local pit manager chips in some money to get things started. Players sign on and help clear a plot of land, known as Kelly's Paddock, for a football field. A set of rules and balls are obtained, and an all-white playing kit is agreed upon. Thus, the Minmi Rangers are born, the first football club in the Newcastle district.

* * *

The Minmi origin story, even if a little embellished, became something of a template for other clubs being formed in Newcastle. A group of miners would meet, a pit manager, happy to see the men engaged in a healthy (and sober) activity away from the workplace, would tip in some funds and a football club would spring up.

The city of Newcastle, situated about 150km north of Sydney at the mouth of the Hunter River, has always been an Australian football heartland. Football there was characterised by its coal mining roots and strong community ties. Playing fields were often rough and became bogs when wet. The locals played the no-nonsense type of football derided by the Sydney press as the 'miner's style'. After all, there wasn't much point playing fancy football when the ball could bobble or disappear down a wombat burrow at any moment.

Early games were fiercely contested and clubs soon looked further afield for competition. In 1887, Newcastle club Hamilton Athletic shocked Sydney football fans by beating Granville 4-1 in the final of the New South Wales knockout cup.

Representative matches between Newcastle and Sydney began in 1886 and became semi-regular fixtures. Minmi Rangers won the Gardiner Cup in 1892 (the New South Wales knockout cup became the Gardiner Cup in 1888) and another Newcastle club, West Wallsend, won it two years in succession in 1900 and 1901.

By the start of the 1925 season, Newcastle clubs had appeared in eight of the previous nine Gardiner Cup finals and won it four times. West Wallsend were the current cup holders, having defeated Woonona 3-0 in the 1924 final.

Since the advent of international football in 1922, many players from Newcastle had represented Australia. Peter Doyle and Bill Maunder played in Australia's first international against New Zealand in Dunedin in 1922. Maunder's name would be forever in the history books as the scorer of Australia's first international goal.

Football fans in Newcastle looked forward to England's visit in 1925. They hoped their local men would put up a fight. In West Wallsend they had arguably the strongest club side in the land, and in Bill Maunder one of its best players. The Newcastle representative team had not lost a match since 1920. One local newspaper columnist suggested New South Wales selectors should have filled their team entirely with players from Newcastle.

As the date for England's first match in the Hunter approached, people talked about football in the coal mines, factories, offices and schools. People who had once pulled on a boot became experts overnight. Those who knew a little about the game became sages. The directors of the city's two rival theatre companies offered a medallion for the best player based on a popular vote. Newspapers with soccer coverage flew off the newsstands. The city of Newcastle was primed to go football crazy.

* * *

England travelled to Newcastle with a depleted squad of sixteen. Injured players Bill Sage and Tom Whittaker stayed behind in Sydney and checked in to Tom Langridge's School of Physical Culture. He would have them right to travel to Brisbane next week, Langridge said.

A good-sized gathering saw England off from Sydney's Central station. An English player asked what kind of city Newcastle was. The slightly cryptic reply "just make sure you wear black collars", was a reference to Newcastle being Australia's largest coal mining centre. Many of the Newcastle players worked in the mines. Jack Coutts, who'd played against New Zealand, China and Canada, accidentally put a pick through his hand earlier in the year. Bill Wells, who represented Newcastle in 1921, was killed in a mining accident in 1924.

At the civic reception in Newcastle, Mayor Morris Light told the audience about an unforgettable experience he had on a trip to the United Kingdom in 1923.

He had purchased a grandstand ticket to the first FA Cup final to be held at the brand new Wembley Stadium, between Bolton Wanderers and West Ham United. He watched in amazement as the ground filled with spectators then overflowed onto the playing arena. Mayor Light, despite having paid 30 shillings for a seat in the grandstand, was forced to stand.

Mounted police, including the famous white horse (actually a grey) named Billy, helped clear thousands of people from the pitch. During the match, players near the sidelines tried to avoid hurting (or being tripped by) spectators encroaching on the field. At half-time, both teams stood in the middle of the pitch, unable to make it to the dressing rooms. Throw-ins were taken from inside the touchlines. Spectators leaned against the goalposts. Light said he could never forget the experience of being in such a large crowd, estimated by some to be as high as 300,000.

John Lewis was pleased that the Newcastle Rugby League were co-operating with the local football association. This was in marked contrast to what he called the 'unfriendliness' of the NSWRFL in Sydney.

* * *

As facilities at the Newcastle Show Ground were far from luxurious, England changed into their kit prior to leaving their accommodation at the Criterion Hotel. Alec Boyd, who had travelled with England and was staying at the same hotel, was struck by how dead the centre of Newcastle was. It was only when the motor-car cavalcade carrying the English team neared the Show Ground that he could see the city was well and truly alive.

Spectators had begun pouring into the ground three hours before kickoff. The northern mail train brought a load of fans from Sydney. Special trains brought people in from the surrounding coalfields.

Local supporters were disappointed when news reached them that Bill Maunder would not be playing due to his persistent knee injury. Australian and New South Wales representative Percy Lennard was also left out of the team.

Maunder's centre-forward position was taken by his West Wallsend teammate, Jack McCroary. The Maunder family was still represented - Bill's brother Henry was selected at fullback and named captain. Probably the most popular selection was Sandy Wells of the Kurri Kurri club, brother of the recently deceased miner, Bill.

Very few people gave the locals a chance. The exception was *The Newcastle Sun,* which boasted: "We have the speed merchants, and hope to be the first to wallop England."

Saturday, 13 June 1925, Match 11: England v Northern District, Newcastle Show Ground

Elevation, or rather the lack of it, is one of the more annoying things for spectators fast filling the Newcastle Show Ground. There are no embankments or terracing. Other than two small grandstands, a few cattle sheds and outbuildings, there's nothing to give a good view over the person in front. Like all Australian grounds, the arena at the Show Ground is oval-shaped, meaning that spectators standing behind the rail are a long way from the action.

Towards the end of the preliminary match, people begin climbing over the rail and hopping down onto the grass surface of the Show Ground. Thousands of fans follow their lead. Some make for the already full grandstands while others converge on the pitch. Soon, the entire playing surface is covered with spectators. The few police and stewards on hand have no chance of holding them back. It takes until half-time for backup to arrive.

Alec Boyd and the English team arrive at the ground to a chaotic scene. Bert Batten, England's captain for the day, stands on the bonnet of one of the cars and tells Boyd: "They might have left us some place to play."

The press tables on the sidelines are too tempting for people seeking elevation and they clamber on top of them in their muddy boots. The tables soon give way and snap into so much kindling. Most of the pressmen move to the halfway line at the front of the surging crowd. Boyd, along with Lewis, Frowde, Atherton and the non-playing members of the English team, take refuge in the pavilion, where they watch the match standing on chairs on the verandah.

At kickoff time, the Newcastle Show Ground is a shambles. Some people have climbed onto the roofs of the grandstands, others have scaled signboards. Dozens of people perch precariously on the livestock sheds scattered around the ground. Spectators in the lower levels of the grandstands cannot see over the heads of the crowd. Only people right on the touchlines have a decent view. Most will only see the ball when it pops up above the heads of the spectators.

After a great deal of effort, police and football officials shepherd the fans off the pitch and back to the touchlines. A wall of spectators marks the boundary of the field. Some fans lean against the goal posts. The scene is reminiscent of Mayor Light's description of Wembley in 1923.

With police forcing a passage through the crowd, Henry Maunder leads the Northern District team onto the field first. They wear a black and white striped kit like Newcastle United in England.

The wailing of a bagpipe band heralds the entry of England onto the field. The crowd encroaches even more. Police and officials struggle to clear a path for pipers and footballers. Spectators roar "like a hurricane", according to one witness.

The pitch, when the players get to it, is slippery underfoot. Two preliminary matches have turned the surface into a muddy morass. The few patches of grass that have survived haven't seen a mower for a long time.

Concerned for their own safety and that of the spectators, England are reluctant to start the game. The Sydney referee, Mr Wright, convinces them to play.

Newcastle's Jack McCroary, the late replacement for Bill Maunder and still pinching himself that he is here as a player rather than a spectator, has the game's first touch. One of his club mates bellows from the sidelines: "You got your touch, Jack."

With the ball wet and heavy, it doesn't take England long to stamp their mark on the game. Two minutes in, Hamilton passes to Simms, who takes it past his marker and crosses to Bert Batten. The Plymouth Argyle man smacks a first-time drive that beats Bob Austin in the Northern District goal and gives England a 1-0 lead. Jack McCroary then gets his second touch.

Northern District skipper Henry Maunder, receiving the ball at the back, swings a pass out to Roy McNaughton.

He crosses and McCroary's eyes light up. As he lines up a shot the ball stops dead in a puddle and England's keeper Teddy Davison picks it up calmly.

Any time the ball goes out, generally by means of hitting a spectator, the throw-in is taken from within the field of play. England winger Charlie Hannaford has a tough time avoiding spectators, including one who keeps trying to shake his hand. After ten minutes of this, Batten has had enough. He signals to the referee his intention to take his men off the field.

Standing. J.Nicholson(Lines) J.Beddow, P.Doyle, A.Harris C.Coutts, H?Maunder(Capt) L.Brown, R.Austin, J.Sanderson(Lines)
Seated W.A.Wright(Ref) F.Coolahan. R.Wells. A.Cameron J.McCroarey, N.Price, R.McNaughton

The Northern Districts team that played England

Referee Wright practically begs the supporters to move back and eventually room is cleared and play gets underway again. A few minutes later, the spectators push forward anyhow. The entire game continues in this manner, with play constantly being halted while fans are moved back.

Then another England move finds the ball at Charlie Hannaford's feet on the left. His pinpoint cross picks out Ernie Simms, who makes no mistake with a header. England are 2-0 up.

Hannaford, despite having to negotiate the human touchline, is playing a brilliant game, always threatening with his pace and skill. Once again, he receives the ball on the wing. Avoiding spectators, puddles, and a few rash challenges he takes the ball downfield before cutting in towards goal. Northern District goalkeeper Austin advances. Hannaford lets fly with a delightful curling shot from a seemingly impossible angle. Austin can only watch as the ball sails into the goal. It's 3-0 to England.

A few minutes later, England come forward again. Northern District centre-half Peter Doyle concedes a corner and Jimmy Walsh trots up to take it. There is no room for him to approach the ball. With cajoling from the referee and officials, a narrow, curved lane is cleared. Walsh cautiously runs in. He sends in a perfect corner and Simms scores England's fourth goal with a powerful header.

Just before half-time, a mighty crash is heard from one end of the ground. Ambulance staff run through the crowd towards the commotion. They find one of the cattle sheds has collapsed. More than a dozen spectators who had been sitting on the roof are sprawled on the ground. Although a little stunned, most suffer only a few cuts and bruises. Two people are taken to hospital with non-life-threatening injuries.

Mr Wright blows the half-time whistle with England leading 4-0. England's keeper Teddy Davison is conspicuous in his near-pristine canary yellow jersey. His Northern District counterpart Austin is covered head to foot in mud. Just like the Wembley final of 1923, players have no choice but to stay on the field during the interval.

A few minutes into the second half, Batten slots in a goal from close range. It is disputed by the locals. They claim the final pass has not come from an Englishman but was tapped back into the field of play by a spectator. The referee ignores them and awards the goal.

Peter Doyle, the Northern District centre-half is the busiest of the local players. The Australian International chases down everything, at one stage sliding yards through the slush and giving the spectators a good laugh. Another of his slide tackles takes out a woman watching from the sidelines. Doyle apologises profusely and goes back to chasing down Englishmen.

Bert Batten is enjoying the muddy conditions. He fires in another shot that appears to be going wide. Suddenly a young boy leaning against the goalpost sticks out a foot and deflects it into the net. Referee Wright is about to signal a goal but Batten stops him and a goal kick is awarded instead.

Stan Charlton, England's right-back, begins another move from inside his own half. He plays it to Billy Caesar, who passes to Batten, the ball then booted out to the left wing and Hannaford. With deft footwork, Hannaford beats Coolahan and Maunder, then with Austin coming off his line, hits a perfect lob that ends up in the back of the net. The visitors now lead 6-0.

England's physical play takes its toll on the locals. Henry Maunder comes off with a leg injury, as does Sandy Wells. Northern District are down to nine players and the no-substitute rule once again is a talking point.

Near the end of the game, another fierce shot by an English forward misses the goal but smacks a woman in the face, knocking her out cold. Ambulance officers attend to the woman and she, too, is taken to hospital.

At full-time, the spectators again close in and England have to fight their way to the awaiting motor cars.

* * *

Charlie Hannaford had been the pick of the England players, scoring two goals and showing great dexterity on the ball. This had all been done while trying his best to avoid injuring the spectators along the touchline.

The Northern District player of the match was voted on by spectators at the ground. At a function at Fuller's Theatre, Peter Doyle was presented with the medal donated by the theatre manager. The home team's captain Henry Maunder said they were outplayed by the better side: "They were far too good, but better control should have been kept of the spectators."

England's captain Bert Batten said: "The game was spoilt by the encroaching spectators, and the management neglected to control the crowd. Under the conditions neither side had a fair chance."

Football officials blamed the police for not having the numbers to control such a big crowd. The police blamed football officials for bad management.

The official crowd estimate was 15,000 but good judges suggested the true figure was in excess of 20,000. It was a record crowd for a football match of any code in Newcastle. By way of comparison, the biggest crowd at a football match in Sydney on the same day was 15,000 for the rugby union match between New South Wales and the

All Blacks. Incidentally, two of the spectators at the rugby were recuperating English footballers Tom Whittaker and Bill Sage.

* * *

England was entertained at Scottish House in Newcastle following the match. Guests applauded the customary speeches celebrating sportsmanship, the bonds of empire and the suggestion that a football version of the Ashes would soon come into being.

Syd Storey was also there to represent the CFA. He had been disappointed by the gate in Newcastle. The takings of £1,042 represented about 10,000 paying customers, approximately half the crowd in attendance. The gatekeepers had been overwhelmed and the fences a little too porous. The two late injuries to local players had the public talking once more about the merits of substitutes.

In Storey's mind, as well as many in the Australian press, the substitute rule was the biggest impediment to the continued financial success of the tour.

If Storey and Lukeman were a little sheepish at Scottish House, they had good cause. During the evening the CFA cabled the Football Association in London about the use of substitutes. Its tone pointed to Syd Storey being the author. By appealing to the governing body over the heads of the tour management, it was going to put a heavy strain on the relationship.

The next day, readers of Sydney's *The Sun* newspaper had the opportunity of seeing the text of the cable sent to the FA for themselves:

'Australian public strongly resent action of your representatives declining allow substitutes for injured players in the first half only. We must insist this be allowed. Tour prejudiced. Please cable Lewis accordingly.'

15
Bush Rats And Pineapples

20 September 1924, Brisbane Cricket Ground

The whole season had come down to this one game. Dinmore Bush Rats, the famous old club from Ipswich, were playing Pineapple Rovers from Brisbane for the right to be declared winners of the Queensland Football Association (QFA) competition.

Any contest between teams from Ipswich and Brisbane had an extra edge.

The Bush Rats had already won the knockout Tristram Shield by defeating Pineapple Rovers 4-2 a few weeks previously.

Pineapple Rovers only needed a point to secure the premiership. A win for the Bush Rats would result in a three-way tie at the top of the table, forcing a round of playoffs.

After 25 minutes, the Bush Rats drew first blood when a Rovers defender deflected a cross into his own net.

Shortly after, Pineapple Rovers keeper Joe Hamilton fumbled a shot into the path of a Bush Rats' forward. Players from both sides charged towards the ball. Suddenly, Tedman of the Rovers and Jack Potts of the Bush Rats began trading blows. Order was only restored by the referee with the aid of a police sergeant.

Pineapple Rovers equalised and held on for a 1-1 draw, claiming the premiership in the process. With a Brisbane side winning the league and an Ipswich side the cup, honours were even for 1924. With England due in 1925, football fans looked ahead to an even more intense rivalry between Ipswich and Brisbane, one that had been a staple of Queensland football for more than 30 years.

* * *

As was the case in Newcastle and the Illawarra, Ipswich's place as a football stronghold owed much to geology. Coal had been discovered near Ipswich in the 1820s and the first mine opened in 1843. In the 1870s, Welshman

Lewis Thomas established mines at Bundamba and Dinmore and coal production soared. Immigrants from Scotland and Wales were prominent among the miners heading to the Ipswich coalfields and in their wake came the first football clubs.

Ipswich club Bundamba Rovers played Brisbane side St Andrew's in 1886, going down by 7-0. In 1889, Bundamba made the final of the Anglo-Queensland Football Association competition also going down to St Andrew's, this time 5-1. A representative team from Ipswich was hammered 8-2 by Brisbane in 1891.

The standard of football in Ipswich improved from the middle of the 1890s. This coincided with the emergence of the Bush Rats club of Dinmore. In 1894, a big crowd of their supporters travelled by train to Brisbane to watch them play in the Queensland Challenge Cup Final. Homing pigeons were released at strategic intervals to relay progress scores to eager fans in Ipswich. The following year the Bush Rats went one better, winning the cup for the first time.

In 1921, the QFA competition was revived after a long break due to the First World War. Clubs from both Ipswich and Brisbane took part. The competition was won by Ipswich clubs for the first three years before Pineapple Rovers' success in 1924.

When Australia made their international debut against New Zealand in Dunedin in 1922, they were captained by Alec Gibb, a Bundamba Rangers player. His selection was affirmation of Ipswich's role as a nursery of football in Australia.

* * *

Due to the promotion of Ipswich side Blackstone Rovers, the 1925 QFA first division consisted of three clubs each from Ipswich and Brisbane. The QFA had a lease on the Brisbane Cricket Ground (aka the 'Gabba'), and to make up a weekly quota of double headers at the venue, required Ipswich clubs to give up some of their home matches.

The Ipswich clubs objected. It was hard for players to make the early match when so many were miners who worked a half-day shift on Saturdays. Secondly, playing less than an equal number of home matches gave Brisbane clubs an advantage.

QFA officials held a crisis meeting to heal the dispute. The Ipswich delegation was led by ex-Australian captain Alec Gibb. A compromise proposed by the QFA was rejected by Gibb and the Ipswich clubs withdrew from the competition. Doubling down, the QFA fined the clubs and threatened them with suspension, which could bar Ipswich players from playing against England. A furious Gibb told a reporter: "We are right up against it with that mob down there." He promised to "fight them, if I had anything to do with it".

One football supporter, named 'J.M.D', took to poetry to express their concerns:

Soccer Dispute

Delegates are flying round,
Bitterness is most profound,
For the Rangers and the Rovers
Want more games on Ipswich ground;
And the angry Bush Rats say
They'll defy the Q.F.A.,
If they have to go to Brisbane
Every time they want to play.

The timing of the dispute was unfortunate. Just as the sport was coming into its biggest season, the Ipswich and Brisbane rivalry threatened to disrupt it. The *Queensland Times* opined: "It is to be deplored that the crisis has arisen at this time, for with players showing improved form and a team from England on its way to Australia, prospects for the code in Queensland were never brighter."

An eleventh-hour intervention by Ipswich politician, J Gledson MLA, managed to smooth things over. The compromise meant that Ipswich and Brisbane would run separate club competitions. For Ipswich, this proved problematic as they only had three senior clubs. They needed to find at least one more to have a workable competition. Players from the Railway Workshops were asked to form a team. What they needed was an experienced player to organise them. And so it was that Gibb was lured out of retirement to captain the newly established Ipswich City club in 1925.

* * *

15 June 1925, Ipswich & Brisbane

The platform at Ipswich railway station was busier than usual. Despite the chill of a wintry evening, a big gathering of local citizens patiently waited for the mail train bearing the English football team on their way to Brisbane.

When the train arrived, the crowd surged forward. Passengers alighted but there was no sign of the Englishmen.

It took a few minutes to find them. They were sitting in their lighted compartments, smoking and playing cards and showing absolutely no signs of greeting the good folk of Ipswich. Eventually, John Lewis was coaxed out and the crowd swarmed around him. "Three cheers for England. Hoo-rah! Hoo-rah! Hoo-rah!"

The mayor of Ipswich gave a little speech welcoming the tourists to Queensland. As John Lewis was about to reply, the railway porter bawled "ALL ABOARD!" The only person from the touring party to get a word in was Syd Storey. He called out from the carriage doorway as the train gathered steam: "There is nothing like them in Australia."

Ipswich Team photo

The crowd shuffled away, peeved the tourists didn't greet them. For their part, the English players had already been mobbed at Warwick and Toowoomba stations and were looking forward to checking in to their Brisbane hotel.

When the train pulled in to Brisbane's Central station, people were lined the length of the platform. Enthusiastic football supporters entered the carriages and searched for the touring party. John Lewis emerged to three enormous cheers. The players were mobbed like conquering heroes and had a hard time forcing their way through the hand-shaking, back-slapping throng.

One of the English players told *The Brisbane Courier* they had "never had a more enthusiastic reception. We are looking forward to our games here". Outside the station, the team stopped for a flashlight photograph before being whisked away to the Windsor Hotel. One reporter described the moment as "unparalleled in Queensland sport".

17 June 1925, Ipswich

England took the 45-minute train trip from Brisbane to Ipswich on Wednesday, 17 June for their match against the local district team, Ipswich and West Moreton. At the Railway Workshops, the Englishmen were given a quick tour of the facilities before being served lunch in the dining room by grumpy staff, upset they hadn't been given the afternoon off to attend the match.

In the town, parents were delighted to see how bright and chirpy their children were. They had no problems getting them to school on time. The children skipped little lunch and by noon were allowed to go home before heading off to the game.

Coal miners downed tools in the early afternoon. One woman was surprised that "the baker and butter man, who usually drifted up my back steps sometime during the afternoon, chased each other through the gate well before lunch". Even her hen laid breakfast eggs an hour early. Shops closed in the afternoon, their staff hurrying off to the game. By 3pm, the centre of Ipswich was a ghost town.

Ipswich football supporters were surprised at how easily England had beaten Illawarra and Newcastle (Northern District). Locals felt an affinity with these regional centres and by performing better than the 8-0 and 6-0 defeats in those games they would have bragging rights over their coalfields' cousins.

In Alec Gibb, Ipswich had a crafty coach who trained his players hard. The locals hoped that the dry pitch and their miner's style of play might catch England off guard. As Gibb gruffly said to one journalist: "Wait till they play us."

Wednesday, 17 June 1925, Match 12: England v Ipswich & West Moreton, North Ipswich Reserve

The Ipswich team step out onto the field to generous applause from a crowd of over 3,000 people. The team look the part in their black and gold hooped jerseys, black shorts and matching socks, though 'Sammy' Teasdale is conspicuous in his light blue socks.

England, arriving at the ground already stripped in their playing gear, can't find a gate to get through. They are forced to make an undignified entrance by hopping over the fence. Aside from a few chuckles, they get a rousing welcome. The crowd make a collective wince when the two teams line up side by side. England's Jack Elkes, Jimmy Hamilton and Billy Caesar are built like rugby forwards.

The North Ipswich Reserve is in poor condition. The pitch is hard and bouncy. It is uneven and riddled with ruts: the worst pitch England had encountered on tour, according to John Lewis. England will have trouble controlling the ball. Another impediment to their play is that the field has been marked very narrow.

Jack Potts kicks off for Ipswich and the locals make a raid that is shut down by Charlie Spencer, playing out of position at fullback.

Within minutes, England take control of the game but find it tough to string their passes together on the bumpy pitch. Jack Elkes provides the early entertainment, twisting this way and that, with the ball seemingly on a string. His odd combination of feints and clumsy running style are enthusiastically cheered, especially when he takes on, and beats, anyone who comes near him.

Ten minutes into the game, Stan Seymour breaks free on England's left wing. His accurate cross finds Elkes, who lashes a goal-bound shot that strikes Ipswich defender 'Fatty' Williams square in the face. His namesake for England, West Ham's Billy Williams, is quick to pounce and lays the ball back to Elkes to slam home a shot from 25 yards. England leads 1-0.

The game settles into a pattern of England pressing and Ipswich chasing. England spend longer on the ball than usual because of the hard surface, while their shooting is erratic. Ipswich, rallying behind the inspiring play of Teasdale, hang in bravely.

Ten minutes before half-time, England put on another good passing move. Billy Williams receives the ball from the right wing, strides towards goal, dribbles past Routlege and Burns then hits a fearsome shot to put England two up.

Shortly after, Ipswich's Wally McDowell goes down with a leg injury and is assisted from the field. The spectators, well aware of the substitute controversy, anxiously wait to see how he responds to treatment. His knee comes good and he's able to retake his place on the field. A few minutes later, the half-time whistle blows with England ahead 2-0.

In the second half, Ipswich play with more confidence. In a swift counterattack, Jack Potts beats Hamilton and fullback Charlton before being blocked by Spencer. The ball ricochets to Artie Williams, who crosses into the area. England keeper Harry Hardy punches the ball but it falls into the path of Jack 'Toddy' Edwards. Suddenly, Edwards is presented with the rare sight of an open English goal but his volley goes agonisingly wide.

England fullbacks Charlton and Spencer are playing a robust game and more than once charge Ipswich's forwards, sending them sprawling to the turf. When the Ipswich men do stay on their feet, they get caught in the expertly applied offside trap.

With just over ten minutes to go, England press through Billy Williams. His powerful shot is turned past the post by goalkeeper Les Halls. Walsh swings in the corner and Williams lashes the ball in from close range to score his second of the day.

Ipswich don't give up. In the dying moments, they take a corner that drops into the penalty area. In the scramble, Artie Williams shoots but the ball cannons off the upright.

* * *

Elkes had lived up to his reputation as the star attraction of the tour and was voted player of the match. One newspaper reporter called him the "prettiest exponent of ball control seen in Queensland".

Ipswich could hold their heads high. They had out-performed Newcastle and Illawarra. Alec Gibb coached his side well, especially the defence. Sammy Teasdale, in his powder blue socks, played a big part in keeping the scores down, completely putting England's champion left-half Len Graham off his game. Wally McDowell was selected as Ipswich's best player by members of the English team.

England were disappointed with their unspectacular 3-0 victory. They hoped the heavy rain that greeted them on their return to Brisbane would continue. The more it softened the pitch at the Exhibition Ground the better.

16
That Murray Boy

c.1914, Brisbane

The boys from Brisbane Normal School can't wait for lunchtime. As soon as the bell rings, a group of them fly out of the schoolyard and sprint down Edward Street. There's no time to waste. They have to be back through the school gate in one hour, or else.

The schoolboys, around 11 years of age, with one of them carrying a soccer ball, skedaddle down Edward Street, cross Alice Street and emerge into the open space of the Botanic Gardens. Their haste isn't just to get in as much play in as possible but to reserve a spot ahead of the students from the Technical College.

One of the first boys to arrive is Albert Murray, known to everyone as Bert. Sometimes words are exchanged with the Technical College students and it's Bert Murray who is the chief spokesman for the schoolboys. The boys play a rough and tumble game of soccer before running back to school in time for afternoon lessons.

* * *

It was in those tough lunchtime games in the Brisbane Botanic Gardens that Bert Murray developed his strong defence, great positional play and a fierce determination to succeed. With the football matches and the one-kilometre run from school and back, Murray developed into a fine athlete. Everyone knew Bert Murray could run all day.

Murray played his club football with Latrobe, making his senior team debut in 1923. He was always involved in the action and centre-half was his natural position. He was a tenacious defender but also worked on the attacking side of his game, always looking for an opportunity to set up his forwards. In 1924, at the age of 21, Murray realised one of his great ambitions when he was selected to play for Queensland against New South Wales.

His athleticism was one of his great strengths. In 1924 and 1925 he won the 440-yard race in a footballers'

Bert Murray (on the ball) for Queensland

sports day. 'Energetic', 'speed and stamina', 'the mainstay of the Latrobe defence', was how Murray was described in press reports during the early part of the 1925 season.

Murray's chief rival for a Queensland berth was the Thistle club's centre-half, Charlie McGovern. With experience playing for Montrose in Scotland, McGovern was a clever player with the ability to pick out a forward with a precision pass.

In the first inter-city trial between Brisbane and Ipswich in 1925, McGovern played centre-half for Brisbane while Murray was a reserve. McGovern couldn't come to terms with the terrible surface at Ipswich and his passing game was ineffective. After the 4-0 loss, Brisbane selectors brought Murray into the team for the second match, picking him at left-half alongside McGovern in the centre. But McGovern pulled out with an injured knee and Murray was moved to centre-half. Despite losing 3-1, Murray was Brisbane's best player and was rewarded with selection in the Queensland team to play England.

***

Brisbane was awash with rain in the days leading up to the match between England and Queensland. Despite this, the city's enthusiasm for the English football team was in evidence everywhere. A journalist for the *Daily Standard* despaired that "in the trams and trains this morning, respectable and intelligent-looking citizens were actually discussing the visit of the English footballers, as though politics didn't matter".

The offices of the *Daily Standard* were overrun with entries in the weekly football-tipping competition. Reflecting the demand from its readers, the prize for the soccer-tipping was £30, double the amount for the rugby league one. Advertisements in newspapers reminded readers of the great crowds that had seen the other-worldly football skills of men like Elkes and Seymour.

50,000 will be there - be one of them!

Although the consensus was that England would win the match, the result in Ipswich had given Queensland supporters a glimmer of hope. The match was billed as a game between the 'dash and enthusiasm' of the locals against the 'science' of England. As Queensland's manager, ex-Australian International Johnny Peebles said: "Queensland is putting its best team on the field and hoping to put up a good fight."

Building on the surge of interest, local football writer, GR 'Dick' Tainton put together a 36-page souvenir programme of the Queensland leg of the tour. It included articles such as 'Will Soccer sweep Australia?' and 'No longer a Chummy game', challenging the myth that soccer was a sport played by immigrants only.

There was one curious item published in Tainton's programme. It was the words to an aboriginal war-cry that would be performed by the Queensland team at the start of the match.

The origins of the war-cry were sketchy. It was said to have come from the Bloomfield River region of North Queensland. Accompanying the war-cry was a message stick with the words engraved on an attached silver plaque.

The message stick was from Taroom, nearly 400km north-west of Brisbane. The Taroom Aboriginal Settlement was a government-run institution, and its residents, referred to as 'inmates', had been forcibly removed from their traditional lands, and all aspects of their lives were under the control of the government.

At the QFA rooms in Albert House, Brisbane, the Queensland players spent the Friday evening before the match rehearsing the war-cry under the tutelage of elocutionist, H. Barrodale.

In the lead-up to the match against Queensland, the English tourists were guests of the Tivoli theatre management for a screening of the movie *The Lost World*.

Queenslanders could not get enough of the film. Screenings would begin at 9am and continue until late in the evening. Moviegoers queued down the street outside the Tivoli waiting to buy a ticket. Some would sit down on the footpath waiting for the next session to start.

Based on a story by Sir Arthur Conan Doyle, *The Lost World* was one of the original blockbuster movies and featured cutting-edge 1925 special effects. Nobody could disagree with the catchphrase from the trailer: "It was made for your amazement!" The film starred Bessie Love and Lloyd Hughes in the leading roles, with a large cast of minor characters, including Jocko the monkey played by himself.

Queensland vs England

Moviegoers watched in awe as animated dinosaurs battled each other to the death. The humans did their best to keep out of the way but found themselves trapped on a plateau in the jungle, seemingly for eternity. Without giving too much away, the day was saved by the level-headed Jocko the monkey, who climbed down to the valley and returned with some rope.

In keeping with the epic scale of the movie, the English players, whose fame in Queensland was by now bordering on the epic, were shepherded to the front of the stage and introduced to an appreciative audience.

The Tivoli management were great friends of football. They donated a trophy worth five guineas for Queensland's best player in the match. The Shafston Rovers football club similarly donated prizes for the best English player.

On the eve of the England vs Queensland game, it was more than the terrors of *The Lost World* that was keeping Syd Storey awake. It had rained almost the entire week in Brisbane and had turned torrential over the last two days. All other sports had already been cancelled for the weekend. The QFA, with Storey's approval, defiantly announced on Friday morning that the game would go ahead no matter what.

Most people expected England would win easily. One exception was 'Glug', who had the following lines published in *The Daily Mail*:

From Perth around to Sydney town,
In every State they've won renown,
And gave our teams a dressing-down-
    We weren't in it.
But in this mimic winter war,
Shone out each English Soccer star;
They haven't lost a game so far-
    But wait a minute!

Our Queenslanders have done the same
In many a willing southern game;
Up here it won't be quite as tame
    When our boys play;

All Brisbane will be outward bound,
And all the ladies winter-gowned,
Will throng to the Exhibition Ground
    Next Saturday

The rain did not relent. On the morning of the match, people living along the Brisbane River were advised to prepare to evacuate to higher ground. Syd Storey and officials from the QFA ventured out to the Exhibition Ground early. As the deluge continued, the turnstiles stayed silent.

About an hour before kickoff, the rain stopped miraculously. This was the monkey with a rope moment Storey had been praying for. Football officials in their suits and ties grabbed buckets and any containers they could find and, rather comically, began to bail out the mini-lakes on the Exhibition Ground. "They might as well have tried to empty the sea with a tea cup," said *The Truth*. The public of Brisbane, many of whom had given up getting into a session of *The Lost World,* figured they had enough time to get to the football match. The turnstiles began to crank into action.

In the Queensland dressing rooms, players received some last-minute bad news. The two best players in the midweek game in Ipswich, McDowell and Teasdale, had been forced to withdraw through injury. They were replaced by two Brisbane players, Jimmy Robertson and Charlie Scone, both from the Thistle club. Even though Ipswich had won the two trial matches by an aggregate of 7-1, there were just three Ipswich players in the Queensland team. To Ipswich supporters, this was further evidence of poor treatment from the QFA.

Queensland waded out to the middle of the Exhibition Ground through ankle-deep water. Rather foolishly, the QFA had not cancelled the preliminary games and the parts of the ground that weren't under water were a quagmire. What good was 'speed and dash' in conditions like these?

Saturday, 20 June 1925, Match 13: England v Queensland, Exhibition Ground, Brisbane

Queensland pose for photographers, resplendent in their maroon jerseys with a white 'Q' on their left breast. At the centre of the lineup, Bert Murray cuts a striking figure. With his dark complexion, inherited from his Jamaican grandparents, he stands there with his collar unbuttoned, sleeves rolled up, tight shorts far shorter than his teammates, and sporting a jazz-age swept back hairstyle.

Queensland vs England

England wade out onto the wet and muddy pitch to great applause. The crowd has grown considerably in a short space of time.

'Kalalgumm! Jenung! Balaibalier! Yana!' echoes out across the Exhibition Ground as the Queensland team recite the aboriginal war-cry. Queensland's captain Edgar Rigby presents his English counterpart Charlie Hannaford with the Taroom message stick.

Under dark clouds, Jack Potts kicks off for Queensland. The locals dash downfield in a good passing movement that breaks down in a mini-lake. England take over possession and begin to stroke the ball around. The surface, although muddy, is true, and just to England's liking. It's only the determined centre-half play of Bert Murray that prevents England from scoring in the opening minutes.

In the 12th minute, after clever play by England's inside forwards, Jack Elkes draws and beats three defenders before slipping the ball across the goalmouth. Bert Batten steers it home from close range and gives England a 1-0 lead.

As another downpour begins, Bert Murray shows that he's up for anything, evading three English defenders before being checked. Charlie Hannaford brings the ball back, bounding past Jack White before passing to Elkes. The Tottenham star is faced with three defenders. No problems for the gangly Elkes, who twists left and right before setting up Batten to score England's second goal.

Soon after, Liverpool's Jimmy Walsh gets away down the wing. He sends a dangerous cross into the penalty area that stops dead in a puddle. Batten is on hand to stab it in the net. England are 3-0 up after 20 minutes and Batten already has a hat trick.

Ernie Simms, England's inside-right, passes to Walsh in the outside-right position. Walsh beats a man and takes it down the sideline. He brings the ball all the way to the corner flag, takes a moment to hitch up his shorts, then sends in a curling cross that Charlie Hannaford heads in for England's fourth goal.

The combination play between Caesar and Walsh on England's right creates havoc for Queensland. The two set up another move down the right and play Simms through on goal. Ted Owen, the Queensland keeper, advances and Simms takes an angled shot that bursts through his hands and into the corner of the net. It's 5-0 to England and they are revelling in the heavy conditions.

England make it six when Batten heads in another cross from Walsh. The half-time whistle blows soon afterward. Although the game isn't in any way competitive, the crowd have been thrilled by England's superb exhibition and give the tourists a great ovation all the way to the dressing rooms.

The entertainment doesn't stop during the interval. A spectator climbs over the fence and stumbles onto the Exhibition Ground arena. Described by one newspaper as a "worshipper at the shrine of Bacchus", the man trots onto the field and begins a shadow display of intricate football skills, dummying and twisting over an imaginary ball.

"He's imitating Jack Elkes," says a spectator.

"No, he's just drunk," says another.

A soccer ball suddenly appears from the crowd and the man continues his solo, dodging run towards the goal at one end. He lines up the ball, shoots, and the spectators burst into applause when it goes in the net (it is the only time a Queenslander has scored after all). But the effort is too much and the man's legs go out from under him. He lands flat on his back in the mud. The crowd's howls of laughter change to jeers when the police constables finally take action. The man gives the audience a bow then runs for the fence with two policemen on his tail.

Ted Owens, having learned the hard way, sports a pair of gloves when he returns for the second half. He doesn't need to wait long before Batten tests them out with a fierce drive.

A rare Queensland attack follows. Bert Murray shuts down an England move and sends a clever through ball, cutting out three English defenders. Jack Potts of the Bush Rats gathers it and passes to Nicholson, who shoots, forcing a full-length diving save from England's custodian Teddy Davison.

Around the 60-minute mark, Batten lashes in another fierce shot that beats Owen pointless. An eighth goal follows soon after when Simms clinically heads in a cross from Walsh.

Billy Caesar, the amateur from Dulwich Hamlet, who has been using his weight to send many Queenslanders into the Exhibition Ground slush, now gets his name on the scoresheet with a blistering drive into the net. Owen is a mere observer. Ernie Simms brings his own tally to three with another well-taken header from a corner. England has reached double figures for the second time on tour.

Shortly before full-time, Billy Caesar robs Queensland's Jack Potts and plays a long ball down the right wing. Walsh controls it beautifully, shakes off his markers and scampers off down the sideline. He crosses into the path of Batten, who hits a first-time shot that gives Owen no chance. England win the match 11-0, their biggest victory of the tour so far.

* * *

Given the weather, the crowd at the Exhibition Ground was far beyond the expectations of Queensland football officials. Over 15,000 fans paid more than £1,000 at the gate, justifying the decision not to cancel the game. The crowd enjoyed themselves, despite the mismatch. They applauded the skill of England, but encouraged Queensland every time they went forward. They particularly enjoyed seeing the players fall face first in the mud.

The Shafston Rovers trophy for the best English player was awarded to Billy Caesar. Bert Batten and Ernie Simms each earned an Akubra hat for their efforts.

The only player to show promise for the home team was Bert Murray, who won the Tivoli prize for the best Queensland player. He was in everything and finished the game soaked in the Exhibition Ground mud. His work rate, tenacity and spoiling tactics were acknowledged by all pundits at the game. When Australia's team for the first Test was announced, Bert Murray was the only Queenslander picked.

20 June 1925, Bundaberg

The brave residents of the progressive regional city of Bundaberg stand on the corner of Balfour and Bourbong Streets, watching time go backwards.

A shrieking wind howls through the streets. People stare up in awe at the south-western face of the Post Office clock tower, where the hands are being blown anti-clockwise by near cyclonic winds. Old timers cannot recall such an occurrence. It feels like an omen. Maybe it has something to do with the upcoming visit of the all-conquering English football team, who on that very day put eleven goals past Queensland in Brisbane. Bundaberg might be a rugby league town but they aren't going to let that get in the way of turning out the welcome mat for an English sporting team.

The Queensland team to play England

Wednesday, 24 June, Match 14: England v North Queensland, Bundaberg

A firm pitch greets England at Bundaberg's West End Reserve. The North Queensland players are mainly drawn from the towns of Bundaberg, Maryborough and Howard. The one exception is goalkeeper Joe Hamilton, who has been lured up from the Pineapple Rovers club in Brisbane. Special trains from Maryborough and Howard have boosted the attendance to a healthy 3,000 for the midweek fixture.

England are caught napping at the outset. The North Queensland forwards take the ball downfield and Cox's shot is saved by Teddy Davison at full stretch. England soon settle down, although they find the light ball difficult to control.

It takes ten minutes for England to open the scoring. A long-range shot from Norwich City's Joe Hannah proves too much for the extremely nervous Hamilton, who gets a hand on it but can't keep it out.

England's outside-left Stan Seymour passes to Ernie Simms, who cuts infield. Dribbling around two defenders, he strikes a sizzling shot that hits the crossbar. While the locals stand around gawking at the ball, Batten pokes in the rebound to give England a 2-0 lead.

A few minutes later, Seymour sets off down the left wing. His accurate cross finds Bert Batten, whose firm header flashes into the net.

Seymour is playing well and local defender McIntosh resorts to a foul to stop him. Seymour curls the free-kick into the path of Ernie Simms, who heads it in to make it 4-0 to England.

Spectators are still applauding when England strike again. Seymour's cross finds the ever-reliable Batten, who notches up his hat trick.

West Ham's Billy Williams exhibits great skill by beating a number of the North Queensland players. His powerful strike hits the upright and falls at the feet of Seymour, who steers it into the net. England go into the half-time break up by six goals to nil.

England fly out of the blocks in the second half. Stan Seymour, who can barely put a foot wrong, sends another perfect cross for Batten to knock in England's seventh goal.

Simms adds to his tally a few minutes later, his long-range effort giving Joe Hamilton no chance. Shortly afterwards, a scintillating movement featuring most of the team ends with a successful strike by Batten. England has scored three goals in ten minutes and with over 30 minutes to go are on target to break their tour record score. But the visitors take it easy and wind the game down, happy to entertain the crowd with flashy play.

The match finishes 9-0 to England.

It's been a profitable week for Bert Batten: with 11 goals in his last two games, he tops England's scorers with 27, ahead of Ernie Simms on 21 and Billy Williams on 14.

* * *

The Bundaberg trip served as a pleasant interlude for the tourists. They were treated to some good old-fashioned country hospitality. The St George Society put on a dinner and dance in a hall bedecked in red, white and blue. Not to be outdone, the local Catholic Society put on a Mah Jong night for the tourists. John Lewis also accepted an invitation to address the local Temperance Society.

The players were given a tour of the Bingera sugar mill. In their swell suits, hats and ties, the Englishmen walked over the lush cane fields that stretched for 80 kilometres in every direction. They chewed sugar cane while being shown around by mill manager A.L. Gibson (no relation to the unfortunate goalkeeper Sid), who also happened to be the patron of the Bundaberg Football Association.

Bundaberg was a turning point for the tour in more ways than one. It would be the furthest north the tourists would travel. From now on, they would, roughly, retrace their steps through the state capitals before eventually arriving in Fremantle where they would board the ship for home. It also marked the next stage of the football side of the tour, with five Test matches against Australia to be played over five weeks.

For John Lewis and Mark Frowde, there was more on the line now. If England was to suffer a reverse against the Australian national side it would damage the team's reputation back home. The England players took great pride in playing for their country and were getting sick of the never-ending jibes by Australians about the failure of England's cricket team in the recent Ashes series.

England took the 8am train from Bundaberg for the 500km, 11-hour journey back to Brisbane on Thursday, 24 June. The weather had improved and there was every possibility the Exhibition Ground surface would be firm and the ball light - conditions more suited to the Australians. England also knew that with an influx of New South Wales players, Australia would be a far tougher proposition than Queensland. With good crowd support, the match would not be without its challenges. What England hadn't counted on, was that after nearly fifty years of waiting, and months of preparations for this inaugural match between the nations, the Australians, at the very last minute, would shoot themselves squarely in the foot.

Part III
The Test Matches

17
The First Test

When Syd Storey and Ern Lukeman reached a compromise with rebellious Illawarra players at Bode's Oval on 6 June 1925, they must have wished that disputes over player payments would go away. But money was on everyone's mind.

Ever since 10,000 people watched the first match of New Zealand's tour of Australia in 1923, followed by the 40,000 who saw the Chinese team that same year, the potential financial reward from international football was apparent to all followers of the sport. That investors in the Chinese tour, many of them football administrators, had made a tidy profit, made people wonder whether the players should also get a cut.

The standard allowance of 10 shillings per day hadn't changed since international football began in 1922. For the higher-profile English tour, the football association in Newcastle wanted this amount doubled to £1 (20 shillings) per day clear of expenses. The CFA, cautious about the massive cost of the tour, decided to keep the rate at 10 shillings.

The players' consolation was to be given a football education by English professionals. Those advocating for better pay for players pointed out that Syd Storey had been granted full payment for lost wages during the tour. Why should the players always be considered last?

Sydney's *The Labor Daily* opined in January 1925: "If the manager must not lose on the trip then why should the players lose?" Presciently, they added: "To evade the players' allowance clause is only putting off trouble which might come at a very inopportune time."

That inopportune time was right before the first Test match.

The most vocal proponent of better reimbursement for players was Sid Cope, who had been secretary of the Illawarra District Soccer Association from 1919 to 1922. He not only believed representative players should get a bigger slice of the pie but pushed for the introduction of professional club football in Australia. To Cope, football in

Australia on its current trajectory would not keep pace with the increasing professionalism of world football. A push to create a professional league in New South Wales in 1925 had been defeated by the Sydney association, which was busy getting its district competition up and running.

Illawarra didn't play under the district system. There was no residential qualification such as that in Sydney. A player could play for whatever club he wished. The introduction of the district system in Sydney saw some good players stuck in reserve grade because they couldn't play for a weaker team in another district. Some of these players were open to the possibility of playing for clubs in the Illawarra. Three Sydney players were lured south: Burns and Fitzpatrick to Thirroul and Forrester to Coledale. It was an open secret that these players were being paid up to 30 shillings a week to play.

In the Gardiner Cup, Metropolitan clubs refused to play against Illawarra teams fielding players who lived in Sydney. The NSWFA came down on the side of the Metropolitan Association, threatening to expel Illawarra clubs unless they stood down their Sydney players.

Cope, who had recently been reinstalled as the secretary of the Illawarra association, had no intention of banning the Sydney players. Illawarra would go it alone, he said, and would begin a professional competition that year. Clubs from Sydney and Newcastle would be invited to join. He argued that crowds would flock to see top football, and players would be earning £5 per week within a few years. Cope withdrew Illawarra's affiliation with the NSWFA.

The NSWFA took a hard line on what they saw as the beginnings of a rebellion. They issued an ultimatum to the players: anyone who turned out for an Illawarra club on 20 June would be ineligible for Australian selection. As a sweetener, Storey and Lukeman announced that Australian players would now get a £1 per day allowance.

After the Australian selectors watched Queensland get demolished by England on 20 June, their interest turned towards news from the playing fields of the Illawarra. They were almost saved by rain as it appeared some matches might be cancelled. But the rain held off enough for Judy Masters and Tom Thompson to turn out for Balgownie Rangers. As if to rub it in, Masters was in sparkling form, netting both goals in a 2-1 win against Thirroul. When Australia's squad for the first Test against England was announced, the names Masters and Thompson were not on the team sheet.

* * *

Judy Masters' omission left a huge gap in the Australian lineup. Even putting aside his leadership abilities and box-office appeal, he was the only centre-forward in the country with form on the board. Australian players had scored just three outfield goals against the Englishmen and two of those were by Masters.

The man closest to Masters in ability was Bill Maunder but he hadn't played a minute's football since injuring his knee in Melbourne. Enquiries found him with a bunch of mates up the country at Narrabri. He considered going to the game but only as a spectator.

Selectors settled on Newcastle centre-forward Jack McCroary. His form for his club side Weston was good: he'd scored 11 goals during the season so far. A bustling type of player, McCroary played for Northern District in their 6-0 loss to England but most of his touches were from the kickoff spot. Although sometimes described as 'The Judy Masters of the north', it was also suggested 'he was no Judy Masters'.

Tom Thompson was also going to be missed. His combination with Masters had been reckoned as Australia's greatest attacking weapon.

Another loss was left-half Harry Spurway, who declared himself unavailable for the match. There were mixed reports about his reasons. Work commitments was one, but another was his disappointment with the allowances paid to New South Wales players on the King's Birthday holiday. Match allowances were reduced on public holidays since players were deemed not to be losing any wages.

The good news for selectors was the recovery from injury of goalkeeper George Cartwright. He had declared himself fit and was eager to do battle with England. Although Cartwright had competition for the position, including Jim Robison from Victoria, the selectors stuck with the man who had played more times for Australia than anybody else.

The Australian selection committee of Lukeman (NSW), Storey (NSW), Hildreth (Qld), Dockerty (Vic) and Holiday (SA) chose the following team on Saturday evening, 20 June:

Gil Storey

Goalkeeper: Cartwright (NSW)
Fullbacks: Robinson (NSW); Faulkner (Tas)
Halves: Gil Storey (NSW); Edwards (NSW); Murray (Qld)
Forwards: Grieves (Vic); Lennard (NSW); McCroary (NSW); Les Brown (NSW); McNaughton (NSW)

On the Monday, both Grieves and Faulkner withdrew from the team. Faulkner, who had played well for Australian against Canada in 1924, had recently moved to South Australia from Tasmania and was unable to get time off work. Two Sydney players were drafted in as replacements: Stan Bourke, from Granville, took Grieves' position at outside right, and the nuggety Frank Gallen, of Balmain, replaced Faulkner at left back. It meant that Bert Murray, carrying the hopes of the Queensland sporting public, was the only member of the team not from New South Wales.

* * *

At 1pm on Monday 22 June, three young men met up under the grand clock tower at Sydney's Central railway station. They were George Cartwright, Sid Robinson and Alf Edwards, members of the Australian football team. Joining them on the overnight mail train to Brisbane was trainer extraordinaire, Tom Langridge. When the train stopped at Newcastle, four more players joined the entourage: Roy McNaughton, Les Brown, Percy Lennard and Joe McCroary. The seven players were on the ride of their life, about to play for Australia against England in football for the first time.

The following day, Stan Bourke, Frank Gallen and Gil Storey also caught the train from Sydney. By Wednesday evening, the entire squad had assembled at the Australia Hotel in Brisbane.

The team trained at the Gabba wearing the maroon jerseys of Queensland. Watching the players intensely and putting them through their paces was Johnny Peebles, the former Australian player. The players' fitness and massage needs were taken care of by the hard-working Tom Langridge. Alf Edwards, appointed captain in the absence of Masters, was upbeat. He told reporters: "Australia are training hard. They are in the pink of condition." He speculated that if the weather stayed dry, Australia's speed and dash could come into play and they might pull off a grand upset.

Peebles, originally despondent after the Queensland match, gradually grew more confident. The enthusiasm of the New South Wales players began to rub off on him. The weather during the week was balmy and, once again, the idea took root that a pacy team of locals on a hard pitch could cause England problems. Peebles began to tell anybody who would listen that this team was capable of winning.

There were a few question marks over some of the Australian selections. Gallen had been overlooked for both the New South Wales games. All three of the half-backs were specialist centre-halves, meaning that Gil Storey and Bert Murray would be playing out of position. Up front, McCroary and Brown were newcomers to the international arena.

Australia's key attacking weapon was outside left Roy McNaughton. He had played four times against England already and his pace and crossing ability had caused the tourists' problems. If Australia was to have any hope, they needed McNaughton to be at the top of his game.

Another key player was inside-right Percy Lennard from the Cessnock club. Lennard was an experienced international, and Brisbane fans well-remembered his stunning goal against New Zealand in 1923, the first ever by an Australian in an international on home soil.

Harry Hardy was England's goalkeeper. The backs were Poynton and Charlton. The squad's other fullback, Whittaker, could still barely walk.

England chose their three best halves, with Len Graham on the left, Charlie Spencer at centre-half, and Jimmy Hamilton on the right.

Both England's star forwards, Bert Batten and Ernie Simms, would play. Centre-forward Batten had scored 27 goals on tour, while inside-right Simms was not far behind, with 23. Jack Elkes, the dribbling wizard, was at inside-left, while Charlie Hannaford and Jimmy Walsh were selected at outside-left and outside-right, respectively.

On the eve of the match, John Lewis delivered a lecture on the laws of the game at the Oddfellows Hall in Brisbane. Lewis levelled harsh criticism at local referees. He was still bitter about the Whittaker injury and said the referee should have sent Thompson from the field. He implied that all Australian referees were not enforcing the rules. His discourse bordered on bizarre when he accused local referees of allowing one-handed throw-ins, something nobody in the room had ever seen happen. Lewis told the audience he would report the Australians' disregard for the rules to the FA in London.

Saturday, 27 June 1925, Match 15: England vs Australia, First Test Match, Exhibition Ground, Brisbane

Glorious sunshine brings hordes of spectators to the Exhibition Ground. Even though they have to sit through four preliminary matches, the organisers have for once put on a contest that warms up rather than bores the crowd. It's a match between the best club side in Brisbane and the best club side in Ipswich. The teams are Pineapple Rovers and the Dinmore Bush Rats. The match doesn't disappoint, Rovers winning 3-2 after going behind twice.

The playing surface of the Exhibition Ground resembles a billiard table. With the prospect of a bouncy pitch, John Lewis requests that the St. Peter's match ball be soaked in water to better suit his players. Referee Mr Donellan,

The crowd for the First Test at the Brisbane Exhibition Ground

who had probably attended Lewis' lecture the previous evening, refuses the English manager's request.

England are forced into making a last-minute adjustment. Jimmy Walsh, who picked up a knee ligament injury in Bundaberg, is ruled out. Charlie Hannaford is moved from outside-left to outside-right and Stan Seymour is brought into the team at outside-left.

Alf Edwards emerges from the Exhibition Ground grandstand into a wall of noise from over 30,000 Queenslanders. The whirr of wooden rattles, something new to Brisbane football, adds to the racket. The crowd includes many newcomers to the game who want to see what all the fuss is about.

The Australians wear dark green jerseys with a single gold 'V'. The kits, supplied by Murdoch's sports store in Sydney, include white shorts and green socks with gold tops.

The roar swells when England come out, led by skipper Ernie Simms. Every vantage point in the arena is filled with spectators. Despite Queensland's heavy defeat the week before, Brisbane football fans have come out in record numbers. In Bert Murray, standing tall in the Australian lineup, with arms folded and chest puffed out, Queenslanders have one of their own to cheer for.

Edwards wins the toss and chooses to defend the Machinery Hill end. Australia will start with the sun in their faces and running into a light breeze. England's centre-forward Bert Batten stands poised over the ball. The referee's whistle blows. Batten kicks off in the first-ever football Test match between Australia and England.

England struggle with the light ball in the early stages and the play is scrappy from both teams. Five minutes in, Spencer plays Hannaford into space on England's right. He leaves Murray in his wake and sends a low cross into the area. Australian keeper Cartwright dives but cannot hold on. The ball sits up for Batten, who fizzes a shot towards goal. Gil Storey, Australia's right-half, sticks out a leg and the ball deflects onto the upright and back into the field of play, where Cartwright drops on it. Australia plays on but referee Donellan, positioned near the goal line, awards a goal to England.

Around the twelve-minute mark, Spencer starts another move, passing to Hannaford on the right touchline. Once again, Hannaford brushes aside Murray before sending in a perfectly weighted cross. England's captain Simms heads the ball past Cartwright to put his team 2-0 ahead.

England's wingers are having no trouble getting the better of Bert Murray and Gil Storey. Only the tigerish play of centre-half Edwards and right back Gallen keeps England at bay. Australian hearts sink when Edwards is forced off with a leg injury but recovers after receiving treatment from Tom Langridge.

Edwards then traps a clearance from a goal kick and attempts a pass to Bourke but Jack Elkes is awake to it and intercepts. He switches play to Seymour at outside-left, then it's on to Hannaford, who runs downfield and crosses into the middle. Batten sticks out a foot and misses but Simms is waiting at the back post and drives in a firm shot past Cartwright. With 25 minutes gone, England lead by three goals and Australia face the prospect of a heavy defeat.

England fullback Cecil Poynton goes down after a heavy challenge, clutching his back. There's speculation he might be taken off but he plays on, running less freely than before. With Poynton in discomfort, Australia play some of their best football of the half and force two corners in quick succession. Stan Bourke swings the corners in deftly and on one of them Harry Hardy, out of character, mistimes his punch, the ball bobbing around the area. It just requires a touch from an Australian boot but the opportunity is missed.

England soon bring the ball downfield through Hannaford on England's right. Hannaford's cross finds Batten, who hits a powerhouse first-time drive. The crowd wait for the net to bulge but the large frame of George Cartwright flies through the air and turns the ball past the post. Half-time comes with England leading 3-0 and very much in the ascendancy.

Australia come out for the second half to plenty of encouragement from the crowd. Their passes begin to stick; they find some rhythm. On the flanks, McNaughton and Bourke find some room. Poynton, England's injured fullback, struggles to keep up.

Les Brown, almost invisible until now, works a nice move with McNaughton on Australia's left. McNaughton's accurate cross picks out Percy Lennard, who heads towards goal. The crowd rise and groan as the ball just goes over the bar.

AUSTRALIAN XI.

P. Lennard, R. McNaughton, L. Brown, F. Gallen, S. Bourke, —, McCroary, A. E. Murray, S. Robinson, G. Cartwright, G. Storey, A. Edwards.

The Australian Team for the First Test

At the 50-minute mark, McNaughton takes possession and skilfully beats England's right-half Jimmy Hamilton. He zips down the touchline as England's defence give chase. McNaughton's cross is well placed, and McCroary lunges with his head but fails to make contact. The ball continues past both English fullbacks and comes to Percy Lennard at the far post. With just Hardy in front of him, Lennard drives a low shot for the corner. The ball ripples the back of the net and the crowd roar like mad. It's England 3 Australia 1, with 40 minutes left. Can Australia do something miraculous?

McNaughton and Bourke are greeted with cheers from the 30,000 spectators every time they get near the ball. With Poynton flagging, England are under as much pressure as they've been all tour. Bourke sends in a cross that is once more mishandled by Hardy. The Australians pounce and from a goalmouth scramble the ball is hacked out by England. A few minutes later, Bourke takes the ball down the line again. His cross evades Hardy's grip.

THE ENGLISH XI.

S. Charlton, C. Spencer, L. Graham, H. Hardy, C. Hannaford, E. Simms, J. Hamilton, J. Elkes, H. G. Batten, S. Seymour, C. Poynton.

The England Team for the First Test

The Australian team with officials

McCroary heads towards an undefended goal but the ball goes just wide.

Even Bert Murray is gaining in confidence and doing much better against Hannaford. Securing the ball, Murray beats his man only for Hannaford to trip him. The crowd responds with loud jeers.

After nearly 20 minutes of sustained pressure, Australia begin to run out of steam. Their speed and dash disappears and England wrestles back the initiative. Tom Langridge might have got the Australians fit but the English professionals have more stamina.

Nearing the end of the game, Seymour crosses from the left. There's a miscommunication between Cartwright and the Australian defence and Simms darts in to score England's fourth goal. A few minutes later,

Hannaford crosses to Batten, who smashes in a stinging shot past Cartwright. The match finishes 5-1 to England.

The full-time whistle is a signal for supporters to pour onto the field. They charge towards the match ball. One youngster picks it up and takes off with it, chased by a mob. Police retrieve the ball, which will eventually be autographed by players from both teams and presented to England as a memento.

* * *

England's half-back trio of Hamilton, Spencer and Graham outplayed their Australian counterparts, with only Edwards showing good form for the home team. Both England wingers, Seymour and Hannaford, had sensational matches. Batten and Simms were at their devastating best, even if the light ball caused them problems at times.

England's fullbacks, Poynton and Charlton, had the Australian attack in hand most of the time. Even when Poynton was injured, the pair's positional play helped them deal with the majority of threats. Possibly the only English player not up to form was goalkeeper Hardy, who made more errors in this one game than he had all tour.

The Australians put up a courageous effort, especially during the 20-minute spell after the interval, when McNaughton and Bourke lit up the Exhibition Ground. Australia's inside forwards were ineffectual - Brown barely had a touch and McCroary's finishing let him down. Many judges thought Masters would have put away at least one or maybe two of the chances McCroary had. At the back, Edwards and Gallen were the pick of Australia's defence.

At the post-match function, England had some encouraging words for the locals. Stan Seymour said Australia had wonderful raw material that just needed good coaching to turn into the finished product. Mark Frowde said Australia

Action from the First Test

really extended England for a while. The score was not a true reflection of the game and Australia could have had a few more goals with a bit of luck.

The politicians were less concerned with the result than with the English team's role as de facto immigration agents. Tell the people back home how good Australia is, they said. Tell them about Queensland and the abundant sugar cane. Tell them about the wide-open spaces just waiting for good hard-working Englishmen to develop it.

Gifts were showered on the visitors. They were presented with a set of serviette rings from Ipswich, boomerangs from the Queensland Home Secretary, and every player received a silver-mounted walking stick, courtesy of the Queensland government.

Cecil Poynton received the McWilliams trophy for the best English player while Len Graham was awarded a Sovereign hat for the next best. Frank Gallen was deemed Australia's best and received a pair of Hotspur football boots. Edwards picked up a Sovereign hat as Australia's next-best player. Bert Murray was also presented with an

Bert Murray in action for Australia

award in front of his peers for being Queensland's best player against England the previous week. He also took home a rose bowl and a gold watch donated by a mysterious 'admirer'.

As was customary, the English management presented their blue enamel FA badges. A few eyebrows were raised when long-term Queensland official John Hildreth was overlooked.

Sometime during the evening, a light-fingered intruder thieved a pair of Jimmy Walsh's trousers from his hotel room. The trousers were later found but £15 and a gold ring were missing. The entire English party chipped in to make good Walsh's loss.

* * *

Monday, 27 June 1925. Match 16: England vs Toowoomba, Toowoomba Show Ground

Local schools and shops close early, and a surprisingly good crowd files into the Toowoomba Show Ground. Many of the locals in what is very much a rugby league town, have never seen a game of football before, yet they've been caught up in the mania surrounding the English visitors to Queensland. Among the spectators are most of Toowoomba's rugby league players and officials.

With Poynton recovering from the back injury he picked up in the first Test, England go into the game without any specialist fullbacks. Stan Seymour plays inside-left instead of his usual outside-left.

Usually, both teams would pose for a photograph on the field at the start of the game but this time England refuse. One of the players says they are here to play football and "not look pretty for a photograph".

The match is even in the early stages. Toowoomba employs a kick-and-chase game while England struggle with the poor surface. Several shots by England are skied over the bar. Indeed, the first chance of the match falls to Toowoomba's Kennedy, whose shot beats Hardy and narrowly misses the goal.

Twenty-five minutes into the game, Jack Elkes finds himself on the ball after good lead-up play by England's halves. The gangly Tottenham man passes to Charlie Hannaford on the right wing. Hannaford crosses to Seymour, who finishes the move with a splendid header to put England 1-0 up.

A few minutes later, England attack again with a fine passing move between Batten and Williams. Batten's searching pass finds Seymour, who strikes it well to give England a 2-0 lead. With a first-half brace, Seymour is enjoying his move to inside-left. A little while later, Seymour falls heavily and has to be treated by trainer Mo Atherton. He is able to carry on and the English management are spared further injury worries.

Charlie Hannaford is giving the Toowoomba players headaches with his pace. As half-time approaches, he goes for another dash down the wing. Spotting keeper Langton off his line, he chips a long-range ball into the net and gets a great round of applause from the spectators.

On their way to the dressing sheds at half-time, England are stopped by the photographer. The players tell him they have never been presented with a team photo all tour and have had enough. The photographer assures them a photo will be sent, and England relent and allow him to take their picture.

England dominate after the resumption. Early in the second half, Hannaford passes to Batten, who hits a tremendous shot that flies into the net.

Minutes later, Batten scores his second goal to give England a 5-0 lead. Elkes completes the day's scoring after an interchange between Seymour and Graham. England takes care to avoid further injuries, and plays out the remaining minutes cautiously for a 6-0 victory.

* * *

England's short stay in Toowoomba was a popular one. Almost 4,000 people watched the game and most enjoyed the spectacle. In a review of the match in the *Toowoomba Chronicle and Darling Downs Gazette,* the reporter was so moved, he felt England's visit might usher in an era of world peace: "When all nations of the earth commingle together in sport, and learn to 'play the game' in the true sporting spirit, then we might hope for peace and unity and world-wide brotherhood."

While at Toowoomba, Syd Storey passed on a complaint from the Queensland Football Association to the England team management. The Queenslanders were indignant that John Lewis didn't present an enamel badge to John Hildreth, who had done such a fine job for many years. Over the next few days, Queensland recipients of the badges indicated that they would return them unless Hildreth was presented with one (although no one appears to have actually sent back a badge).

The matter was serious enough for Lewis to write to Brisbane's *The Daily Mail* to clarify his position. He regretted there was a perceived slight to Hildreth and noted that he was only acting on information given to him. He didn't see how England's management could be blamed and very much hoped he could put the matter right at a later time.

Even when England arrived back in Sydney ahead of the second Test, Frowde was quizzed about the badges and explained that no offence was intended. One letter writer to a Brisbane paper opined: "Why all the fuss over a badge, it makes them look like children quarrelling over an apple."

18
'The Greatest Test Match In Australia'

Ever since England employed their physical tactics in Sydney, supporters at club games had taken to calling out, 'Play the English style' when they wanted their team to rough their opponents up. Some referees, second-guessing themselves after the public debates about charging, began to take a lenient view of the practice, and matches had become rougher as a result.

On 27 June, the Granville club of Sydney, once proud exponents of the scientific style, were playing very much in the English style against Eastern Suburbs. The main target of their roughhouse play was Easts' new centre-forward Jack Smith. Fresh off the boat from England and playing only his fourth match in Australia, Birmingham-born Smith had created a sensation in the Sydney premiership.

Smith stood like a colossus on the field. At 185 centimetres and tipping the scales at nearly 85 kilograms, Smith was not built like the usual whippet-thin Australian centre-forwards. Although on the slow side, he possessed good ball control and a fearsome shot, but best of all, he was happy to throw his bulk around in the penalty area.

In his second club game, he scored four goals in Eastern Suburbs' 5-2 win against Pyrmont Rangers. He also scored the following week against the crew of the British cruiser *HMS Concord*, handing the bluejackets their first defeat in Australia.

The game between Granville and Eastern Suburbs was one of the most physical games seen in years. Smith came in for heavy punishment and was fouled repeatedly. Tempers flared in the second half when Easts' fullback Booth laid out Granville's Dunn with a right hook after copping a high boot to the face. The 'English style' appeared to be having a detrimental effect on local football. Smith played well, setting up his side's only goal in a 4-1 defeat. With the second Test in Sydney just a week away, every club player was making an extra effort to be noticed by selectors.

* * *

Australia made a change in the fullbacks for the second Test, with Faulkner back in to replace Robinson. A week had made all the difference to Faulkner's South Australian employer and he had been given the all clear to play.

Tasmania's Len Norman was chosen at right-half in place of Gil Storey. Unfortunately, Norman was unable to take time off work so selectors settled on the reliable Charlie O'Connor from Sydney's Eastern Suburbs club.

Bert Murray was another casualty and was replaced at left-half by Harry Spurway from the Gladesville-Ryde club. Spurway was a product of the Granville schools' system and had the Australian characteristics of speed and fitness to go with a sound tackling technique and the ability to win the ball in the air.

Up front, selectors couldn't decide between St. George's injury-prone Harry Sherringham or Cessnock's Alex Thompson. Both players were bracketed against the inside-left position with a final decision to be made on match day.

The crucial centre-forward position was giving the selectors headaches. Bill Maunder was initially pencilled in but withdrew due to his injured knee. With Judy Masters unavailable because of the Illawarra dispute, the selectors hit upon an unusual idea: why not fight fire with fire? Get a big English-style centre-forward to batter the English backs. And that was how 26-year-old Jack Smith suddenly found himself reporting to Langridge's School of Physical Culture alongside his new Australian teammates after only having played four senior games in the country.

* * *

The English team arrived in Sydney on Wednesday after a 24-hour train journey from Toowoomba. On the Queensland leg of the tour, the team had covered over 2,500 km, won all five matches and scored 34 goals with just the one against. Four injured players were waiting for their teammates at Central station: Whittaker and Walsh, as well as Poynton and Caesar, who had skipped the Toowoomba match to get in some extra conditioning time at Langridge's.

When the tired, unshaven touring party went to retrieve their luggage, they couldn't find it anywhere. Their bags had gone missing somewhere between Toowoomba and Sydney. After such a gruelling trip and the disappointment of the luggage, the team were only too happy to spend some time in the Turkish baths in Elizabeth Street, where they chatted about sugar cane, pineapples and the wonderful Queensland hospitality.

England checked back in to the Bondi Hotel and trained at Waverley Oval. The press and the English management both predicted Australia would be stronger in the second Test. England had a high regard for Spurway and thought he was a good addition for Australia. One unnamed English player said that most of Australia's defensive problems were tactical. In England, it was common practice for fullbacks to take the inside forwards and for halves to take the outside men. Although some clubs reversed this strategy, the point was that it was determined before the match started. The Australians, he said, were making things up while the game was in progress.

On the eve of the second Test, John Lewis spoke to a gathering at Sydney University. Disappointed to learn that private schools and universities in Australia hadn't taken up football, he was happy to accept the university's invitation. But Lewis, rather than promote the game, used the occasion to attack local football officials. Australian referees were not up to scratch and were allowing rough play to go unpunished. Once again, he said Australia's position on substitutes was wrong, and the practice of allowing substitutes in competition matches was against the laws of the game and would be reported to the FA in London.

Lewis took aim at Syd Storey. He said Storey should have at least cabled the FA his request for substitutes prior to the tour rather than deliver it to him dockside at Fremantle. Not stopping there, Lewis criticised the payments made to the Australian players. Australians were receiving an allowance of £1 a day on top of expenses, and what's more, he recently heard a rumour that Australian players were to be paid a bonus of £5 for each Test match they played in. This was preposterous. True amateurs were only eligible for expenses. Lewis, whose players were being paid a weekly wage from the proceeds of the tour, claimed Australia was in breach of their amateur status and this would be brought to the attention of the authorities in London.

If John Lewis was put out by the ensuing storm of press criticism over his Sydney University lecture, he wasn't showing it. He was in positively grand spirits. He had just received a telegram from his old club, Blackburn Rovers, congratulating him and the team on their performances and wishing them good luck for the rest of the tour.

On the morning of the second Test, England players either soaked up the sun along the promenade or dipped their toes in the ocean. Trainer Mo Atherton's worst fears were realised when Poynton had to withdraw from the match due to his back injury. With Whittaker already out, England had only one specialist fullback. Charlie Spencer was moved from centre-half to right-back, with Jimmy Hamilton taking the centre-half position. Jimmy Walsh was another late injury withdrawal and Stan Seymour came in at outside-left.

Australia's final selection decision was to play Sherringham at inside-left ahead of Alex Thompson. Taking a leaf out of England's book, Australia changed into their kit at Langridge's so as to arrive at the ground ready for action. Tom Langridge was feeling confident. He thought Australia should have drawn the first Test and believed the changes made would be enough to give the home team the win.

Nothing could illustrate the reason why football authorities had tried so hard to secure the Sydney Cricket Ground more than the poor playing surface at the Sydney Show Ground. The ground's primary purpose was for agricultural events, and the Annual Sheep Show had been held during the week. After being trampled by farm animals for two days running, the final component of the Sheep Show, the sheepdog trials, had taken place the very morning of the second Test. It was only at midday that the last of the sheep and dogs had been herded off the arena. Fortunately for the international players, it was the schoolboy footballers in the preliminary matches who would encounter the sheep dung at its freshest.

* * *

Saturday, 4 July 1925, Match 17: England vs Australia, Second Test Match, Sydney Show Ground

An icy wind greets the players as they line up at halfway. They are presented to Governor-General Lord Forster, the visiting governor of Tasmania Sir James O'Grady, and New South Wales' premier Jack Lang. Lord Forster is coming to the end of his tenure as Governor-General and is performing a kind of farewell tour. Regarded as being a champion of Australian sport, it has taken a visit from England for him to attend his first football game in an official capacity.

As radio station 2FC begins another of its live broadcasts, Ernie Simms wins the toss and chooses to defend the Paddington end and run into the wind. As usual, England are much bigger than the locals but this time there is an exception. Australia's centre-forward Jack Smith is as big as any of the opposition. His selection is a long shot but the Sydney crowd will keep an eye on his bulky frame. There's a fine sense of anticipation as the big crowd settles in and players take up their positions.

Lord Henry Forster, Governor-General of Australia, meets the England team at the Second Test

Jack Smith passes to Percy Lennard at the kickoff. The Australian forwards make good progress and it takes a strong challenge from Charlie Spencer for England to gain possession.

The light ball gives England problems and their usual fluency is missing. Charlie Hannaford has his opinions of Harry Spurway confirmed when the Australian left-half coolly dispossesses him.

In the fifth minute, Stan Seymour receives the ball on the left and sends it across to Charlie Hannaford on the opposite wing. Hannaford plays a first-time cross and Bert Batten heads the ball towards goal. A yellow blur flashes through the air and palms the ball away to safety. George Cartwright's impossible save is wildly applauded.

Australia now go on the attack and Jimmy Hamilton handles the ball in a dangerous position. The crowd rise in anticipation as two Australians stand over the ball and consider their options. Roy McNaughton taps the ball to Stan Bourke but he blasts his shot high over the crossbar.

England left back, Stan Charlton, conscious of Spencer's inexperience at fullback, plays the one-back game perfectly, springing the offside trap a number of times. England begin to control the game and from the 20-minute mark enjoy most of the possession.

A dazzling move between England's star goal scorers, Batten and Simms, ends with a pass played into the path of Elkes. Cartwright, showing his usual courage and some unusual agility, dives at the Tottenham man's feet and prevents a certain goal.

With five minutes remaining in the first half, an unmarked Charlie Hannaford receives the ball on the right wing. From near the corner flag he whips in a cross towards the far post. Seymour heads across goal and Simms rises up to head it into the back of the net. For a moment, there is confusion in the crowd. The ball had passed through a hole in the net and bounced away. But the goal is awarded and England are up 1-0.

With the half-time whistle imminent, Australia makes one last push. Roy McNaughton, who has been struggling against the England defence, receives the ball on the left. Looking up, he spies Bourke in the penalty area and plays it to him. Bourke taps it around the floundering Spencer and hits a shot that Teddy Davison can only parry. Players pile into the goalmouth as the ball bobbles around. Fortunately for Australia, the big body of Jack Smith is lurking nearby. With his centre-forward's instinct, Smith makes a rush at the ball and tumbles into the netting. After a moment's confusion the crowd cheer when they realise the ball has also ended up in the net.

In that one piece of bustling play, Smith has earned his place in the team. The crowd are still cheering as Australia heads into the dressing sheds with scores level at 1-1.

The crowd are entertained by the Westmead Boy's Band in the interval but the show is stolen by two bulldogs chasing a ball around the field. Spectators laugh and clap at the dogs' high jinks, the music providing a colourful backdrop. Play is held up while the dogs are removed and the band complete one of their numbers. This is all rather onerous for John Lewis, who has previously complained about the overly long half-time breaks in Australia.

In the second half, the pace of the game doesn't slacken. England still has the best of the opportunities but the Australian defence stands strong. Frank Gallen is in great form and stops any move that threatens on the right. Faulkner, at left-back, settles down after a nervous start and does a good job keeping Hannaford quiet.

For once, Jack Elkes struggles to make an impact on the game. The rough surface is not to his liking and he and Batten can't seem to steer the ball on target. Then Elkes receives a cross with his back to goal. Showing marvellous dexterity for a big man, he hits his overhead hook shot sweetly. Cartwright makes a stunning save.

Harry Sherringham, Australia's inside-left, is struggling to keep up. Early in the second half, his knee begins giving him trouble. He leaves the field and Tom Langridge frantically applies his magic touch. Sherringham returns after five minutes but is limping noticeably.

Action from the Second Test

Around 75 minutes into the game and with the scores locked at 1-1, Australia are still successfully fending off England's blows. Cartwright is having a brilliant game, while Spurway and Gallen provide the steel to Australia's defence. The exhausted Australians are reduced to the occasional counterattack, only flankers Bourke and McNaughton posing any real threat to England.

Stan Bourke is the instigator of one such counterattack. Receiving the ball in the outside-right position he gets the better of Charlton and sprints down the touchline. His waist-high cross is a tricky one for the English defence. Spencer, beaten badly for the first goal, can't resist and punches the ball with his fist. Appeals go up from the Australians. The referee, Mr Wright, points to the spot. Penalty!

Action from the Second Test

England have never been behind during the second half in any game on tour. Here, with just 15 minutes to play, is a golden opportunity for Australia to set up a win and level the series. Alf Edwards, the captain, now has a decision to make. If only Judy Masters was playing, it would be all so simple. He mulls it over. Should he give it to the new man Smith, who has already scored today? As captain, should he step up and take it himself? Stan Bourke is another with penalty taking experience. No. Edwards hands the ball over to Roy McNaughton, the Cessnock flyer and constant thorn in England's side.

All eyes turn to the penalty spot. Young McNaughton places the ball and retreats back several paces.

He stops.

An unbearable silence descends on the Sydney Show Ground.

Nobody sits.

The 20-year-old Australian amateur sizes up the 37-year-old professional goalkeeper from The Wednesday club in Sheffield.

The crowd takes each step of McNaughton's run up with him. He strikes the ball well. Davison is frozen on his line. Alas, the net doesn't ripple. McNaughton's penalty is struck so well it goes sailing over the bar and lands in the part of the Show Ground near the pen where the sheep had been kept earlier that morning.

To make matters worse for Australia, Sherringham's knee gives out completely shortly after the penalty miss. He is taken from the field and Australia will have to play the last fifteen minutes one man short.

England are shaken into action. With a man advantage, they stroke the ball around more freely. In the 80th minute, Seymour floats a cross into the area. Bodies pile in. The ball rolls to England captain Ernie Simms. His close-range shot is well saved by Cartwright but it rebounds to Elkes, who pokes out a toe and the ball rolls into the net. England have the lead.

There are fears that the final 10 minutes could become a rout. Batten bursts through and is about to take a shot when Cartwright and Gallen dive at his feet. Although Cartwright has made another courageous save,

Action from the Second Test

the referee spots a foul by Gallen and awards a penalty to England.

Jack Elkes steps up to take the kick. He strikes it well but Cartwright makes a spectacular diving save.

With a few minutes remaining, Stan Charlton goes down with an injury. England trainer Mo Atherton takes him from the field and Elkes is temporarily moved to left back. No further scoring occurs and England finish 2-1 winners.

* * *

After the game, an English player said: "For a time I thought we were gone." The spectators had been gripped by a stirring contest. Although the crowd was smaller than those for the New South Wales matches, the 25,000 fans loved every minute of the game. The press called it "The greatest Test match in Australia".

George Cartwright played his best international game and was many people's pick as player of the match. One English player said: "… that goalkeeper would break the heart of any forward". Other players to receive special mention were Gallen at fullback, Spurway in the halves and Bourke at outside-right.

The weaknesses for Australia were O'Connor at right-half and Sherringham up front. Even allowing for his

Jack Elkes of Tottenham Hotspur scores England's winning goal

injury, Sherringham had done little. Jack Smith, despite bagging a goal, was unable to bring his wingers into the game and was found wanting in pace.

Alec Boyd said England's halves - Sage, Hamilton and Graham - were superior to Australia's and that was the key to the tourists' victory. His pick for player of the match was Stan Charlton, who not only had to deal with the pacy Bourke but had to cover for Spencer, who was playing out of position. The late injury to Charlton was of great concern to the English management as it meant all three of their specialist fullbacks were out of action.

Syd Storey was pleased with the gate of £1,400, although he would have hoped for more. With £15,900 total gate takings, the tour looked likely to make a profit but nothing was certain. The figure of £18,000 quoted for expenses was, after all, only an estimate.

The next item on Storey's list of problems was the rupture in relations with the Illawarra association. More Sydney players had been rumoured to have signed on with Illawarra clubs. There was talk of whole clubs shifting camps to the new professional competition. St. George was the first Sydney club to form a team with the express purpose of taking part in the new league.

On the Friday evening before the second Test in Sydney, CFA officials agreed to Storey's request to pay Australian players a £5 bonus for each Test match. This worked out at £55 a match or £275 in total. Although margins were tight, Storey felt the risk was worth taking. Without the bonus, more of the best players might be tempted to join the Illawarra professional competition.

Syd Storey was cagey when Lewis made his accusation about the bonus payment at his Sydney University lecture. He initially indicated they were only considering the idea but later admitted they had made the decision. As it was an honorarium to be paid at the end of the tour, Storey didn't regard it as affecting the players' amateur status. After all, he said, the Australian cricket team had played under that scheme for many years.

Lewis replied that the FA took a different view of amateurism than England's cricket authorities at the MCC. England's amateur definition for football was very strict and was a bone of contention between it and the more liberal football associations of Europe.

Storey again lashed out at Lewis over the substitute rule. He said the Australian sporting public had been "disgusted" over England's attitude. Perhaps what irked Storey most was that he had recently received the formal response from the FA to his telegram insisting Lewis relent over substitutes. The FA advised: "Confirm the action of our representatives in not allowing substitutes."

* * *

England's midweek engagement was in Newcastle. After the crowd debacle earlier in the tour, local authorities wisely changed the venue from the Show Ground to the Newcastle Sports Ground. The Sports Ground could not hold as many people but provided better accommodation for spectators.

The local team was selected from players representing the Newcastle city clubs of Adamstown, Newcastle, New Lambton, Wallsend and West Wallsend. The local footballers had a strong incentive to play well as there were still spots up for grabs in Australia's third Test team the following Saturday.

England only arrived in Newcastle at noon on the day of the match. When Charlton's chest injury prevented him from playing, England drafted in two specialist halves, Joe Hannah and Charlie Spencer, as fullbacks. Billy Williams went from centre-forward to inside-left and Bert Batten, due to stand down for the game, was brought in as centre-forward.

Wednesday, 8 July 1925, Match 18: England v Newcastle, National Sports Ground, Newcastle

England's Harry Hardy is the first keeper to get his hands on the ball when he comes out to gather a cross from Newcastle winger Dunn. Hardy's clearance finds Jimmy Hamilton, who passes to Ernie Simms. In typical English style, the inside man switches to the wing and Jimmy Walsh floats in a cross. Batten meets the ball with a firm header only to see the ball clear the crossbar.

Newcastle's other winger, Johns, then crosses the ball into England's goalmouth. Charlie Spencer heads it unconvincingly and Hardy is forced off his line to punch clear under a robust challenge by two Newcastle forwards.

The game see-saws and England's next attack starts near the touchline, with outside-right Jimmy Walsh playing in Ernie Simms. Hands shoot up from the defenders attempting to copy England's offside trap. There is no whistle and Simms plays in Bert Batten to pulverise the ball past Newcastle keeper Jordan and give England a 1-0 lead.

England struggle to find their rhythm against a willing Newcastle team employing the physical 'English style'. Fullbacks Art Lambert and Arch Harris do a good job emulating England's offside trap, frustrating the tourists' forwards. At half-time, England lead by just the one goal.

The second half becomes a grind as Newcastle challenge ferociously and stifle England's passing tactics. Newcastle's Peter Doyle and England's Jimmy Walsh carry on a battle of their own, and in one challenge both go somersaulting across the turf. When Walsh gets up, the crowd hoot. Doyle plays the rest of the match favouring his right leg.

Hardy has a torrid afternoon in the English goal, doing his best to avoid a number of feet-first challenges. Referee Tom Crawford has words with several of the Newcastle forwards but doesn't take any other action.

The visitors retaliate to some of the rough play. This is the most aggressive team England have encountered all tour. With around 10 minutes of play left, Batten finally beats Lambert's offside trap and charges through on goal. Inside the penalty area, Lambert lunges and brings Batten down. England claim a penalty but referee Crawford plays the advantage and Seymour steers the loose ball past the advancing keeper into the goal.

A few minutes later, Walsh centres but Newcastle fullback Harris clears. The ball comes to Jimmy Hamilton who shoots, only for Lambert to block the ball with his body and send it well outside the area, where Sage drives it first-time. The ball flies through the air like an artillery shell into the back of the net.

* * *

The match finished 3-0 to England in fading light. The game had been dull, marred by rough play, too many fouls and offsides by both teams. England were concerned about sustaining more injuries and at times looked to be playing within themselves. They didn't appreciate the vigorous tactics of the home team and were surprised at how well Newcastle applied the offside trap.

* * *

As expected, O'Connor, Smith and Sherringham were dropped from Australia's third Test team. Early in the week, selectors picked just eight players - with the final three to be named after the midweek game in Newcastle.

These eight players, along with four emergency replacements, went into training at Langridge's School of Physical Culture on George Street. On Tuesday evening, the Australian players working through their fitness routines nearly dropped their barbells when Judy Masters and Tom 'Titch' Thompson moseyed on in through the front door.

19
Judy's Back

After the second Test, the *Sydney Sportsman* pulled no punches with its headline: "With Masters and Thompson Australia would have won". A series tied at 1-1 going into the third Test would have done wonders for ticket sales. As it was, Ern Lukeman estimated the tour had lost £500 in revenue by not having Judy Masters in the team.

With Storey and Lukeman both in Sydney, they set about trying to resolve the ongoing rift between Illawarra and the NSWFA in order to get the two Balgownie Rangers men into the Australian side.

Applying a creative interpretation of the rules, Storey announced that although Illawarra had withdrawn its affiliation, the NSWFA had not formally *accepted* it. Storey and Lukeman got to work. A deal was brokered by which the Sydney Metropolitan association approved the transfer of the three rebel players to Illawarra in the best interests of the game.

The machinery of 1920s football administration moved slowly. Now it was up to the Illawarra District Soccer Association to agree to re-affiliate and heal the rift. They were given until the Wednesday evening before the third Test to make their decision.

When the deadline approached, Sid Cope, now secretary of the Illawarra Association, told Storey and Lukeman that he couldn't arrange a meeting until the following week. This played nicely into Storey's hands. On Thursday, Storey announced that since the NSWFA had not yet accepted Illawarra's withdrawal, Masters and Thompson were eligible for the Test team. They were immediately reinstated, though, truth be told, they had already been training at Langridge's with the team since Tuesday. The dispute had not been settled, but it had been delayed long enough to allow Australian football's biggest drawcard to play.

* * *

It would be fair to say that most of the English touring party had never heard of the town of Maitland. Situated on the Hunter River, 35km north-west of Newcastle, it had historically been overlooked as a venue for Test matches in favour of its more populous neighbour. That Maitland was chosen to host the third Test was testament to the enthusiasm and hard work of the local football community.

Football in the Newcastle region came under the overall banner of the Northern District British Football Association (NDBFA). It consisted of two geographical areas, one based around the city of Newcastle itself, and the other around the coalfields further inland. The coalfields clubs had their own association, the South Maitland British Football Association (SMBFA), but all senior clubs played in the NDBFA competition.

With its ties to the coal-mining communities that gave birth to football in the district, the SMBFA regarded itself as a spiritual home of Australian football. But Newcastle also had a rich history and one of its clubs, West Wallsend, was the current Gardiner Cup champion. Both districts boasted their own star players: Bill and Harry Maunder from West Wallsend were Newcastle men, while Roy McNaughton and Peter Lennard of Cessnock were from South Maitland.

When the English tour was announced, the New South Wales Football Council agreed that one of the Tests would be played in the area controlled by the NDBFA.

To decide if the match would be played in Newcastle or Maitland, a conference was held in Sydney. Each group had the support of their local councils. Three of the coalfields' clubs sent letters in support of the South Maitland bid. The South Maitland faction included Mr Hoskings, manager of the Hunter River Agricultural Society, who explained the benefits of playing the game at the Maitland Show Ground. The argument that swayed the day was financial: The Maitland Show Ground had a cheaper rental and didn't issue free tickets to members.

* * *

Alec Boyd felt the third Test was Australia's best chance to win a match. The team selected was the strongest yet, and Tom Langridge had them in superb condition. As captain, Judy Masters would be a great inspiration for the team, and Edwards, now relieved of the captaincy, should have a big game. According to Boyd, if Australia did spring a surprise, millions of people around the world would be searching for Maitland on a map.

England arrived in Maitland at midday on Friday, 10 July. Despite the lengths the SMBFA went to secure the fixture, it was surprising, and a trifle embarrassing, that no local football officials met the train or turned up to the

Grandstand at Maitland Show Ground still stands today. This photo was taken in 2023.

civic reception. When J.W. Earp of the SMBFA arrived much later in the day, he was at a loss to explain how the mix up could have happened.

Mo Atherton's major concern was the fitness of England's fullbacks. Earlier in the week, a Sydney doctor examined Tom Whittaker's knee and pronounced him unfit to play for the rest of the tour. Cecil Poynton was already out with a back injury and Stan Charlton was doubtful after taking a knock in the second Test in Sydney.

Buoyed by Masters' return, Australia trained hard under the watchful eye of Bill Carroll, one of the great Australian footballers of the pre-war era, while Tom Langridge took charge of the team's physical fitness. Langridge's School of Physical Culture was a busy place, with recent arrivals the New Zealand rugby league team among the many visitors.

Langridge travelled to Maitland with the Australian team. Boyd phoned him at the hotel on the eve of the third Test. "We shall win alright on Saturday," the ever-hopeful Langridge said. The phone was passed to George Cartwright: "I like our chances."

With Masters and Thompson back and the possibility of playing an England without any specialist fullbacks, the Australians were quietly confident. If only the weather held and the pitch stayed dry.

On the afternoon before the match, showers set in. They continued all night and into the early part of the next morning. News also came through that England fullback Stan Charlton had been passed fit to play. Judy Masters was still in a good frame of mind, saying: "Our team has a great chance of winning".

* * *

11 July 1925, Match Day, Maitland

Outside Maitland's High Street station you could barely move. Each of the specially run trains that came in from the coalfields or Newcastle were bursting at the seams with football fans. People wended their way through the usually sleepy streets that were now clogged with traffic, including motor buses packed to the rafters with football supporters.

The No. 1 grandstand had sold out a week ago. There were still tickets available for the Show Ground's other grandstand but you'd better get in quick.

The gates opened to queues of supporters at 10am. An hour before kickoff, an estimated 10,000 spectators were inside the ground. The fans included football first-timers, English supporters, and locals excited by the prospect of Australia fielding their best team of the series. Those from the coalfields were eager to see how their two local heroes, Roy McNaughton and Percy Lennard, would fare against the Englishmen.

Besides police on foot, there were mounted police patrolling the venue. Authorities wanted no repeat of the chaotic crowd scenes at England's first match in the Hunter a month ago. One spectator was so excited that he over imbibed and spent the entire match snoring loudly under the grandstand.

As kickoff time approached, the breeze picked up but the sun poked through murky clouds. Both grandstands were completely full. People had scaled the outbuildings and were sitting on the rooftops.

Saturday, 11 July 1925, Match 19: England vs Australia, Third Test Match, Maitland Show Ground

England run out to sustained applause. After clattering across the abrasive speedway track, their boots find the comforting squelch of a muddy playing surface.

It's a special moment for Judy Masters when he leads Australia out as captain against England for the first time. The hosts get a wonderful reception and there's no doubt Australia has the majority of the support. Local stars McNaughton and Lennard get the biggest ovation of all. When Masters wins the toss, the crowd cheer as though Australia has scored a goal. Masters chooses to run with the wind.

England's Bert Batten kicks off to Elkes, who turns it back to Graham. The ball goes out to Hannaford on the wing. He takes it to the vicinity of the corner flag and crosses to the feet of Batten. It sits up nicely on the gluey surface and Batten smashes it into the back of the net. England lead 1-0 in the first minute.

Australia creates a number of opportunities in the first 20 minutes. The forwards use their speed to advantage even if their ball control is lacking. When Percy Lennard cleverly turns Stan Charlton, the crowd roar him on. The Cessnock man dashes towards goal. As Seymour comes across to close him down, Lennard unleashes a powerful shot. Teddy Davison dives and the crowd rise in unison. The ball zips inches past the upright and the crowd sit down again.

Rain begins to fall and England click into gear. Batten makes a run into the penalty area and is tripped by Faulkner. He sits in the mud looking hopefully to the referee but the penalty is not forthcoming.

Cover of the Third Test programme

Nearly 30 minutes into the first half, Jack Elkes receives the ball from an England throw-in. He passes to the speedy Charlie Hannaford in the outside-right position. Frank Gallen tries to intercept but Hannaford beats him easily and sends the ball skidding across the area. Ernie Simms hits a firm low shot into the corner of the net to give England a 2-0 lead.

Barely a minute later, Liverpool's Jimmy Walsh outpaces Australia's halves and probes towards goal. He passes to centre-forward Batten, who crashes in a strike that beats Cartwright easily. England are now up 3-0 and are relishing the slippery conditions.

Australia attempts to hit back but a tame shot from Judy Masters is easily collected by England keeper Teddy

Action from the Third Test - Roy McNaughton for Australia and Jimmy Hamilton (Crystal Palace) for England

Davison, who clears downfield. Hannaford traps the clearance, goes around Gil Storey and Frank Gallen before unleashing a shot that deflects in off the far post.

Not long after England's fourth goal they attack again through Joe Hannah, who sends a neat pass to Batten. There is a smart one-two between Batten and Walsh before Batten fires a stinging shot that gives England a 5-0 lead.

Australia responds by sending the ball to McNaughton on the wing. The Cessnock man outpaces Jimmy Hamilton and gallops down the touchline. His cross finds his Cessnock teammate Percy Lennard, who shoots on the run. Davison is beaten and the Maitland crowd go berserk when the ball ends up in the back of the net. The half-time whistle sounds with England leading 5-1.

Two minutes after the resumption, Ernie Simms lays off the ball to Batten, who sends it flying past Cartwright for another English goal.

Charlie Hannaford continues to cause trouble for Australia. After a good team move, he sends a pinpoint cross to Simms, who heads towards the corner of the goal only for Cartwright to pull off a spectacular one-handed save. As he does, he collides with the goalpost. A stunned Cartwright is treated by Tom Langridge. He is soon put right and a disastrous change of goalkeeper is averted.

After having a seemingly good goal disallowed for offside, Elkes puts on some of his jazzy tricks for the crowd.

As a couple of defenders box him in, he flicks the ball out to Ernie Simms to drive it into the back of the net from 30 yards out. England now lead 7-1 and the Australians long for the sound of the full-time whistle.

Completely outplayed, Australia still shows some fight. Masters, briefly shaking off Spencer's shackles, sends a ball wide to the left. McNaughton controls it and jinks past Hamilton. His cross finds Percy Lennard with his back to goal but he twists and shoots. Davison makes a good save but cannot hold onto the ball. Tom Thompson gets to the rebound first and stabs it home to score Australia's second goal.

Bert Batten, with four goals already, is still not done. Receiving the ball near halfway he beats the offside trap and brings it towards the Australian goal. The ever-willing Cartwright charges off his line but Batten coolly eases the ball past him to score England's eighth.

The final whistle blows moments later and England have walloped Australia 8-2, taking an unbeatable 3-0 lead in the five-Test series. The action doesn't end there. Spectators, officials and players make a dash to souvenir the match ball. One spectator is carrying it away when Jack Elkes upends him in the grandstand and claims the ball for England.

* * *

Bert Batten was the outstanding player of the match. His five goals brought his tour tally to 38. England outshone Australia in every department. Their forward play was sparkling, the halves far superior, and their defence was sound.

Judy Masters failed to make an impression on the game. He was shut out of it due to the close attention of Spencer, who had learned much from his first encounter with Masters in Sydney. The Australian backs failed to live up to their previous week's form, and Cartwright had an off day. Edwards played his worst game of the tour, too often going to ground in defence. McNaughton and Lennard were the only Australian players to come out of the game with any credit.

"They were much too good, everywhere," Masters said.

* * *

England didn't have far to travel for their next match. Located around 30km south-west of Maitland, the mining town of Cessnock was, in the words of Shire President John Brown at the official reception, "the capital city of the coalfields." The England squad was given a tour of the coal mines and got a first-hand view of the working conditions of many of the district's players.

The strength of football in the coalfields was underlined by the fact that five of the local team were Australian representatives. These were Bob Austin, Cec Williams, Jack McCroary, Roy McNaughton and Percy Lennard. The local paper, *The Cessnock Eagle and South Maitland Recorder* wasn't particularly confident, predicting that "although Cessnock does not expect to be victorious, the players will show that they can take defeat in a real sportsmanlike manner".

Wednesday, 15 July 1925, Match 20: England v South Maitland, Cessnock Show Ground

People from all over the coalfields descend on the Cessnock Show Ground. Many of the local pits shut early for lack of miners to work them.

The playing surface is not in the best of shape, the grass overly long. Liberal doses of sand have been spread around to hold the surface together after it had been trotted on by horses, cows, sheep, pigs, dogs and other farmyard animals. A good midweek crowd of around 5,000 sits patiently behind the roped off playing field, enjoying the winter sunshine.

Jack McCroary kicks off for South Maitland. The locals absorb early pressure from England while proving dangerous on the counter. Early on, Bill Sage holds back Jack McCroary and concedes a free-kick. McCroary quickly takes it and passes to Roy McNaughton on the wing. McNaughton crosses but none of his teammates can get a touch on it.

England's ground-passing game is hampered by the long grass and the eager locals intercept many of their efforts. South Maitland's left-half Avis gains control of a wayward English pass then beats Jack Elkes before passing to McCroary then on to Percy Lennard, who steers his shot just wide.

With the fans shouting encouragement, the locals take the game to the visitors. England are almost embarrassed when McCroary swoops on a back pass from Billy Caesar. Only Sage's last-ditch challenge clears the danger.

England hit back through Bert Batten, whose angled shot is saved by South Maitland's keeper Bob Austin. The rebound comes to Elkes, and Austin again saves his point-blank effort. Football supporters in Newcastle have long felt that Austin is every bit as good as Cartwright and should have been in the Australian Test team. Next, a long-range effort by Billy Caesar looks certain to dip under the bar but Austin pulls off a spectacular diving save to deflect it for a corner.

Shortly before half-time, England's goalkeeper Harry Hardy kicks downfield. South Maitland right-back 'Ginger Mick' Farrey controls the ball and passes to Avis, who rapidly transfers it to McNaughton. The Cessnock flyer centres to McCroary, who traps the ball and turns brilliantly, opening up the goal. His right foot shot from in front sails over the bar and is met with ironic cheers.

At half-time, the score stands at 0-0. Not many teams had kept England goalless in a half. Although their teamwork has lacked the finesse of the visitors, South Maitland have chased down every ball and contested every challenge.

England change their tactics after the interval, favouring a longer passing game better suited to the surface. Around five minutes into the second half, Charlie Spencer robs Lennard of the ball and clears downfield. Elkes is on the receiving end and sends an accurate long pass to Billy Williams, who steadies and blasts a left-foot drive that beats Austin to give England the lead.

Soon after, England go on the attack through Stan Seymour at outside-left. Another of his precision crosses beats everyone and ends up in the back of the net, registering England's second goal.

South Maitland work hard to get back into the game. Jack McCroary, having a fine game, is played through and steers the ball past the advancing Hardy. The ball rolls towards the goal, and the England keeper scampers back and hacks it off his own line. Spectators claim the ball had gone over the line but the referee rules play on.

England then bring the ball forward through Billy Williams. His centre finds Billy Caesar, who lashes the ball past Austin to put England 3-0 up.

South Maitland refuse to give up and they find an outlet through the always-eager Roy McNaughton at outside-left. Getting away down the wing, he sits up a cross to the back post. Hardy comes out but misjudges the flight. Percy Lennard, coming in at pace, thrusts out a leg. As he falls to the turf, he hears the crowd's joyous cheers. The ball has ended up in the net and South Maitland have become the first regional team to score against the tourists.

The locals are spent. Some of the players had worked a shift in the mines until noon that day. Their strenuous efforts to keep up with the Englishmen have worn them out. When Seymour has the ball at his feet near the end of the game, he looks up to see exhausted men in front of him. Drawing several players, Seymour slips the ball to Elkes. With room to move, the gangling Elkes takes it around a few defenders before hammering in a long-range shot that is too hot for Austin and puts England ahead 4-1.

The full-time whistle sounds with Elkes on the ball, and for the second match in a row, he souvenirs it.

* * *

The match had been scrappy due to the poor surface but the crowd went away happy with the good showing put up by the home team. England outclassed the locals but only after a torrid first half. Proud local football supporters could reflect on a performance that was better than Australia's in the third Test. They could also put one over their local rivals, since the crowd of 5,000 with a gate of £403 was significantly higher than the coalfields the previous Wednesday.

England left Cessnock for Sydney that evening. By Monday morning, while English players strolled along Bondi Beach, many of the spectators and players at Cessnock were back underground working at the coalface.

20
Daylight Robbery

England's crushing victory in Maitland gave them an unassailable 3-0 lead in the five-match Test series. Syd Storey had a recurring nightmare of Roy McNaughton's penalty sailing over the bar in the second Test. Judy Masters might have returned to the fold like a knight in shining armour but his white charger dumped him unceremoniously in the Maitland mud.

Reminders that the fourth Test was a dead rubber could be found everywhere. Newspapers contrasted the football series to Australia's 1924 Ashes-winning rugby league and 1924/25 Ashes-winning cricket teams. By inference, it was suggested that Australia should stick to sports they were good at. And although there was no officially designated trophy for the football series, newspapers knew readers would understand headlines such as: 'SOCCER TEST: ENGLAND TAKES THE ASHES' in *The Labor Daily*, and 'ENGLAND TOO GOOD. SATURDAY'S SOCCER TEST: ENGLAND WINS ASHES' in *The Newcastle Sun*. Alec Boyd writing for the *Sunday Times* noted: "England would take the Ashes with them".

With Sydney having already hosted two interstate matches, a Metropolitan XI game and a Test match, there was only so much football goodwill, not to mention spare change, that the city's sporting audiences could invest on the English tour. Early ticket sales for the upcoming fourth Test in Sydney weren't encouraging.

The New Zealand rugby league team were busily capturing the attention of the sporting public. Now training with Tom Langridge, they were competing well in Australia. In a tough game against New South Wales at the Sydney Cricket Ground, one New Zealand player ran on to the field for the second half with his arm dangling limply by his side. New South Wales captain Reg Latta sportingly allowed New Zealand to make a substitute. This was not according to the official rules but was publicly lauded. *The Sun* newspaper opined: "After all football is a game - not a business, and the pity is that Latta's action could not be copied by the England Soccer manager, Mr John Lewis, who refused to allow a New South Wales substitute in a recent match for an injured man in the first half of a game."

Not that the substitute rule was as important now since Australia had never asked for substitutes in the Tests. But the bad blood it had stirred up already, along with the series being decided, and Australia's seemingly impossible task of defeating England, made it difficult to garner public enthusiasm for the fourth Test.

Storey could certainly do without any other distractions to a potential audience for the last big tour game in Sydney. But distractions were arriving from all quarters, including by air and by sea.

17 July 1925, Distractions by Air, Sydney Harbour

On the shores of Farm Cove, thousands of faces gaze at murky skies to the south. At 2pm, four RAAF planes scout to the south and west. Finding nothing, they fly back to base. An hour later, some people traipse home. Others start to worry. The waiting dignitaries, including the Italian consul, prominent Italian citizens, Australian politicians and representatives of the armed forces, shuffle their feet and chatter nervously.

RAAF Squadron Leader Lawrence Wackett dramatically hops aboard a motor boat and speeds to one of the Royal Australian Navy ships in the harbour. On his return, he assures the people on the foreshore there is nothing to worry about - the great airman has been sighted over Jervis Bay.

Just after 4pm, the ever-vigilant Squadron Leader Wackett points to a tiny speck in the sky. "There they are," he says. People all over the eastern and southern suburbs of Sydney also look up when they notice the plane. The Australian football team, training at the Show Ground for the fourth Test, are among those casting their eyes to the heavens.

When the waiting crowds at Farm Cove see the plane for themselves, a loud cheer goes up. The seaplane circles the warships in the harbour and lands with a gentle splash not far from *HMAS Sydney*. As the plane taxies towards Farm Cove, the sailors lining the decks of the warships yelp and wave their caps. Sirens and horns blare from boats, ferries and yachts. The band on *HMAS Adelaide* strikes up the Italian anthem.

Squadron Leader Wackett is rowed across to the plane and passes up a tow line. The two airmen, pilot Wing Commander Francesco Di Pinedo and mechanic Ernesto Campanelli, hop out onto the seaplane's floats and nonchalantly light up cigarettes.

On shore, the men remove their overalls. The 34-year-old Di Pinedo, tall, handsome and quietly spoken, is wearing a grey golf suit, Campanelli, a plain suit. Two youngsters from the local Italian community, Miss Rossi and Master Loschiavo, are ushered forward and hand the pair a large bouquet of flowers.

Di Pinedo had left Rome on 21 April with the ultimate goal of reaching Tokyo. This flight is meant to prove the utility of seaplanes for long-distance travel. Di Pinedo believes that seaplanes are the future of international travel as they don't require expensive airports.

The Italian consul can't stop shaking the airmen's hands. Press photographers, reporters and spectators jostle each other in their eagerness. The welcome has to be cut short so police can force a path through the throng to whisk the airmen away to a waiting vehicle for a reception at Government House.

* * *

The same afternoon that Di Pinedo landed in Sydney, Australia's football hierarchy were on a train bound for Wollongong. Anxious to shore up the loyalty of Masters and Thompson, Syd Storey, Ern Lukeman, and Stephen Stack of the Sydney association, travelled to a meeting with Illawarra football officials.

Storey wasn't giving much away. He believed the concession of allowing the rebel Sydney players a transfer was enough and that Illawarra needed to stay affiliated with the NSWFA. It was up to Illawarra to rejoin the fold. Storey wasn't prepared to make any further concessions.

Illawarra's Sid Cope was not impressed. He'd put a lot of effort into setting up the professional league. He was not about to postpone it under duress from nit-picking curmudgeons from Sydney. Ern Lukeman, taking a more conciliatory tone than Storey, said that the NSWFA weren't opposed to professionalism as such, but for it to succeed, it needed a united approach and only a league involving clubs from Sydney, Illawarra and Newcastle could hope to be successful. Lukeman said that playing against England was a lifelong dream for Judy Masters and the action of the Illawarra clubs had caused him much distress.

Although appreciative of the diplomatic efforts of Lukeman, Cope felt that the NSWFA had not addressed any of their grievances. After the three Sydney men left, the Illawarra clubs voted on a proposal to re-affiliate with the NSWFA. The clubs rejected the proposal but to Cope's surprise, two clubs, Balgownie Rangers and Corrimal, voted for it. Cope believed he'd been double-crossed. It was a heavy blow to the strength of the proposed new competition.

The real cause of the about face by Balgownie and Corrimal was soon revealed. Both clubs were reinstated to the Gardiner Cup as a reward for not joining the professional league. Cope suspected that while in the Australian camp, Masters, who was also an official of Balgownie Rangers, had been won over by the silver-tongued Syd Storey.

* * *

Australian selectors made wholesale changes in light of the debacle in Maitland. In the backs, Gallen was axed and Faulkner was unavailable as he had to get back to his employer in Adelaide. Alf Edwards, Australia's captain in the first two Tests was another casualty. Perhaps the biggest surprise was the dumping of outside-right Stan Bourke, who had performed well in the first two Tests and was starved of the ball in the third.

Victoria's William Aiken was originally slated in at left-back but had to refuse due to work commitments. Sid Robinson of Pyrmont was called up for Aiken, while 19-year-old Arch Harris, who had played well for Newcastle against England, took the right-back position.

Art Lambert of the Adamstown club in Newcastle replaced Edwards' at centre-half, while Bourke's position on the wing was taken by Allan Burns of the Canterbury club in Sydney. The choice of Lambert at centre-half was odd since he played fullback for his club and it was in this position that he and Harris effectively employed the one-back game against England.

England's injury toll had grown to six. Tom Whittaker had already been ruled out for the tour, and Mo Atherton was working overtime getting Spencer, Sage, Hannah, Hannaford, Poynton and Charlton fit. Apart from Harry Hardy replacing Teddy Davison in goal, England went with the same outfield players from the third Test in Maitland. Charlton was a 50/50 proposition and several payers would likely be playing while nursing injuries.

Mo Atherton, at least, had an assistant now. When Stan Seymour needed a rub down after one of the games, Tom Whittaker, feeling idle after his injury, obliged. Seymour told Whittaker he was a natural. From then on, Whittaker helped in masseur duties and preparing the team. It was a lesson that would serve him well in the years to come.

On the morning of the fourth Test, the English team watched the shimmering Pacific Ocean from the balcony of the Bondi Hotel. After breakfast, most of the players strolled along the beachside promenade. Down on the sand, Charlie Hannaford practiced ball work under the watchful eye of Mo Atherton. But it was no good. His hamstring was not up to it. Hannaford's name was scratched from the team sheet and West Ham's Billy Williams' added to it.

18 July 1925, Match 21: England vs Australia, Fourth Test Match, Sydney Show Ground

Like in the first New South Wales game on 30 May, Judy Masters captains the locals and Len Graham captains England. Both teams get a great ovation as they enter the arena from a moderate-sized crowd. Once again, the Sydney Show Ground surface is in poor condition, with many bare patches.

Fresh from welcoming Di Pinedo at Government House the previous day, New South Wales Governor Sir

Dudley de Chair is introduced to the teams before kickoff by the football-loving politician Hugh McIntosh.

There is a light breeze and the sun is shining. Jack Elkes says: "If this is winter what is summer like?"

Masters gets the ball rolling but Charlie Spencer checks the initial attack and sends to Bert Batten down the centre. Arch Harris, Australia's newest fullback, takes his first touch in international football, a rugged challenge on England's star centre-forward.

England pressures Australia's goal and Harris, Robinson and Lambert are kept busy. Len Graham dispossesses Burns and plays a good through ball for Jack Elkes in the inside-left position. Elkes skilfully evades the Australian defence before passing to Jimmy

George Cartwright making a save in the Fourth test

Walsh on the wing. Walsh skips free of a challenge and lobs a cross to the far post for Ernie Simms to head firmly into the back of the net. England lead 1-0.

The crowd barely take their seats before they are off them again. Elkes starts the move by passing to Batten, who sends it across to Simms. Seeing Batten's run, Simms plays him in with a perfectly weighted diagonal ball. Batten outmuscles the backs and slots the ball into the bottom corner as Cartwright comes off his line. It is 2-0 to England with just five minutes gone and Australia's chances of getting anything out of the game already look unlikely.

At the 15-minute mark, Bert Batten receives Len Graham's throw-in and turns towards goal. He works a one-two with Elkes and hits a shot on the run from nearly 35 yards out that sails into the top corner of the net. Batten's spectacular goal is met with great applause from the crowd.

Just a minute after the third goal, Batten bears down on Cartwright. Batten strikes another thunderbolt and

Australia's Harry Spurway vs Jimmy Walsh (Liverpool) of England in the Fourth Test

Cartwright flings himself across goal and tips it over the bar with one hand.

Elkes, the provider for the first two goals is giving the Australian defence headaches. Receiving a ball from Batten, he runs downfield, feinting and dodging as he goes. With his back to the goal and hemmed in by the Australian defence, he suddenly turns, dribbles past Gil Storey and Harris then blasts a shot that Masters said later reminded him of "Beachy Bill", the notorious Turkish gun battery at Gallipoli. It's 4-0 in just 20 minutes and England look set to outdo their feat in Maitland.

Despite a number of close scrapes, Australia manages to hold England out for the rest of the half. Harry Hardy has barely had a touch in the England goal and the second half bodes ill for the home team.

With no band booked, Mr Bendrodt's bulldogs are let loose at the interval with some balloons. The bulldogs show remarkable skill in keeping them off the ground. One spectator yells: "Why don't you play them against the Pommies? We might have a chance then."

For the second half, Thompson and McNaughton swap places, with Thompson now playing outside-left and McNaughton at inside-left. As both players rarely touched the ball in the first half, it seems a strange move.

But the move almost immediately bears fruit. After an interchange of passes with Masters, Roy McNaughton shoots but it goes just wide. There are some encouraging cheers from the stands.

Sitting on a 4-0 lead, England pass the ball around to take the pace out of the game. When Elkes beats a few players and shoots well over the bar, one of the spectators shouts: "Are you trying?"

Both Thompson and McNaughton get more involved in the play. Thompson dribbles neatly for about 20 yards but his long-range shot is easily held by Hardy. McNaughton and Thompson then put on a good passing move and Thompson's cross to Masters is plucked out of the air by the England keeper.

After saving a long-range effort from McNaughton, Hardy launches one of his massive punt kicks down the field. Jack Elkes plays the ball to winger Williams, who beats his marker and crosses into the middle. An unmarked Ernie Simms heads it in from close range, making it 5-0 to England.

The visitors are happy to see out the rest of the game with a bit of showboating thrown in for good measure. Elkes has the crowd in stitches as he makes sport with the Australians. Elkes would dribble around a few defenders before retreating and taking them on again. He goes around in circles but the crowd enjoy it.

The full-time whistle blows at 5-0 to the tourists.

* * *

It was a dominant England performance and the scoreline of 5-0 flattered the locals. England outplayed Australia in every position but particularly in the halves, with Len Graham being the pick. Jack Elkes was superb, playing one of his best games of the tour.

The Australians were dreadful. The gamble on Art Lambert was a failure. He roamed out of position and couldn't

England score their fifth goal in the Fourth Test

cope with the skill of Elkes and Batten. Arch Harris was overawed by the occasion, although he showed resilience after taking some heavy knocks early on. Australia's forwards barely got the ball. Roy McNaughton was the best of them. Masters bustled hard but was again well-covered by Spencer.

Burns, as outside-right was a poor selection. He lacked the pace of Bourke and played so wide that one reporter said he could have been mistaken for a linesman. George Cartwright was down on form. Questioning his continued selection, the Sydney Sportsman rather unkindly noted that "the only way Cartwright could lose his place was if he died".

The novelty of the England tour was wearing off. The relatively small attendance of 14,000 made for gate takings of £950, taking the total for the tour to just over £18,000. While it appeared the tour would not lose money, hopes for a big profit were fading. Syd Storey knew that every last shilling of revenue was important. What he heard at the end of the game would have had him tearing his hair out.

Near full-time, the bags holding the change from the turnstiles were handed over to Sydney football officials Stephen Stack and Frederick Packer, who took them to the finance room in the grandstand. When they left the room to watch the remainder of the game, they didn't store the bags in the safe provided. Instead, they literally hid them under the mat. When Stack and Packer returned to the finance room the bags were gone. A light-fingered spectator had made off with £185, or roughly 20 per cent of the takings.

"Soccer officials are careless with money," wrote the Evening News. Stephen Stack duly reported the matter to the Darlinghurst police, who assigned plain clothes officers to the case. They didn't have much luck. A month later, a red-faced Stack was compelled to offer a £50 reward for information. The reward went unclaimed.

21
Distractions By Sea

20 July, At Sea, off Gabo Island
On a pitch-black evening off the Victorian coast, the most powerful armada ever assembled in the Pacific battled gale force winds and mountainous seas. All up, 57 warships of the United States Pacific Fleet bore down on the east coast of Australia in the worst conditions they'd experienced since leaving Pearl Harbor a few weeks before.

The cruise was an exercise to help cement relations between the United States and Australia as well as a means of testing out operational procedures in the event of a future Pacific war.

With special correspondents on board, Australians had been following the ships' progress in minute detail. A near mania for all things American gripped the Australian public as the fleet, carrying 25,000 US navy personnel, drew closer. Nearly 30 nautical miles east of Gabo Island, radios crackled and signal lights flashed. The mighty armada split in two. The larger contingent, aboard the *USS Seattle* and under Admiral Robert E. Coontz, headed southwest towards Melbourne. The smaller contingent, aboard the *USS California* and under Admiral Samuel Shelburne Robison, headed north towards Sydney.

* * *

On the Tuesday following the fourth Test, England journeyed to Parramatta to play their only tour match against a club side.

Granville in Sydney's west was one of Australia's oldest and strongest football districts. Centred on the heavy engineering works at Clyde, Granville had been formed from its workforce of mainly Scottish immigrants in the 1880s and the game had continued to be popular among their Australian-born descendants.

Playing in a black-and-white strip and known as the Magpies, Granville had a proud record in the Sydney competition dating back to 1885. They had won the league for the past two seasons and were leading the competition again in 1925.

The organizer of the tour fixture was Fred Barlow, a one-time engineer at the Clyde Engineering Works who had been with the club since the 1890s. Barlow was a great servant of football as an administrator for the Granville club, the NSWFA and the CFA. Barlow was often called 'the grand old man' of football in Australia.

Tuesday, 21 July 1925, Match 22: England v Granville, Parramatta Oval

Motor cars provided by the Granville club pick up the English team from Bondi and take them to Parramatta. A big contingent of schoolboys are in the crowd. Football has always been popular in schools in the Granville district and the English tourists are impressed with the standard of play in the schoolboys' preliminary match.

Despite a cold westerly, a good midweek crowd of over 3,000 are on hand. Schoolboys cheer loudly for England but make an even bigger noise for the local team. Shouts of 'Go the Magpies' are heard from different parts of the ground.

England find the early going tough against a committed club side. Granville's halves, including recent Australian captain Alf Edwards, combine well, while the backs are on the alert, too. One of the first chances falls to Granville when Hele plays in Flynn down the left flank. Flynn's ball across the goalmouth reaches Stan Bourke, who beats Charlton and lashes in a shot that brings out a good save from England's keeper Teddy Davison.

For nearly half an hour, the play see-saws, with Davison getting as many touches as his Granville counterpart Ted Atchison.

Then Len Graham, England's elegant left-half, gets his team moving. His delightful pass finds Bert Batten, who charges past three defenders before striking a powerful shot that gives Atchison no chance.

A few minutes later, England's left-back Stan Charlton gets the visitors underway again. He passes to Batten, who swings it out to Billy Williams on the wing. Williams takes it down the touchline and chips into the centre. There's a moment's hesitation between Atchison and his fullbacks and Ernie Simms pounces and lobs the ball neatly over the stranded keeper's head. The half-time whistle sounds with England leading 2-0.

At half-time, Fred Barlow is happy with the solid effort Granville has put up. A recent recipient of one of the little blue enamel FA badges, Barlow is very much enjoying the occasion. Rugged up in blankets, he and John Lewis, the 'grand old men' of Australian and English football, chat away like they've known each other all their lives.

In the second half, Granville continues to take the game to England. Rigby, Granville's right back, plays a good ball to Stan Bourke, Australia's outside-right for the first three Tests. Bourke makes a good run before cutting in and striking a clean shot. Davison dives but can only parry the ball. A group of players scramble for the ball and it falls to Harold Winter, who smashes the cover off it. The shot rattles the net and the schoolboys shriek in jubilation. It is now 2-1 to England and the game is in the balance.

England attempt to hit back quickly. Liverpool's Jimmy Walsh raids down the flank and crosses to Williams, whose first-time shot is blocked by Atchison. The ball pops up and Simms heads it into an open goal to restore England's two-goal advantage.

Shortly after, Edwards concedes a free-kick outside the Granville penalty area. Jack Elkes floats it into the middle. Simms rises above the defence and heads it into the net to bring up his hat trick. England are now 4-1 up.

Batten then receives a pass near halfway and proceeds to run through the locals' defence. As Atchison advances, Batten slams the ball home to give the tourists a 5-1 lead. Soon after, Len Graham sets up another scintillating attack, shifting the ball out to Walsh, who passes inside to Elkes. The Tottenham man twists and turns, dribbles past three players before playing it to Graham. The ball is laid off for Batten to score England's sixth goal and register his own hat trick in the process.

* * *

23 July 1925, Distractions by Sea, Sydney Harbour

Crowds had been flocking to the harbour since before dawn. Many were aboard the flotilla of ferries, chartered boats and private vessels. The New South Wales government declared a public holiday - 'Fleet Day' - for the arrival of the US fleet, and the harbour foreshore was the place to be for a great view of the show.

On Sydney Harbour's South Head, people scanned the misty ocean for any sight of the American visitors. Then the *USS California* appeared out of the mist like a breaching leviathan. Soon, all ten battle cruisers and three auxiliary ships of the squadron could be seen in line-ahead formation.

The ships glided into the harbour amid a mass of humanity on the foreshore. Admiral Robison had never witnessed such a crowd in his life. Civil authorities estimated there were close to one million people watching from vantage points on the harbour.

RAAF seaplanes soared above the ships in welcome. As if that wasn't enough of a spectacle, Francesco Di Pinedo suddenly swooped out of the sky, putting on his own display for the visitors. Di Pinedo had planned to leave for Brisbane earlier in the week but engine trouble delayed him. His many Italian friends urged him to stay on for the arrival of the US fleet.

The US sailors marched through Sydney in a parade that brought the city to a standstill. Many VIP guests, including the English football team, were invited by Premier Jack Lang to watch the spectacle. It is unclear whether any of the English team watched the parade as they had to play a match that afternoon.

Sydney football administrators tried hard to arrange a match with the sailors but the only football the crews were familiar with was the American version. There were rumours that the *USS Colorado* could field a team and a match was tentatively pencilled in for the weekend.[1]

US Fleet arriving in Sydney Harbour

[1] The *USS Colorado* game didn't come off but a game with the American fleet did eventuate on 1 August between a team from the Rose Bay Tram Depot and the crew of the *USS Oklahoma* at Rushcutter's Bay Oval. The Tram Depot won by 6 goals to 3.

Hoping to cash in on the Fleet Day public holiday, Syd Storey and CFA officials organised a different kind of match. It had grown from an idea suggested by a member of the public in Newcastle. Why not split England into two teams and give them a few Australian players to make up the numbers? This would give the public a chance to see a good contest and at the same time give local players experience playing alongside skilled professionals. With interest in the tour waning, it seemed like a good idea.

The original game set down for Fleet Day, another England vs New South Wales fixture, was cancelled and the exhibition match put in its place. Both England goalkeepers would captain their sides and consequently the teams were called Hardy's XI and Davison's XI. With many visitors in the city to see the US sailors, a big crowd was hoped for. A good gate would go some way towards easing the embarrassment caused by the robbery.

* * *

Thursday, 23 July 1925, Exhibition Match: Hardy's XI vs Davison's XI, Sydney Show Ground
The teams are:

Hardy's XI (red and black): *H Hardy (Eng), J Hannah (Eng), S Robinson (Aus), G Storey (Aus), C Spencer (Eng), L Graham (Eng), C Hannaford (Eng), P Lennard (Aus), J Masters (Aus), J Elkes (Eng), R McNaughton (Aus)*

Davison's XI (blue): *J Davison (Eng), S Charlton (Eng), E Pont (Aus), W Caesar (Eng), J Hamilton (Eng), H Spurway (Aus), J Walsh (Eng), E Simms (Eng), H Batten (Eng), A Phillips (Aus), W Williams (Eng)*

The Show Ground's surface is even worse than before. The field is dry and strewn with bare patches. A strong breeze whips up clouds of dust.

Despite hopes to the contrary, the crowd is miniscule. Most football fans are next door at the SCG for the rugby league match between New Zealand and New South Wales.

Three minutes into the game, Jack Elkes sets up Roy McNaughton. McNaughton outpaces the defence and crosses to his Cessnock club mate Percy Lennard. Drawing his man, Lennard lays the ball into the path of Judy Masters, who reacquaints himself with what it's like to score against an English goalkeeper. It's 1-0 to Hardy's XI.

Harry Hardy is forced to save shots from Ernie Simms and Billy Caesar, while Teddy Davison has to stretch to keep out Hannaford's effort. For the first time on tour, the English keepers are getting a workout.

Roy McNaughton is playing superbly. After a good run, he crosses to Percy Lennard, who sends it out to Elkes. Standing on the ball around 30 yards from goal, Elkes sums up his options. Surprising everybody, he lobs the ball into the top right corner of the net past a stunned Davison.

At half-time, the score is 2-0 in favour of Hardy's XI.

Shortly after the restart, Clapton Orient's Charlie Hannaford makes a dash down the wing. He crosses to Percy Lennard, who controls the ball, cleverly beats Spurway then tucks the ball into the bottom corner of the net. Hardy's men are now 3-0 up.

Davison's XI eventually get on the scoreboard a few minutes later, when Bert Batten heads in a cross from Ernie Simms.

Hardy's men strike back almost immediately. This time, it's a fine effort from Roy McNaughton that restores his team's three-goal advantage.

There is more goalmouth action at the other end as Davison's team try to get back in the game. After a scramble in the penalty area, the ball comes to Albert Phillips from the Kurri Kurri club. His rattling strike beats Hardy and it's now 4-2 in favour of Hardy's XI.

Charlie Spencer makes it 5-2 with a long-range effort that gives Davison no chance. Spencer jokingly apologises to Davison for the goal. Harry Hardy at one stage takes off for a long run downfield. The English players are having a bit of fun. Bert Batten barely raises a sweat. One fan says Batten and Simms should be arrested for loitering.

Judy Masters scores his second for Hardy's XI a few minutes later. Near the end, Simms and Batten shake off their lethargy and Batten scores from Simms' cross. The final score is 6-3 in favour of Hardy's XI.

* * *

Roy McNaughton was the best forward on the field and relished the service provided by Elkes. England co-manager Mark Frowde said McNaughton was the best player in Australia: "Should he ever decide to come to England, he would not have very much trouble in winning a place in any of the big First League teams."

Reporters had mixed feelings about the game. *The Labor Daily* called it a "fine exhibition" and it was "football as it should be played". In the *Arrow*, Alec Boyd saw the game as passionless and dull. He called it "a dreary display and nobody was sorry when the final whistle sounded". At one point, he noted, "a woman was seen to be reading a book".

* * *

The last week of England's Sydney stay was a busy one off the field as well-wishers were determined to give them a fitting farewell.

John Lewis and Mark Frowde were guests at a lunch put on by Reg Browne, a well-known philanthropist and New Zealand rugby supporter. Suspended over the tables was a ball used in one of the Test matches in a garland of jonquils and violets, representing the English colours. Lewis and Frowde were also treated to a lunch at Parliament House, courtesy of Jack Lang, the New South Wales Premier.

The team enjoyed dinners and race meetings. Top billiards player Walter Lindrum, who the footballers had watched several times, shouted the team to a function at the Palais Royale on the eve of their departure. Lindrum promised to catch up with Billy Williams in London the following year.

England's departure would mark the end of the tour for Syd Storey. His period of leave without pay from the Railways Department had expired, and he wouldn't be travelling on to Melbourne. It had been a trying few months for Storey, and no one could say his role had been a sinecure. He'd always put Australian football first, even if it meant stepping on the toes of the English team management.

Ern Lukeman was another official who had spent time with the tourists in New South Wales and Queensland but wouldn't be travelling any further. John Lewis was disappointed Lukeman couldn't get time off work to continue with the team as the pair had struck up a good rapport. William Lincoln from the NSWFA took the role of CFA liaison for the Melbourne leg of the tour.

Immediately after the exhibition match, the English tourists caught the overnight train to Melbourne. Despite the festivities of Fleet Day still going on all around Sydney, the team were astonished by the large gathering of football supporters at Central Station to see them off. As the train pulled out, the entire length of the platform was thick with well-wishers. People raised their hats and shouted: "Hip-hip hooray! Hip-hip hooray! Hip-hip hooray for the English team."

22
The Vics Stand Tall

Friday, 24 July 1925, The Grand Parade of the US Fleet, Melbourne
For weeks, Melbourne has been preparing for the arrival of the US fleet. Other than a brief aeronautical infatuation when Di Pinedo passed through the city the week before, all eyes are now on the sea.

The flotilla of 43 vessels under the command of Admiral Coontz aboard the *USS Seattle,* arrived in Port Phillip Bay on 23 July.

The next day, the American sailors march through the city. Despite it not being a public holiday (school children have been given the afternoon off), hundreds of thousands of people line the route of the parade. People crowd the footpaths, lean out of windows and stand on the rickety iron verandahs above the shopfronts. Bunting adorns every balcony. Everywhere people are waving miniature American flags. The city is awash in red, white and blue.

A detachment of mounted troopers on white horses leads the parade, followed by Marines and bands from the warships and finally by the sailors themselves. Crowds edge forward as cheers reverberate through the city's streets.

In Bourke Street, Clarence Newbould, secretary of the Footscray (Australian Rules) Football Club, is standing under the cantilevered verandah of Hoyt's Picture Theatre with a crowd of people waiting for the parade. Just after the leading elements of the band march past, he steps out from underneath the verandah to get closer to the street. From behind him comes a gigantic crash and the crunch of twisting metal. Looking around, he sees the verandah perched at a precarious angle with parts of it nearly touching the ground. From underneath the collapsing structure, people scream and cry for help.

Bystanders frantically begin clearing away the debris. The American sailors stop marching and rush to help. Ambulances and commandeered private motor vehicles transport people to nearby hospitals. A temporary first aid station is set up at Bourke and Swanston Streets, where nearly 300 people are treated for minor injuries.

Miraculously, despite 150 people being taken to hospital, only eight are critically injured. One person, Eva Pearce, a 19-year-old saleswoman from the Myer Department store, later dies from her injuries.

On the streets of Melbourne, rumours of large numbers of casualties sweep through the crowd. When the sailors resume their march and salute Australian Prime Minister Stanley Bruce on the steps of Parliament, it is in front of a subdued audience.

* * *

It was in this unsettled atmosphere of a celebration gone awry that the English footballers checked into the George Hotel in St Kilda. John Lewis was not happy with the travel arrangements. He had been against playing the exhibition match on Thursday as it meant arriving in Melbourne just a day out from the fifth Test match after another long train journey.

* * *

In the early years of international football in Australia, it was difficult for players to take time off work to travel to matches in another state. It was common for at least a few players from the host city to be picked in Australian sides as a matter of convenience and a way of bolstering local support.

Collapsed balcony on Bourke Street

Four Victorian players were selected in Australia's team for the fifth Test. Jim Robison, goalkeeper for second division club Northumberland and Durham, took the place of George Cartwright. He had played against England in both the earlier tour matches in Melbourne. Journalist JO Wilshaw, writing in *The Herald,* said that he'd be surprised if England "can get the ball past the greatest of Australian goalkeepers".

Footscray Thistle's William Aiken would play left back. He had played against the Englishmen three times already and his inability to travel to New South Wales and

Queensland had cost him a place in the Australian team earlier in the tour.

Preston's George Eccles replaced Burns at outside-right. Eccles had been a centre-forward but moved to the wing in 1925. A speedy player, he made the outside right position his own and had been selected for the fourth Test but couldn't take time off work to travel to Sydney.

The other Victorian was Harold Morrison, the Prahran City centre-half who would play right-half for Australia. Morrison had played once against England, for the Australian XI in Melbourne on 23 May.

South Australia provided one player for the Australian team, Port Adelaide right-back Jack Mitchell, who had already played three times against England. Mitchell would be renewing acquaintances with Aiken, who he had partnered with for the Australian XI in Adelaide and Melbourne.

New South Wales supplied two halves and four forwards. Harry Spurway had to pull out of the Melbourne trip at the last moment, his place at left-half taken by Charlie O'Connor.

Albert 'Dutchy' Phillips, from Newcastle club Kurri Kurri, was a surprise selection. He hadn't played against England at all but could boast of scoring against an English keeper, a feat he achieved for Davison's XI in the exhibition match on Thursday.

England manager John Lewis left it late to choose his team's goalkeeper. Hardy and Davison had played two Tests each, and Lewis couldn't decide between them. He left it up to the two players. In democratic spirit, they tossed a coin for it. Hardy won and elected to play but on the morning of the match he was not feeling well and Davison took his place.

The Melbourne soccer press talked up the game. *The Argus* expected "there will be many converts to the round-ball code" as a result of the match. It was hoped the appearance of Victorian players in the Australian team, as well as it being the last opportunity of seeing the Englishmen in action, would help draw a big crowd. With many visitors in the city to celebrate the US fleet it seemed possible, according to JO Wilshaw, that the 30,000 capacity of the Fitzroy Cricket Ground could be tested.

Saturday, 25 July 1925, Match 23: England v Australia, The Fifth Test, Fitzroy Cricket Ground, Melbourne

Rain during the week has turned the Fitzroy Cricket Ground muddy and the cricket pitch area in the middle is a quagmire. Australia runs towards the Brunswick Street end. The hoped-for 30,000 fans have stayed away. Instead,

Advertisement for the Fifth Test in Melbourne

Judy Masters kicks off in front of a sparse crowd.

England starts well, with Jack Elkes looking lively. He puts in the first cross of the game but Australian keeper Jim Robison gathers safely. Elkes then follows it up with a booming drive that tests Robison once more. With the ball seemingly glued to his toe, Elkes then dashes through several opponents before side-footing the ball just beyond the post. Robison's muddy jersey is testament to how hard he is working.

England put the ball in the back of the net via a Bert Batten header but Ernie Simms is ruled offside. Billy Williams then attacks down the wing. The West Ham man centres to a group of players in the goalmouth. As the ball bounces, William Aiken stretches out a hand. The referee, W.A. Palmer, has no hesitation in pointing to the penalty spot.

England captain Stan Charlton signals Bert Batten to take the kick. The Plymouth Argyle scoring machine calmly approaches the ball. A loud 'Ooh!' escapes from the crowd when his kick goes wide of the goal.

England's heavier forwards are combining well, and only desperate defending from Aiken and Mitchell and good goalkeeping by Robison keeps them at bay. Elkes is the biggest danger, either drawing men and passing or taking it around three or four at a time. The crowd applaud every time he gets the ball.

At the 25-minute mark, Jack Elkes again slips past several defenders. Aiken mistimes a challenge and brings down the big Tottenham man in the area. Referee Palmer blows for penalty number two. Stan Charlton isn't keen on giving the ball to Batten this time, and steps up to take it himself. He tucks the ball into the corner of the goal to put England 1-0 up.

There's barely a moment's let up as England pound Australia's goal. In quick succession, Robison makes four brilliant saves from Simms, Batten, Graham and Elkes. The Victorian is proving that he deserves his Australian jersey.

A short time later, Elkes is again brought down in the area, this time by Jack Mitchell. England has its third penalty of the first half. Now, Robison has to stare down Millwall's Len Graham, still yet to score on the tour. True to form, Graham blasts the ball over the crossbar.

Gaining confidence from the penalty misses, Australia attacks through George Eccles. From the wing, he centres to Judy Masters, who expertly guides it on to 'Dutchy' Phillips. The Kurri Kurri inside-right beats Caesar and passes to Roy McNaughton, who sends the ball into the English penalty area. With the goal at his mercy, Tom Thompson hesitates and is closed down just as he's about to level the scores.

The half-time whistle blows soon after, England leading by just the one goal.

Jimmy Walsh, England's outside-right, comes to life at the start of the second half, setting up a chance that Batten heads over, then winning a free-kick after an excellent run. Billy Caesar shoots directly from the free-kick but Jim Robison saves superbly.

After soaking up the early pressure in the second half, Australia attacks on the counter. Judy Masters breaks into clear space and passes to his Balgownie teammate Thompson. Thompson's shot from 15 yards looks to be going in but Davison dives and makes a fine save. The England keeper boots the ball a long way downfield where it is controlled by Len Graham. Graham passes to Batten, who shoots from outside the area. Robison appears to have it covered but inexplicably the ball bursts through his hands and into the goal. After such a heroic performance, it's a pity that one mistake has proved so expensive.

Australia's defence is outstanding as England continue to press. Jim Robison puts the mistake behind him and pulls off a number of saves that prevent England running away with the match. The full-time score of 2-0 to England represents a fine effort by Australia.

* * *

The Victorian and South Australian representatives in the team all played well. Fullback William Aiken just shaded Jim Robison as Australia's player of the match. The hosts' halves were overshadowed by England's once more, but up front, Judy Masters had his best game of the Test series.

Jack Elkes was the best player on the field. England's record in the five Test series was outstanding, winning all five matches while scoring 22 goals and only conceding four.

Only 5,000 people attended for a gate just shy of £400. The lure of the interstate Australian Rules match between Victoria and Western Australia at the MCG had been too powerful, drawing a crowd of 45,000. Besides, many people seemed happier watching American sailors play baseball than the Australian team playing football against England.

* * *

England did get to meet some of the American sailors in Melbourne. At a function put on by the Brunswick (Australian Rules) Football Club on Sunday, the Englishmen and officers from the *USS Oklahoma* viewed the club's new grandstand at Brunswick Park.[2]

On Monday afternoon at 4:30pm, England boarded the train for the final leg of their tour. They would do it without one of their most popular players. Billy Caesar headed to Sydney to embark on the *SS Manganni* to America to visit friends on his way home. Caesar had enjoyed his time in Australia. He even gained weight during the tour, tipping the scales at over 95kg on his departure.

A big crowd of football supporters saw the English team off from Spencer Street station. The cross-continental journey ahead was a mammoth one. It would take four days to reach Perth.

---

[2] On 1 August St Kilda played an American fleet team at Middle Park. The match was drawn

23
Once More, For The Lads

South Australian football officials Wolfram Bellis and Bob Holiday had travelled to Melbourne hoping to arrange another tour fixture in Adelaide but a mix up saw England booked on the train for Monday not Saturday. Despite this missed opportunity, a big group of football supporters waved farewell to England as they stopped briefly in Adelaide.

The East-West express reached the gold mining town of Kalgoorlie in the Western Australian hinterland on Thursday, 30 July. The local Mayor and the town's sporting dignitaries entertained England during their five-hour stopover before the team headed to Perth. Players and management were given a reception in Kalgoorlie's sumptuous Edwardian-era Town Hall, that Lewis said was the finest he'd seen in Australia.

The Western Australian team for the final match, Fremantle.

Some of the Englishmen were given a tour of the South Kalgoorlie gold mine. John Lewis was more than happy to see it - he just happened to be a shareholder.

At Kalgoorlie, Lewis told a reporter that he would be "very guarded concerning his public utterances as to the treatment of the team in the eastern states". He would give full disclosure when he reported to the FA in London. There were some gripes he had to get off his chest, however. He was "not too well pleased with the manner of their reception as a whole". He went on at length about his quibbles with the eastern states, the foul on Whittaker being one of the main ones. Whittaker had been deliberately fouled, and Australian referees were far too lenient on 'jumping' at the man. One referee, Tom Crawford in Newcastle, had publicly declared that many players were ignorant of the rules and should not be penalised unless it was with intent, something that infuriated Lewis.

Lewis criticised New South Wales officials for their tinkering with the rules of the FA. Their cavalier approach to substitutions, including their use in competitive fixtures in domestic competitions, was something he would also bring to the attention of the FA. Lewis also spoke out against the payments made to Australian players, which, in his book, made them professionals.

The England team for the match vs Western Australia, Fremantle.

He also complained about the travel arrangements. Travelling from Fremantle to Bundaberg and back again had taken its toll on the players. He noted the inadequacy of an 18-man playing roster for such a long tour. Playing the five Test matches over five consecutive Saturdays, with travel to regional venues for midweek games in between, was far too onerous on the players.

These comments were not well received in the eastern states. *The Australian Worker*, noting that the comments were made at Kalgoorlie, said "his complaint looks like a squeal at a safe distance". *The Newcastle Sun* wrote: "Had his men had to do a shift in the pits as some of the Maitland and Newcastle men did before they were free to play, then John Lewis might have had cause to complain."

* * *

At 9:45 am on Friday, the last day of July, the Englishmen stepped off the overland express in Perth. The team had enjoyed the tour but were aching to return home. Fatigued from the trip, the players headed straight for the showers when they reached their lodgings at the Savoy Hotel. Only eleven players were free from injury and there were still two games to play. Because England had been treated so well on their first leg in Western Australia, Lewis had agreed to a second match on the final leg. The first game was on Saturday at Fremantle and the second two days later at Subiaco Oval.

Western Australian players had been preparing for these matches for months. They were well into their domestic season and their fitness levels were far above what they were when the tour opened. The match fitness of the locals against the fatigue and homesickness of the tourists made a few optimistic supporters believe Western Australia could end England's winning run.

The Western Australian squad was selected nearly a month before the match. They were coached by Laurie Carr and trained by George Stevenson of the Perth Thistle club. Carr lectured the players on tactics, and worked out a match plan that the team revised after each practice session. The training was described as "systematic", a sign that the locals were taking the matches seriously.

The first task for Western Australian selectors was to choose a goalkeeper to replace Boland, who had broken his leg at Fremantle in May. Boland had only just been discharged from hospital after nearly two months recuperating. They settled on George Kirk, formerly of South Australia, who had played against the Chinese and the Canadians.

Saturday, 1 August 1925, Match 24: England v Western Australia, Fremantle

Fremantle councillors look with some glee at the large crowd that has turned out for the penultimate match of the tour. They have come under criticism from the more extreme Australian Rules supporters for allowing soccer to be played on Fremantle Oval. The manager of the Western Australia team that played Victoria in the recent interstate Australian Rules match in Melbourne, has urged the WAFL to only endorse council candidates who support the Australian code and not the foreign British game. But Fremantle council has stood by its decision and the good crowd vindicates their position.

Spectators arriving late find that all the grandstand tickets have sold out. Jock Warden leads out his Western Australian team to enthusiastic cheers. A few moments later, the popular Jack Elkes runs out at the head of his English team to an enormous ovation. The governor of Western Australia, William Campion, takes his seat and fans wait a few more moments for the team photographs and all is in readiness.

Early on, Billy Williams sprints down England's left and sends in a cross that Ernie Simms heads just over the crossbar. Bert Batten has the next attempt, a scorching shot from outside the penalty area that beats Western Australia's goalkeeper Kirk. England is one up with barely two minutes on the clock.

Ten minutes into the game, England's forwards put together a sparkling move that Simms finishes for England to go 2-0 up.

Elkes begins to play up to the crowd. With incredible close control, he dribbles around a handful of players and sets up Billy Williams, who is ruled offside. Simms then plays Jimmy Walsh in on the right wing. Walsh centres beautifully to Batten on the run to head in England's third goal.

Walsh then turns provider, crossing to Simms who makes no mistake from close range. England lead 4-0 at the break and Western Australia's game plan is in tatters.

Andy Gordon has the locals' first chance of the second half. After good lead-up play by Warden, Gordon finds himself one-on-one with England's keeper Harry Hardy. Gordon strikes the ball wide of both the advancing keeper and the goalposts.

Western Australia push forward whenever they can. A great chance falls to Wally Gardner, who strikes a firm drive that Hardy gets a palm to. The rebound comes to Newall who shoots first time only for Hardy to spring up and complete a tremendous double save.

Elkes takes the momentum away from the locals by dancing through the defence again. A woman remarks:

"I do love Elkes' sword dance, it is the funniest thing I've seen in a long time." After receiving a pass from Williams, Elkes zips off again, stepping around challenges with ease before launching a sizzling shot from 20 yards that gives Kirk no chance. The score is now 5-0 to England.

With around ten minutes to go, Western Australia launch a splendid attacking move. All the forwards get a touch and the crowd get behind the home team. Gardner drills a shot along the ground from over 20 yards, beating the diving Hardy. A huge cheer goes up from the crowd. Wally Gardner, the first Australian to score against England on the tour, now has two goals against them.

A late goal for Batten is disallowed for a push by Simms. The match finishes 5-1 to England.

* * *

A smoke social at the Perth Literary Institute after the match on Saturday served as the tour's official farewell. Mark Frowde spoke about some of the important issues facing football in Australia. The disputes over grounds with other sports had been detrimental to the tour. He was disappointed with the bad sportsmanship of other codes, in particular the Rugby League in Sydney for denying them use of the best playing arenas. The answer was that football needed enclosed grounds of its own.

Frowde congratulated his players on their perfect record and excellent behaviour on and off the field. The team were eager to conclude the tour, having won every match. Frowde finished by paying tribute to the work of John Lewis. Although 70 years of age, Lewis had travelled with the team all over Australia with the sole aim of promoting the game of football.

Everyone wanted to hear from John Lewis. When the great man rose to his feet he had to wait while the audience gave him a lengthy standing ovation. "Soccer is not a British game, it's the world game" *(cheers)*; "It is the only true football' *(more cheers)* "It has a future in Australia' *(hear! hear!).*

Monday, 3 August 1925, Match 25: England v Western Australia, Subiaco Oval, Perth

Only a small crowd is at Subiaco Oval to witness England's last match of the tour. England has made two changes to Saturday's team, with Davison taking Hardy's place in goal and Stan Seymour coming in for Ernie Simms. Bert Batten, England's leading scorer for the tour, is rewarded for his efforts by being named captain, while Warden again captains Western Australia.

England come out with all guns blazing. Players are eager to notch up one final goal for the tour. Western Australia's defence works hard to thwart the Englishmen and the harder the tourists try, the more they get in each other's way. Their hitherto wonderful teamwork has deserted them.

Close to half-time, with scores locked at 0-0, Western Australia makes a foray into England's territory. A handy piece of teamwork sees the ball at the feet of Andy Gordon of the Casuals club. He strikes a firm shot that is smartly blocked by Teddy Davison. The ball rebounds straight back to Gordon. He hits the ball again, aiming for the corner. This time, Davison is beaten. The small crowd go wild as Western Australia takes a most unlikely lead.

At the interval, Western Australia lead 1-0. It is the first time on tour that England has trailed at half-time. Their cherished winning record is now under threat. Worn out and with their minds on home, the Englishmen face a prickly challenge. They have to find motivation they've rarely needed all tour. How will the team be viewed back home if they lose a match to a lowly state side?

Stan Seymour is one of the biggest stars of the squad. Famous for the goal that sealed Newcastle United's victory in the 1924 FA Cup Final and regarded as one of the best outside lefts in England, his form on tour has been patchy. Of all the players, he has struggled most on hard grounds. But with the team's reputation on the line, he comes out in the second half in a determined mood.

Gathering the ball at halfway, Seymour bursts into open territory. It's as though he's at St. James' Park with thousands of Geordies cheering him on. At just the right moment, he rips in his cross. Bert Batten, the greatest goal scorer to ever grace an Australian pitch, launches himself at the ball. His header is perfect and Kirk is beaten. England have their all-important equaliser.

Suddenly, the passes begin to stick. The ball is stroked around just like on their best days. Len Graham, who played for England against Scotland in the cauldron of Hampden Park, wakes from his Subiaco snooze and makes a darting run down the left side of the Western Australian defence. He stands up a ball to the far post. Jimmy Walsh, the Liverpool forward who has not scored all tour, makes a beeline for it. His header just creeps in under the crossbar and he narrowly avoids knocking himself out on the goalpost. England take a 2-1 lead and the goal celebrations are among the most exuberant of the tour.

Batten scores England's third with a powerful drive. Seymour then sends in a fearsome shot that hits the crossbar before Batten turns in the rebound, then scores his fourth goal of the game with a cracking shot from distance that fizzes past the hapless Kirk. The full-time whistle blows. England have won their last game of the tour 5-1.

* * *

For 45 minutes, England played at the peak of their form. It was possibly their best half of football in Australia. It was a fitting swan song to an incredibly successful tour. The match finished a little after 5pm. Within the hour, the touring party were aboard the passenger liner *Osterley* at Fremantle, waving to the hundreds of football supporters on the shore.

24

A Breath From Heaven

Monday, 31 August 1925, Russell Square, London

"The Australians have much to learn in regard to Association football. Their biggest problem," John Lewis told his rapt audience at the Football Council, "is that they never stay in their position. Take the halves, they never join the attack and are always too slow to help out their backs. As for the backs, they need to do more than just clear the ball downfield. They don't play as a team, as we know it here. Their forwards are pacy, but they need to work together as a unit. Why, they only need to look at the likes of Elkes, Batten, Hannaford…".

The English team had arrived from their marathon tour the previous evening. Eager to get home, they'd disembarked from the *Osterley* at Toulon, taken the train across France, and after spending the night in Paris, arrived in Dover via the Channel ferry.

Family, friends and members of the FA greeted the team at London's Victoria station. It was a far cry from the scenes at the same place in April, when Gilligan's English cricket team arrived home from their Australian tour. That day, thousands of supporters welcomed them and it took the cricketers nearly an hour to get out of the station. That was despite them losing the Ashes series 4-1. The English footballers, who had made a clean sweep of the Tests and every tour match besides, were almost forgotten. The exhausted players declined the offer of a dinner that evening and headed straight home.

Lewis was proud of his team. Written off as second-rate on their departure, they had overcome the hurdles of long travel, injuries, and a playing roster far too small. Lewis told the Football Council the team had at times played "bewilderingly dazzling football." The team had struggled with injuries, at times having just 13 fit players. But his men didn't complain. They were always willing to play out of position for the sake of the team. Joe Hannah, a halfback, had played the final eight matches as a fullback. Jimmy Walsh, normally a centre-forward, had played most of his matches on the wing. The team played for each other, and, most importantly, upheld the prestige of English football.

"The Australians showed us great hospitality in every centre," he said. "Great crowds attended many of the games in New South Wales and Queensland." He was especially impressed with how well football was going in the schools. Although the sport faced many challenges, he was sure football would eventually become the leading sport in Australia. After this, Lewis presented the FA with the Australian flag given to him in Sydney. The inscription on the silver band read:

"Presented by Sir Samuel Hordern to the first English Soccer football team, on the occasion of their visit to New South Wales, May 30, 1925. The staff of this flag was made from timber out of His Majesty's ship Australia, sunk April 1924."

The flag was gleefully accepted, stored away, and promptly forgotten about.

* * *

In subsequent interviews and in his regular column in the *Lancashire Evening Post*, Lewis recalled some of the vagaries of football Down Under. Refereeing standards were a particularly irksome issue for him. The Australian referees were completely mistaken in their interpretation of the charging rule and often blew for free kicks that would never be awarded in England.

A great story he would tell was of the first tour game in Sydney. When Judy Masters gave New South Wales a 2-1 lead in front of a packed house at the Show Ground, Lewis claimed two of the Australians were clearly offside. The referee didn't blow for it, nor did the linesman signal. What truly incensed Lewis was the linesman waving his flag in joy to the cheering spectators.

Another irritant for Lewis was the leniency shown by referees to inexperienced players. When Charlie Spencer was tripped in a match in Newcastle, referee Tom Crawford said that the offence was done in ignorance rather than intentionally and waved play on. The prone Spencer was reported to have said, "Ignorance be hanged" (with perhaps a few adjectives thrown in). Crawford had quite a run-in with Lewis, and during a lecture of his own, publicly challenged some of Lewis' interpretations.

Match balls were another bone of contention. On the hard grounds they were particularly difficult to control. Lewis claimed (subsequently denied in Australia) that in a match at Newcastle, the cause of a misshapen ball was that a rugby bladder had been inserted into it.

Early in the tour, Lewis was also critical of the way ball boys would have three or four balls at the ready. This was not the done thing in England. But he later changed his tune. On the big cricket ovals and show grounds, it saved a lot of time when the ball boys could give the players a new ball while they hunted down a loose kick that had ended up near the square leg boundary.

One of the main stumbling blocks for football in Australia, he said, was the vast distances between cities and how difficult it was to control the game effectively. He recommended Australia employ a full-time secretary who could give the sport their full attention. Lewis was initially critical that Australia had yet to decide on a competition format for the trophy donated by the FA but mellowed after realising how expensive it would be to run an interstate tournament in such a big country.

* * *

As recognition for their services to English football, the team that toured Australia was chosen as the professional side to play the amateurs in the 1925 FA Charity Shield. John Lewis appreciated the gesture by the FA. He hoped the players would "do themselves credit when they encounter the amateurs on October 5, and thus justify the eulogies they have received in the Press and elsewhere for their magnificent displays in the Commonwealth. The selection will also show our Australian friends that the FA recognise the greatness of the visitors' success on such a long and arduous outing, and thoroughly appreciate the services they have rendered to the game."

The match was played at White Hart Lane, London, on 5 October 1925. Twelve members of the England team that toured Australia took part in the match: the eleven professionals plus Billy Caesar who turned out for the amateurs. At the last minute, the professionals received a severe blow when Bert Batten had to pull out due to injury. The Professionals team that took the field was: Hardy, Charlton, Poynton, Hamilton, Spencer ©, Graham, Hannaford, Walsh, Simms, Elkes, and Seymour. Joe Hannah was a reserve.

The Professionals met with bad luck. Simms, Elkes and Walsh all had goals denied by the woodwork in the first half. Stan Seymour missed a penalty in the second half. Ernie Simms took a knock early in the match that would eventually force him to go off, leaving his team to battle on with 10 men.

The Professionals faded as the Amateurs played what the press labelled the 'Scottish' style. The Professionals were slower to the ball and might have still been suffering fatigue from their arduous tour, made worse by not having had an off season.

The Amateurs overran the Professionals 6-1. Charlie Hannaford scored the only goal for the Professionals. One reporter said the display of the players who had toured Australia "must have come near to breaking the heart of Mr John Lewis".

That evening, a dinner in honour of the English touring team was held at Frascatti's Restaurant in Oxford Street. Despite the loss that day, the players had every right to be proud of their achievements. They had played 25 tour matches, winning them all and scoring 139 goals while only conceding 13. They had upheld England's reputation as one of the great footballing nations and had drawn the biggest crowds in Australian football history. Just over 300,000 Australians passed through the turnstiles during the tour. This was all done while travelling over 45,000 kilometres by ship, rail and motor car.

Charles Clegg, the President of the FA, praised the touring party before making the presentations. Each player not only received a specially struck medal but was presented with an England international cap. One of the lengthiest and most arduous football tours of any era had formally come to an end. In the words of the *Athletic News:* "So closes a great and successful undertaking."

The Australian tour would be John Lewis' last football undertaking. Little over three months later, on 13 January 1926, he died at his home after a short illness.

* * *

Australian club sides met with mixed success when copying the methods of the Englishmen. In a match in Perth in August between Casuals and Rangers, some clever tactics were on display. "The Casuals on several occasions combined nicely," wrote P.S.R. in *The West Australian*, "and gave evidence of the change the visit of the Englishmen has made to Western Australian soccer, the ball being rarely wasted, while quite a lot of back play was indulged in."

If passing backwards, including to the goalkeeper, was one trademark of the English style, robust use of the shoulder and charging was another. In Sydney in particular, matches became rougher as harangued referees put their whistles away and challenges went unchecked, often leading to an exchange of blows and players being sent off.

The technical deficiencies in Australian footballers were going to be hard to put right. Fullbacks needed to learn to pass rather than just hoof the ball downfield. Halves needed to link up better with the backs and the forwards. More switching of the ball across field by the halves was required to bring some variety to the attack. While Roy McNaughton was universally praised by the visitors, one criticism of him was that he always went outside his man and never inside. Despite his great pace, this predictability in his play made the English backs' jobs easier.

The playing arenas in Australia were also not up to scratch. John Lewis said the best pitch they played on was Brisbane's Exhibition Ground with the Melbourne Cricket Ground a close second. The rest had lamentable playing surfaces unsuitable for producing quality football. At all grounds, the spectators were too far from the action and couldn't appreciate the finer points of the game. Australia needed rectangular grounds, not the cricket ovals and agricultural show grounds used in the tour games.

Lewis held out no great hopes for an Australian tour of England. The clubs were too busy and would only field reserve teams against Australia.

The two most crucial things Australia could do, according to Lewis, were to appoint a full-time administrator and to encourage the game in the schools. The school footballers in Queensland and New South Wales had greatly impressed the English touring party. Develop that talent, Lewis said, and Australia's football standards would improve considerably.

Just prior to England's departure, Syd Storey paid a tribute to the tourists in *The West Australian*. He recounted some of the great matches in New South Wales and, once more, rued McNaughton's missed penalty that would have given Australia a 2-1 lead in the second Test with just 13 minutes to play. He was sure Australia had received a great football education and would put the lessons to good use. Even though Storey had clashed with Lewis over substitutes and payment to players, he thanked Lewis, Frowde and trainer Mo Atherton for their hard work on the tour.

Storey called the tourists "the famous English representative Soccer team" and said that they brought great credit to the English Football Association. He added: "Not for many a day will the displays of Batten, Simms, Hannaford, Charlton, or the goalies Hardy and Davison be forgotten."

* * *

The benefits of the tour were to be educational rather than financial. In late 1925, Syd Storey announced that the tour had made a profit of just £76. The expenses had blown out to £20,000, considerably more than the £18,000 estimate. There was still enough revenue for the Australian players to receive their £5 per-Test-match bonus, something that Storey had been determined to do even if it meant crossing swords with John Lewis.

It was the effect of the big gates in the early games that led to the most direct consequence of the tour, namely the breakaway professional competition in the Illawarra district. On 25 July, the same day as the fifth Test was being played in Melbourne, the first openly professional soccer competition in Australia commenced with two matches in Wollongong and one in Sydney.

The new competition had already received a number of setbacks. When the two strongest Illawarra clubs, Balgownie and Corrimal withdrew, along with one of the Sydney clubs, the professional competition was reduced from nine to just six teams.

Illawarra might have had a strong football culture but they couldn't draw big gates to the games. Often, the gates weren't enough to cover the travelling expenses of the visiting team. Sid Cope, the chief architect of the professional competition soon realised the writing was on the wall. By the end of 1925, the league couldn't continue. A compromise was reached with the NSWFA to allow four Illawarra clubs to compete in the Sydney premiership in 1926. The Illawarra clubs proved their class, with Balgownie topping the table and Corrimal finishing third.

The push for a professional league continued, however. It appeared that it might start in 1927 but Storey, who bitterly opposed the idea of the NSWFA losing control of the game, helped thwart the move at the last minute.

At the end of 1927, Sydney's biggest club, Granville, aligned themselves with the professional league movement. It created a domino effect with twelve of the best teams in New South Wales joining them. Unable to reach a compromise, the professional league, known as the State League, commenced in 1928 as a breakaway from the NSWFA. Football in New South Wales was now split between 'loyalists' of the NSWFA and 'rebels' from the State League.

An editorial in the loyalist-leaning publication *The Soccer News* said: "It is indeed a calamity that there should be any division in the control of the game in this State." The inability of the two sides to reach a compromise had a damaging effect on the game. State League players were not eligible to be picked for Australia. The split was not patched up until 1932, stalling much of the momentum the English tour had created.

After the rift was healed, Australia played a home series against New Zealand, their first against their Trans-Tasman rivals for ten years. They also toured New Caledonia in 1933 and completed a successful tour of New Zealand in 1936.

Efforts continued to get an English team to tour again. Although unable to secure a professional team, the FA sent an amateur side to Australia in 1937. Lessons had been learned from 1925. The itinerary was reduced to only 10 games compared to the 25 matches played in 1925. Only three Test matches were contested and only a single match against New South Wales was played. The best grounds in each city were secured.

On 16 July 1937, Australia played the England amateurs in a Test match at the Sydney Cricket Ground. Australia won an entertaining game 6-4. Syd Storey, now the chairman of The Australian Soccer Football Association, must have been exhilarated to see the SCG packed to the rafters with over 40,000 people in attendance. It was like the glory days of 1925 all over again.

Storey's experience in dealing with enigmatic English managers, petulant players, rebellious referees and acrimonious administrators, provided a perfect grounding for a life in the public sphere. Following in his father and uncle's footsteps he turned his hand to politics. In 1941, Storey was elected to the New South Wales Parliament as the Member for Hornsby, a seat he held, with some breaks, for over 20 years.

Storey had a long and distinguished career in football. From organiser of the Balmain Fernleigh Football Club, to being the secretary of the NSWFA, to heading the Australian association, he was involved in football administration for over 50 years and was active up to the year of his death in 1966. He was a man devoted to serving the sport he loved and was inducted into the Football Australia Hall of Fame in 2003.

Many years after Syd Storey's death, his grandchildren were cleaning out the garage of their late father. They came across a horde of material belonging to their grandfather, Syd. In it were mementos of his life in football. A truly remarkable find was a small wooden casket with a silver razor case inside. This was the 'Soccer Ashes' trophy for football matches between Australia and New Zealand that had been missing since the 1950s. The discovery of the trophy was made public on Anzac Day 2023, almost 100 years since it was created. Syd Storey was once more in the news.

* * *

3 May 1952, Wembley Stadium, London

Two smartly dressed managers lead their teams onto the lush turf of the famous Wembley arena. Newcastle United and Arsenal line up in the middle to enthusiastic applause from nearly 100,000 spectators. Striding out with a cane in his hand and sporting his characteristic top hat, Prime Minister Winston Churchill ambles along the ranks of the two teams conversing and shaking hands with the players.

Arsenal had finished third in the league compared to Newcastle's eighth, but with a number of Arsenal players carrying injuries, there is no clear favourite. Both teams had tasted recent FA Cup success - Arsenal in 1950 and Newcastle in 1951.

The first clear chance falls to Arsenal's Doug Lishman. He hooks a shot across his body that flashes just past the post, the keeper beaten. Arsenal are then hit by a number of injuries. First, Ray Daniel is sent to the turf and re-breaks his arm, which had only just been set. Somehow, he manages to play on. Then Walley Barnes badly injures his knee, forcing him to recuperate on the wing.

Barnes can't continue and is assisted to the dressing room. The Arsenal manager, no stranger to severe knee injuries himself, stays with Barnes to console him for the first ten minutes of the second half.

English football still hasn't embraced substitutes and a ten-man Arsenal struggle to contain the Newcastle forwards, who play sparkling football. Ten minutes from time, Newcastle's outside-left Bobby Mitchell crosses into the box and Chilean star George Robledo heads in off the goal post. One goal proves to be enough and Newcastle become the first team in the twentieth century to win the FA Cup two years in succession.

The two managers shake hands warmly after the game. They are old friends. Nearly thirty years before they were teammates on England's 1925 tour of Australia. Newcastle United's manager Stan Seymour says to his Arsenal counterpart Tom Whittaker: "Tom, ours is the cup; yours the honour and glory."

* * *

Stan Seymour returned from the 1925 Australian tour to find somebody else playing in his outside-left position. With typical determination, he forced his way back into the first team. He became an integral member of the Newcastle United side that won the Football League in 1926/27, scoring 19 goals in the season.

Seymour finished his playing career in 1929, having scored 84 goals in 266 matches for Newcastle United. He set up a sports store in Newcastle and tried his hand at journalism. At the end of 1930s he was brought back to the club as a director and eventually became manager, guiding the team to two FA Cup triumphs in 1951 and 1952. Seymour was on the United board right up to his death in 1978. After nearly 60 years with the club, he had earned the nickname 'Mr Newcastle'.

* * *

Tom Whittaker, Arsenal's manager in the 1952 FA Cup Final, had a roundabout ride to one of the most coveted positions in English club football. On board the *Osterley* while sailing back from Australia in 1925, a woman passenger told him about the famous surgeon in Liverpool, Sir Robert Jones, who might be able to help him with his injured knee. Still barely able to walk when he got back to England, Whittaker tracked down Jones, who performed the operation. Although he could now walk properly again, he was unable to continue playing football.

After receiving compensation from the FA, Whittaker was at a loose end. The new Arsenal supremo Herbert Chapman interviewed Whittaker, and, discovering he had some useful skills, kept him on at the club. Whittaker performed many jobs at Arsenal's home ground Highbury, including installing the electric wiring in the new players' gym under the grandstand.

Ever the willing learner and drawing on his knowledge of working alongside Mo Atherton on the Australian tour, Whittaker became an assistant trainer with the club. When Arsenal's trainer was sacked after a dispute with Chapman, Whittaker was offered the position.

Whittaker studied physiotherapy and became a highly valued member of Chapman's staff. Whittaker learned a great deal from Chapman, one of football's great innovators. In 1947, after Chapman's successor George Allison was shown the door, Tom Whittaker was appointed Arsenal manager.

Whittaker led the club to two Football League championship titles, in 1947/48 and 1952/53, as well as winning the FA Cup in 1950 and finishing runners-up in 1952. Whittaker was still serving as Arsenal's manager when he died of a heart attack in 1956, aged 58.

* * *

3 December 1953, Balgownie, New South Wales

The couple welcomed the reporter from *The Illawarra Daily Mercury* into their modest weatherboard home and made him feel at ease. Judy and Frances Masters had just returned from a 10-month visit to the United Kingdom. It was a trip the couple had always wanted to make since settling in Australia after the First World War.

The couple had visited Frances' relatives in England and toured the length and breadth of the British Isles. Judy saw many football matches while in England and Scotland, including the 1953 FA Cup final at Wembley, where Stanley Matthews starred for Blackpool in their 4-3 victory over Bolton Wanderers. Masters, who was a bandsman himself, was thrilled to see the 140 members of the Royal Marines Brass Band performing before the game and at half-time.

Another highlight of the Masters' trip was watching the England vs Scotland game, also at Wembley. Judy thought the atmosphere was superb and was impressed with the passion of the Scottish supporters who had saved up for the trip for two years.

Judy Masters also met fellow-Australian Joe Marston, the Preston North End centre-half. Marston, originally from the Leichhardt-Annandale club in Sydney, signed for Preston in 1950, and in 1954 would become the first Australian to play in an FA Cup Final. Marston was honoured to meet Masters and said: "It was like a breath from heaven to hear our Australian accent again."

At the end of the interview in Balgownie, the reporter left the house, in his own words, 'reluctantly'. Was it just the warm hospitality he received? As he turned to wave goodbye to the couple standing in the doorway, he knew Judy Masters' health was declining. Over forty years labouring in the mines and breathing in coal dust does that to a man.

Judy was certainly in a nostalgic mood that day. He often mentioned old comrades. He called Tom 'Titch' Thompson "the most-versatile Australian I have ever seen". He was sure players like Thompson and Bill Maunder would have thrived in England under good coaches.

As Judy Masters watched the reporter get into his car, who was to say his mind didn't go back to a balmy day in May 1925, when an English football team played in Sydney for the first time. Did the hairs stand up on the back of his neck when he recalled giving his team the lead not just once but twice? He would never forget the noise of the crowd. The sound of 50,000 voices cheering themselves hoarse. Cheering for him.

THE END

Epilogue

Having flirted with the idea of joining FIFA since before the First World War, Australia finally affiliated with the world body in 1956, just in time for the Melbourne Olympic Games. Although knocked out in the second round, the Melbourne Olympics marked Australia's debut in an international tournament.

Australia's first attempt to qualify for the FIFA World Cup was in 1966. Australia was unsuccessful then, but in 1974 they qualified for the World Cup for the first time, featuring a team of semi-professional players with backgrounds reflecting the changing multi-cultural makeup of the country.

Some agonisingly close, yet ultimately unsuccessful World Cup qualification campaigns followed. Australians became used to the quadrennial ritual of having their hopes raised only to be dashed at the final hurdle, including giving up a 2-0 lead late in the match against Iran at the MCG to draw 2-2 and miss qualification for the 1998 tournament.

On a cold February night in 2003, at Upton Park in London, Australia defeated England for the first time. Australia won 3-1, with a team including European-based stars such as Mark Viduka, Harry Kewell, Craig Moore, Marco Bresciano and Mark Schwarzer, who would form the core of Australia's 'Golden Generation.'

It was this Golden Generation who took Australia to the 2006 World Cup Finals in Germany after a break of 32 years. At the tournament, Tim Cahill scored twice in Australia's maiden World Cup finals victory; a 3-1 result over Japan, that helped them reach the knockout stages for the first time.

Perhaps the greatest moment in Australia-England football rivalry didn't occur in the men's game at all. It happened at Stadium Australia in Sydney on 16 August 2023. The occasion was the semi-final of the FIFA Women's World Cup between Australia and England. In the stadium, 75,000 spectators were enthralled by the action. Millions more watched on television at home and at public venues across Australia.

England had gone 1-0 up in the first half and dominated much of the game. In the 63rd minute, a sudden burst by

Australian striker Sam Kerr brought the crowd to their feet. Collecting a pass near the halfway line, she brought the ball towards the England goal with the defence back-pedalling. Her magnificent strike from distance into the top corner levelled the scores and had people screaming in delight from Fremantle to Bundaberg. And although Australia eventually lost the game 3-1, the match had the entire country buzzing.

A football match between Australia and England that had the whole country talking? What Syd Storey would have given to experience that back in 1925.

APPENDIX

Test Matches

FIRST TEST (Tour match 15)

27 June, Exhibition Ground, Brisbane

ENGLAND (3) 5 *(Simms 3, Batten 2)*

AUSTRALIA (0) 1 *(Lennard)*

England: Hardy, Poynton, Charlton, Graham, Spencer, Hamilton, Hannaford, Elkes, Batten, Simms, Seymour

Australia: Cartwright, Robinson, Gallen, Murray, Edwards, Storey, McNaughton, Brown, McCroary, Lennard, Bourke

Crowd: 30,000

SECOND TEST (Tour match 17)

4 July, Sydney Show Ground

ENGLAND (1) 2 *(Simms, Elkes)*

AUSTRALIA (1) 1 *(Smith)*

England: Davison, Spencer, Charlton, Graham, Hamilton, Sage, Seymour, Elkes, Batten, Simms, Hannaford

Australia: Cartwright, Faulkner, Gallen, Spurway, Edwards, O'Connor, McNaughton, Sherringham, Smith, Lennard, Bourke

Crowd: 25,000

THIRD TEST (Tour match 19)

11 July, Maitland Show Ground

ENGLAND (5) 8 *(Batten 5, Simms 2, Hannaford)*

AUSTRALIA (1) 2 *(Lennard, Thompson)*

England: Davison, Charlton, Hannah, Graham, Spencer, Hamilton, Hannaford, Elkes, Batten, Simms, Walsh

Australia: Cartwright, Faulkner, Gallen, Spurway, Edwards, G Storey, McNaughton, Thompson, Masters, Lennard, Bourke

Crowd: 10,000

FOURTH TEST (Tour match 21)

18 July, Sydney Show Ground

ENGLAND (4) 5 *(Simms 2, Elkes 2, Batten)*

AUSTRALIA 0

England: Hardy, Charlton, Hannah, Graham, Spencer, Hamilton, Williams, Elkes, Batten, Simms, Walsh

Australia: Cartwright, Robinson, Harris, Spurway, Lambert, Storey, McNaughton, Thompson, Masters, Lennard, Burns

Crowd: 14,000

FIFTH TEST (Tour match 23)

25 July, Fitzroy Cricket Ground, Melbourne

ENGLAND (1) 2 (Charlton, Batten)

AUSTRALIA 0

England: Davison, Hannah, Charlton, Caesar, Spencer, Graham, Walsh, Simms, Batten, Elkes, Williams

Australia: Robinson, Mitchell, Aiken, O'Connor, Edwards, Morrison, Eccles, Phillips, Masters, Thompson, McNaughton

Crowd: 5,000

Other Tour Matches

Match 1

7 May, Subiaco Oval, Perth

England (4) 8 *(Simms 5, Caesar, Elkes, Sage)*

Perth 0

England: Davison, Charlton, Whittaker, Hannah, Hamilton, Caesar, Hannaford, Sage, Simms, Elkes, Batten

Perth: Marr, Poile, Utting, Gentry, Warden, Davis, Wilderspin, Illingworth, Cruickshank, Newall, Badham

Crowd: 3,000

Match 2

9 May, Fremantle Oval

England (1) 7 *(Williams 4, Simms 2, Hannah)*

Western Australia 0

England: Hardy, Charlton, Poynton, Hannah, Spencer, Graham, Hannaford, Williams, Simms, Elkes, Seymour

Western Australia: Boland, Utting, Boyle, Boys, Finlayson, Martin, Bubb, A Gordon, J Gordon, Gardner, Nesbit

Crowd: 10,000

Match 3

14 May, Adelaide Oval

England (3) 10 *(Batten 6, Williams 2, Seymour, Hamilton)*

South Australia 0

England: Hardy, Whittaker, Poynton, Caesar, Spencer, Hamilton, Sage, Walsh, Batten, Williams, Seymour

South Australia: Gibson, Mitchell, Gibbs, Rennie, Gore, Addie, Nenn, Cameron, Denman, McQueen, Robertson

Crowd: 4,000

Match 4

16 May, Thebarton Oval, Adelaide

England (3) 4 *(Hamilton, Hannaford, Whittaker, Batten)*

Australian XI (0) 1 *(Gardner)*

England: Davison, Charlton, Poynton, Caesar, Hamilton, Graham, Sage, Batten, Whittaker, Elkes, Hannaford

Australian XI: Pilgrim, Mitchell, Aiken, Boys, Gore, Norman, Grieves, Honeysett, Denman, McQueen, Gardiner

Crowd: 3,658

Match 5

20 May, Melbourne Cricket Ground

England (4) 7 *(Williams 4, Seymour 2, Simms)*

Victoria 0

England: Davison, Charlton, Poynton, Hannah, Spencer, Caesar, Walsh, Simms, Williams, Elkes, Seymour

Victoria: Robison, Osbaldiston, Aiken, Harris, Ritchie, G Raitt, Templeton, Church, Hubbard, Orr, Barrett

Crowd: 5,600

Match 6

23 May, Melbourne Cricket Ground

England (1) 5 *(Simms 2, Spencer, Hannaford, Batten)*

Australia XI 0

England: Hardy, Whittaker, Poynton, Hamilton, Spencer, Graham, Hannaford, Simms, Walsh, Batten, Seymour

Australia XI: Robison, Mitchell, Aiken, Bristow, Ritchie, Morrison, Honeysett, W Raitt, W Maunder, Orr, McNaughton

Crowd: 13,000

Match 7

30 May, Sydney Show Ground

England (2) 3 *(Batten 2, Simms)*

New South Wales (2) 2 *(Masters 2)*

England: Hardy, Charlton, Poynton, Hannah, Spencer, Graham, Hannaford, Simms, Batten, Elkes, Seymour

New South Wales: Cartwright, Druery, Leabeater, Coolahan, Edwards, Spurway, Bourke, Lennard, Masters, Thompson, McNaughton

Crowd: 50,000

Match 8

3 June, Sydney Show Ground

England (2) 3 *(Batten 2, Elkes)*

Sydney (0) 1 *(Hancock)*

England: Davison, Charlton, Whittaker, Hannah, Hamilton, Caesar, Hannaford, Sage, Simms, Elkes, Batten

Sydney: Atchison, Gallen, Sid Robinson, O'Connor, G Storey, Peel, Burns, Winter, Alewood, Hancock, Robertson

Crowd: 12,000

Match 9

6 June, Bode's Oval, North Wollongong

England (8) 8 *(Simms 2, Elkes 2, Williams 2, Seymour 2)*

Illawarra 0

England: Davison, Whittaker, Poynton, Hamilton, Spencer, Graham, Elkes, Simms, Walsh, Williams, Seymour

Illawarra: Richardson, Hunter, Druery, Gerling, Creighton, Cheney, Burns, Green, Masters, Mackay, Thompson

Crowd: 7,000

Match 10

8 June, Sydney Show Ground

England (1) 4 *(Batten 2, Seymour, Simms)*

New South Wales (1) 1 *(McNaughton)*

England: Hardy, Charlton, Poynton, Hannah, Spencer, Graham, Hannaford, Simms, Batten, Elkes, Seymour

New South Wales: Cartwright, Leabeater, Druery, Coolahan, Edwards, Spurway, Bourke, Green, Masters, Thompson, McNaughton

Crowd: 40,000

Match 11

13 June, Newcastle Show Ground

England (4) 6 *(Batten 2, Simms 2, Hannaford 2)*

Northern District 0

England: Davison, Charlton, Poynton, Caesar, Hamilton, Graham, Walsh, Simms, Batten, Williams, Hannaford

Northern District: Austin, Harris, H Maunder, Coolahan, Coutts, Doyle, Wells, Cameron, McCroary, Price, McNaughton

Crowd: 20,000

Match 12

17 June, Ipswich Show Ground

England (2) 3 *(Williams 2, Elkes)*

Ipswich & West Moreton 0

England: Hardy, Spencer, Charlton, Hannah, Hamilton, Caesar, Walsh, Graham, Williams, Elkes, Seymour

Ipswich: Halls, Routledge, Burns, Williams, Warrell, Teasdale, Edwards, McDowell, J Potts, Rumble, Williams

Crowd: 3,000

Match 13

20 June, Exhibition Ground, Brisbane

England (6) 11 *(Batten 6, Simms 3, Hannaford, Caesar)*

Queensland 0

England: Davison, Charlton, Poynton, Caesar, Hamilton, Graham, Walsh, Simms, Batten, Elkes, Hannaford

Queensland: Owen, Burns, Rigby, White, Murray, Stone, Edwards, Gibb, J Potts, Nicholson, Robertson

Crowd: 15,000

Match 14

24 June, West End Reserve, Bundaberg

England (6) 9 *(Batten 5, Simms 2, Hannah, Seymour)*

North Queensland 0

England: Davison, Poynton, Hamilton, Caesar, Spencer, Hannah, Walsh, Simms, Batten, Williams, Seymour

North Queensland: Hamilton, Judd, Lord, Wilson, McIntosh, Aikenhead, Barrett, Allan, Putman, Peattie, Cox

Crowd: 3,000

(Match 15 - First Test)

Match 16

29 June, Toowoomba Show Ground

England (3) 6 *(Seymour 2, Batten 2, Hannaford, Elkes)*

Toowoomba 0

England: Hardy, Spencer, Hannah, Sage, Hamilton, Graham, Hannaford, Elkes, Batten, Seymour, Williams

Toowoomba: Langton, Hillocks, Fox, McKewan, McNab, Adams, Jenkins, Oliver, Kennedy, Martin, Lynam

Crowd: 4,000

(Match 17 - Second Test)

Match 18

8 July, Newcastle Sports Ground

England (1) 3 *(Batten, Seymour, Sage)*

Newcastle 0

England: Hardy, Hannah, Spencer, Graham, Hamilton, Sage, Seymour, Williams, Batten, Simms, Walsh

Newcastle: P Jordan, Lambert, Harris, Doyle, C Coutts, Bailey, Johns, Brown, Craig, Cameron, Dunn

Crowd: 3,000

(Match 19 - Third Test)

Match 20

15 July, Cessnock Show Ground

England (0) 4 *(Williams, Seymour, Caesar, Elkes)*

South Maitland (0) 1 *(Lennard)*

England: Hardy, Spencer, Hannah, Graham, Sage, Caesar, Elkes, Williams, Batten, Seymour, Hannaford

South Maitland: Austen, Williams, Farrey, Avis, Hodge, Liddle, McNaughton, Lennard, McCroary, Manion, Williams

Crowd: 5,000

(Match 21 – Fourth Test)

Match 22

21 July, Parramatta Oval

England (2) 6 *(Batten 3, Simms 3)*

Granville (0) 1 *(Winter)*

England: Hardy, Charlton, Hannah, Graham, Hamilton, Caesar, Simms, Elkes, Walsh, Batten, Williams

Granville: Atchison, Rigby, Mace, Hele, Edwards, Hill, Flynn, Waldon, Davis, Winter, Bourke

Crowd: 3,000

Exhibition Match

23 July, Sydney Show Ground

Hardy's XI (2) 6 *(Masters 2, Elkes, Lennard, McNaughton, Spencer)*

Davison's XI (0) 3 *(Batten 2, Phillips)*

Hardy's XI: Hardy, Hannah, Robinson (Aus), G Storey (Aus), Spencer, Graham, Hannaford, Lennard (Aus), Masters (Aus), Elkes, McNaughton (Aus)

Davison's XI: Davison, Pont (Aus), Charlton, Caesar, Hamilton, Spurway (Aus), Walsh, Simms, Batten, Phillips (Aus), Williams

Crowd: 2,000

(Match 23 – Fifth Test)

Match 24

1 August, Fremantle Oval

England (4) 5 *(Batten 2, Simms 2, Elkes)*

Western Australia (0) 1 *(Gardner)*

England: Hardy, Charlton, Hannah, Graham, Spencer, Hamilton, Williams, Elkes, Batten, Simms, Walsh

Western Australia: Kirk, Hinton, Nicholls, Finlayson, Warden, Boys, Gardner, Newall, Smart, Gordon, Wilderspin

Crowd: 8,000

Match 25

3 August, Subiaco Oval, Perth

England (0) **5** *(Batten 4, Walsh)*

Western Australia (1) **1** *(A Gordon)*

England: Davison, Charlton, Hannah, Graham, Spencer, Hamilton, Seymour, Elkes, Batten, Williams, Walsh

Western Australia: Kirk, Hinton, Nicholls, Finlayson, Warden, Boys, Gardner, Newell, Smart, A Gordon, Wilderspin

Crowd: 2,000

England Player Statistics

Sources vary widely for English goal scorers, particularly in the midweek games. The figures quoted are based on newspaper reports of the games.

Player	Club	Tests		Other Matches		Total	
		Matches	Goals	Matches	Goals	Matches	Goals
H Batten	Plymouth Argyle	5	9	16	39	21	48
E Simms	Stockport County	5	8	14	26	19	34
W Williams	West Ham	2	0	12	15	14	15
S Seymour	Newcastle United	2	0	13	12	15	12
J Elkes	Tottenham Hotspur	5	3	16	8	21	11
C Hannaford	Clapton Orient	3	1	11	6	14	7
W Caesar	Dulwich Hamlet	1	0	11	3	12	3
J Hamilton	Crystal Palace	4	0	15	2	19	2
J Hannah	Norwich City	3	0	14	2	17	2
W Sage	Tottenham Hotspur	1	0	7	2	8	2
S Charlton	Exeter City	5	1	13	0	18	1
J Walsh	Liverpool	3	0	12	1	15	1
T Whittaker	Arsenal	0	0	6	1	6	1
L Graham	Millwall	5	0	15	0	20	0
C Spencer	Newcastle United	5	0	14	0	19	0
H Hardy	Stockport County	2	0	11	0	13	0
C Poynton	Tottenham Hotspur	1	0	11	0	12	0
J Davison	Sheffield Wednesday	3	0	9	0	12	0

Australian Player Statistics

Australia's Test Match Players 1925

27 players represented Australia against England in the five Test Matches

Player	State (Region)	Tests	Goals
R McNaughton	NSW (Newcastle)	5	
G Cartwright	NSW (Sydney)	4	
A Edwards	NSW (Sydney)	4	
P Lennard	NSW (Newcastle)	4	2
S Bourke	NSW (Sydney)	3	
F Gallen	NSW (Sydney)	3	
J Masters	NSW (Illawarra)	3	
H Spurway	NSW (Sydney)	3	
G Storey	NSW (Sydney)	3	
T Thompson	NSW (Illawarra)	3	1
W Faulkner	Tasmania/South Australia	2	
C O'Connor	NSW (Sydney)	2	
S Robinson	NSW (Sydney)	2	
J Smith	NSW (Sydney)	1	1

Continued

Player	State (Region)	Tests	Goals
W Aitken	Victoria	1	
A Brown	NSW (Newcastle)	1	
A Burns	NSW (Sydney)	1	
G Eccles	VIC	1	
A Harris	NSW (Newcastle)	1	
A Lambert	NSW (Newcastle)	1	
J McCroary	NSW (Newcastle)	1	
J Mitchell	South Australia	1	
H Morrison	Victoria	1	
A Murray	Queensland	1	
A Phillips	NSW (Newcastle)	1	
J Robison	Victoria	1	
H Sherringham	NSW (Sydney)	1	

All Tour Matches: Appearances and Goal Scorers

Qualification: Must have played at least 3 games against England or scored at least one goal.
NB: A total of 151 Australians played against England

Player	State	Appearances	Total Goals
R McNaughton	NSW (Newcastle)	10	1
A Edwards	NSW (Sydney)	7	0
P Lennard	NSW (Newcastle)	6	3
J Masters	NSW (Illawarra)	6	2
T Thompson	NSW (Illawarra)	6	1
S Bourke	NSW (Sydney)	6	0
G Cartwright	NSW (Sydney)	6	0
H Spurway	NSW (Sydney)	5	0
W Gardner	Western Australia	4	2
W Aiken	Victoria	4	0
H Boys	Western Australia	4	0
F Gallen	NSW (Sydney)	4	0
J Mitchell	South Australia	4	0
G Storey	NSW (Sydney)	4	0
A Gordon	Western Australia	3	1

Continued

Player	State	Appearances	Total Goals
Coolahan	NSW (Newcastle)	3	0
A Druery	NSW (Illawarra)	3	0
T Finlayson	Western Australia	3	0
A Harris	NSW (Newcastle)	3	0
J McCroary	NSW (Newcastle)	3	0
A Newall	Western Australia	3	0
C O'Connor	NSW (Sydney)	3	0
S Robinson	NSW (Sydney)	3	0
J Robison	Victoria	3	0
R Utting	Western Australia	3	0
J Warden	Western Australia	3	0
H Winter	NSW (Sydney)	2	1
F Hancock	NSW (Sydney)	1	1
J Smith	NSW (Sydney)	1	1

Acknowledgements and Bibliographical Notes

In autumn 2024, I ventured down to Wollongong to witness a game of club football. The match, played in misty rain, was between Unanderra Hearts, wearing the maroon strip made famous by the Heart of Midlothian club in Edinburgh, and Balgownie Rangers, sporting a black and white strip that Judy Masters would have approved of.

The match had everything - crunching challenges, good goals and an abundance of aggro. There was even a red card issued at half-time as tempers boiled over outside the dressing sheds. It was refreshing to see that football under the escarpment is still played with the same vigour and verve as it has been since the game was first introduced in the latter part of the 19th century.

My ulterior motive for being at this game was to meet Illawarra and Balgownie Rangers football historian, **Travis Faulks**. Travis has provided me with photos, advice, and information on Illawarra's rich football history and to him I owe a debt of gratitude.

Australia's community of football historians may be small in number but they are large in spirit. I particularly wanted to thank **Tony Smith** for his expertise on all matters South Australian, and his book *The First Sixty Years, Soccer in South Australia 1902-1962,* should be a part of every football historian's library.

In Queensland, **Mark Pringle**, **Neville Cruickshanks**, and **Garry McKenzie** have all provided information either directly or indirectly. For Ipswich football history, Garry McKenzie's website ipswichsoccer.blogspot.com and Neville Cruickshanks' historyofipswichsoccer.net are invaluable resources.

Victorian football history is well served by the work of the Football Victoria Historical Committee on the website footballvictoria.com.au. I could not mention Victoria without acknowledging the fine work of **Mark Boric**. His website melbournesoccer.blogspot.com is a wonderful archive of Australian football history.

ACKNOWLEDGEMENTS AND BIBLIOGRAPHICAL NOTES

Trevor Thompson's *Playing for Australia, The First Socceroos, Asia and the World Football* and *Burning Ambition - The Centenary of Australia-New Zealand Football Ashes* (the latter co-authored with **Nick Guoth**) have both provided context, and indeed inspiration, for this book. I also wanted to acknowledge the work of **Philip Moseley**, in particular his biographical material on John Fletcher and Judy Masters. A well-thumbed copy of Philip's *Soccer in New South Wales, 1880-1980* was always within arm's reach during this project.

By far the biggest source of material for this book comes from the **Trove Newspaper** archive at the **National Library of Australia** (NLA). Trove is free to access and is a national treasure. The NLA also has a copy of *Tom Whittaker's Arsenal Story*, which I made good use of. The British Library's The British Newspaper Archive was an excellent source for British perspectives on the FA tour of 1925.

I spent many an afternoon and evening in the comfy confines of the **State Library of New South Wales** poring over their original issues of *The Soccer News*. There's something about reading the originals of these magazines, many with corrections to team lists noted in pencil, that were small enough to fit into a coat pocket. The staff at the State Library have been unfailingly helpful and their care for their collections is superb.

I used **ozfootball.net** as a source for stats and team line ups. **Andrew Howe's** *Encyclopedia of the Socceroos Centenary Edition, 1922 to 2022* was another essential resource.

Thanks to **Athas Zafiris** who published my first article about the 1925 tour on *Shoot Farken*, which in turn fuelled my fascination with pre-World War II Australian football history.

Thanks also to my creative writing mates **Rob, Eva, Amanda** and **Tracie** at TheMovingPen.com.au for all your encouragement and support along the way.

A big thank you is also due to **Bonita Mersiades** and her team at **Fair Play Publishing** for the wonderful job they do in getting Australian football stories out into the world.

Finally, a great shout out to my friend **Peter Eedy**. Peter is a fine football historian with a special expertise in Queensland. Peter read and commented on the early drafts of many of the chapters of the book. Without his wisdom, insight and encouragement, I doubt this book would have been completed.

More really good football books from Fair Play Publishing

Whatever It Takes

Hear Us Roar

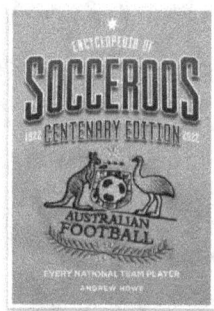
Encyclopedia of Socceroos Centenary Edition

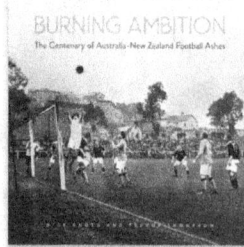
Burning Ambition
The Centenary of Australia-New Zealand Football Ashes

Tales of South American Football

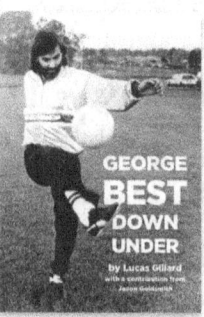
George Best Down Under

The First Matildas

Socceroos A World Cup Odyssey

fairplaypublishing.co.au/shop

FAIRPLAY PUBLISHING

www.ingramcontent.com/pod-product-compliance
Lightning Source LLC
Chambersburg PA
CBHW051351070526
44584CB00025B/3716